SO FAR _{AND} _{YET} SO CLOSE

SO FAR AND YET SO CLOSE

Frontier Cattle Ranching in
Western Prairie Canada and
the Northern Territory
of Australia

WARREN M. ELOFSON

UNIVERSITY OF CALGARY
Press

University of Calgary Press
2500 University Drive NW
Calgary, Alberta
Canada T2N 1N4
www.uofcpress.com

LIBRARY AND ARCHIVES CANADA CATALOGUING IN PUBLICATION

Elofson, W. M., author
    So far and yet so close : frontier cattle ranching in
western prairie Canada and the Northern Territory of Australia
/ Warren M. Elofson.

Includes bibliographical references and index.
Issued in print and electronic formats.
ISBN 978-1-55238-794-8 (paperback).–ISBN 978-1-55238-796-2
(pdf).–ISBN 978-1-55238-797-9 (epub).–ISBN 978-1-55238-798-6
(mobi)

    1. Ranching–Canada, Western–History. 2. Ranching–Australia,
Northern–History. 3. Ranch life–Canada, Western–History. 4. Ranch
life–Australia, Northern–History. 5. Frontier and pioneer life–Canada,
Western. 6. Frontier and pioneer life–Australia, Northern. 7. Canada,
Western–Environmental conditions–History. 8. Australia,
Northern–Environmental conditions–History. I. Title.

FC3209.R3E46 2015   971.2   C2015-902066-2
                                              C2015-902067-0

The University of Calgary Press acknowledges the support of the Government of Alberta
through the Alberta Media Fund for our publications. We acknowledge the financial support
of the Government of Canada through the Canada Book Fund for our publishing activities.
We acknowledge the financial support of the Canada Council for the Arts for our publishing
program.

Alberta
Government   Canada

Cover Image: Canadian cowboy with six-shooter. Tom Graham on horse,
High River area, Alberta, [ca. 1893]. Glenbow Archives, Calgary, NA-237-20.
Cover design, page design, and typesetting by Melina Cusano

For Lily Jane and June Lou

Contents

PREFACE

One finds many points at which the cattle frontiers of western Canada and northern Australia evoke comparisons. First and most obviously they came to life at about the same time – between the late 1870s and the early 1880s. In both cases corporations were heavy investors. The ranches utilized an open range system in which tens of thousands of cattle were allowed to roam over thousands of square acres with little human intervention; as the cattle mingled on the pasturelands they were subject to the depredations of two- and four-legged predators and the ravages of disease – the mange in North America and "tick" or "redwater" fever down under. The ranchers in the two regions faced severe losses from the vagaries of weather – primarily extreme cold in Canada and extreme heat and drought in Australia; they also struggled with the problem of accessing distant markets and they grappled unsuccessfully to produce finished (i.e., properly fattened) beef carcasses in surroundings that were agriculturally marginal. In both societies, a numerical predominance of males among the newcomers helped to create an excessively masculine culture, blur traditional gender roles, and promote interracial fraternization. Ultimately, moreover, a nearly indistinguishable "country" culture developed in these geographically disparate and distant lands the imprint of which was to be unmistakable through to the modern era.

The ranching people in these two societies had their differences too. All the above similarities were in one way or another a reflection of frontier environmental conditions – that is, conditions associated with the very fact of the "newness" of society. But as western Canadians and northern Australians took specific steps to respond to certain natural environmental factors – including vegetation, terrain, soil type, precipitation, and seasonal temperature fluctuations – they had to adopt specific methodologies to sustain their businesses. More than anything else, this accounted for the emergence of the family ranch/farm in western Canada and the maintenance of the most extensive form of animal husbandry known to man in the Northern Territory.

Much of the background information about the western Canadian frontier comes from one or more of the books or articles I have written over the years on North American cattle ranching. In every place in the text where I have used this material I have been able to confirm or clarify it by adding significant new primary source evidence. I gathered most of the information on Australian ranching during trips I was able to make over the course of four years to the repositories in Brisbane, Adelaide, Melbourne, Canberra, and Darwin. Because I was working in a country so distant from my own I often had to go through a wealth of documents at a frenzied pace and thus needed to call upon the librarians and archivists in those cities for considerable help and endless patience. I wish to acknowledge my debt of gratitude to them for their kindness, their efficiency, and their professionalism. The research for the book was supported by a Standard Research Grant from the Social Sciences and Humanities Research Council of Canada.

INTRODUCTION

It can be said with confidence that this study is the first in-depth comparison of the late nineteenth- and early twentieth-century cattle ranching societies in western prairie Canada and the Northern Territory of Australia. The central theme is the impact of the environment on human behaviour. It is beyond doubt that Mother Nature played a major role in sculpting and conditioning virtually all agricultural settlements pretty much everywhere in this world. In the process of delineating that role in these two regions, the pages that follow will also look closely at the power of man-controlled or man-influenced environmental circumstances. At the instigation of ranching in both regions those circumstances reflected a particular stage of development that we usually designate with the term "frontier"; and that refers to the earliest period when the incoming people were relatively unfamiliar with the land and liable to make mistakes, when populations were sparse and labour in short supply, when gender ratios were way out of balance, and when newcomer and Native populations met in relatively large numbers for the first time. In so far as pastoral practices were concerned, it also speaks of a period before basic infrastructure such as fences and barns could be built to enclose and contain the livestock, or roughage could be put up in sufficient amounts to ensure the animals always had a proper food supply, or enough good wells could be drilled to safeguard their drinking water. Factors of these sorts encouraged the first western Canadian and northern Australian graziers to embrace strikingly similar cultural and agricultural ways though they operated a world apart and under very different ecological, climatic, and topographical pressures.

To elaborate on the latter statement is, one hopes, to make a worthwhile contribution to both Canadian and Australian scholarship. Over a century ago, Frederick Jackson Turner in America and, later, Russell Ward in Australia, argued that conditions in a frontier region brought a deterioration in the traditions to which migrating people had been accustomed in their original society.[1] This stimulated new ideas and values that deeply affected the way they went about their day-to-day lives. In its most fundamental form, the two men's common thesis is simply that frontiers alter human behaviour. With respect to the early grazing industry in each of these countries, that line of reasoning is beyond doubt.[2] But in demonstrating that early Anglo society in their West was not merely an expansion of that society found in the United States, Canadian ranching historians have tended to employ a metropolitan analysis that stresses the predominance of Eastern laws, legal agencies, and culture.[3] Down under, ever since Henry Reynolds estimated in 1981 that over one hundred fifty years European invaders killed some twenty thousand Aborigines, researchers have been examining the process whereby indigenous societies were dispossessed of their territory.[4] Some have disputed Reynolds's findings, igniting in the process a heated battle about both numbers and blame.[5] The ensuing controversy has encouraged frontier scholars to concentrate almost exclusively on race. The present study attempts to illustrate how a wide range of "New World" conditions in both countries affected the lives of the first ranchers and gave them a common set of challenges that, for a time at least, they handled in much the same way.

At the operational level, this is discernible in the ranchers' adoption of the so-called "Texas system" to work their herds.[6] That system was the most basic, unrefined, and extensive form of agricultural production in existence. Anglo-Americans originally embraced it after the annexation of Texas from Mexico in 1845.[7] Like the Mexican graziers before them, the Anglo cattlemen allowed their stock to "range indiscriminately over a large surface of country, thirty, forty, and even fifty miles in extent."[8] Key to the system was low costs.[9] Huge spreads of tens of thousands of acres were established with little more capital expenditure than what was required to build the most rudimentary facilities for the cattle and some very modest housing for the workers.[10] Since the stock grazed year round the men who ran the spreads did not have to put up any feed. They did have to round up the cattle twice a year so the calves could be branded and castrated and the big steers could be cut out for slaughter. Thus was born the iconic American cowboy. The business of roundups was "no easy task." Men had to be expert horsemen with loads of "cow sense," and they needed to be able to handle a "lasso," which they carried "at saddle-bow." Their job was to gather the animals into bunches and drive them into hastily constructed pens where some men, working from the backs of their frisky little horses, cut out the fats and roped the calves while others worked methodically with branding iron and knife. Many took pride in "this 'Cow-Boy' life" and "notwithstanding its hardships and exposures, generally" became "attached to it."[11] These men also soon caught the public imagination as the swashbuckling, freedom loving knights of the plains.[12]

It was mainly upon the expertise of these young males, creations of the Deep Southern cattle frontier, that open range grazing was destined eventually to expand north along the edge of the Rocky Mountains all the way to Canada. After a period of stagnation and decline the Texan beef industry experienced growth like never before in the late 1870s and early 1880s. A host of new pastoral companies with wealthy stockholders from the East and Great Britain poured into southern and north-central regions and then entered the foothills country of the panhandle in the northwestern part of the state. Most of the owners were urbanites with little knowledge either of grazing techniques or ecological conditions in the West and they entrusted their stock to the skilled hired men who had cut their teeth on the cattle ranges. As the grasslands of Texas filled, tenderfoot investors were able to take over major regions of Arizona, Colorado, Wyoming, and Montana. Finally some of them entered the plains and foothills of southern Alberta and Assiniboia (which in 1905 would become the southern region of the province of Saskatchewan).[13]

In the beginning the so-called "great ranchers" of western Canada adopted all the assumptions of the Texas system – "profound neglect" of the herds for most of the time, open range, low costs, and large-scale production.[14] The Canadians endorsed this system because it fitted the frontier environment almost perfectly. They were starting up an industry where it had never existed before; and because it would have been costly, and exceedingly difficult without a more substantial labour force, to build fences and barns and put up large amounts of feed, it seemed appropriate to embrace a system that deemed those tasks unnecessary. Unfortunately, this put the ranches into a head-on collision with the natural environment. More than anything else, what was to bring them all down within two and a half decades was the inferior quality of their stock and low reproduction and survival rates due largely to the harsh northwestern climate, the short growing season, predation, and a disease that plagued the cattle as they mingled on the open range. The same ecological forces would ensure that this system and all the ranches that utilized it were to be replaced by a much more intensive, more refined, and smaller-scale family-run agricultural form.

At almost exactly at the same time that the Canadian cattlemen were assembling their ranches on the northern Great Plains of North America, Australian pastoralists were erecting very similar operations in formerly unsettled lands in their Northern Territory. One might be accused of applying the term the "Texas system" to their practices rather loosely since, geographically speaking, they were so far removed from it and, given their natural setting, they almost certainly would have adopted a similar technique even had the Texans never existed. On the other hand, the Texans did implement the system on a wide scale first, and it is clear that the Australians had ample opportunity to read about it, so that initially this must have bolstered their confidence in its fundamental attributes. The best-known agricultural journal in the country, the *Pastoral Review*, carried numerous pieces concerning American beef cattle production from the early nineteenth century on, and regular newspapers often featured Texas ranching in their articles.[15] "From the grassy plains" of Texas "cattle are purchased by men who somewhat resemble the squatters of Australia," pundits informed the general public. They "take up land in ranches and graze over wide regions."[16] It is also to be acknowledged that employing the term "Texas system" here to describe pastoral practices in both countries is a matter of convenience. It enables us to, for one thing, comment on the characteristics of this approach that the Australians and Canadians maintained and, for another, at the same time visualize any specific ways in which they eventually deviated from it. In that sense it is a sort of measuring stick from which to gain a better understanding of how cattle grazing was carried on in both countries.

Australian cattlemen headed to the Territory mainly to expand the land holdings they were already managing in more settled parts of the country. They too were reacting to frontier environmental influences. Open range grazing was the easiest approach for them to adopt in the earliest stage of settlement, just as it was for their Canadian counterparts and for the same reasons – labour was short and infrastructure, particularly in the form of water wells and all the paraphernalia they required, was incredibly expensive. The first Australian graziers misjudged particular circumstances in their new land too and it cost them dearly. However, they were better equipped than the Canadians to understand the natural elements they would have to deal with. Most of them had previously started up successful pastoral ventures when opening hinterlands of South Australia, Queensland, or New South Wales and they had a fairly good grasp of climate and ecology throughout the continent. They felt the large-scale open range approach for which the Texan ranchers were renowned would work in the Northern Territory and they were right. Ultimately, after an initial period of disappointment and failure, this system, with minor adjustments, was to take hold in the outback because the climate, terrain, flora, and fauna were amenable.[17]

An environmental analysis is by definition a "bottom up" rather than a "top down" one. It is interested in how and why men and women and their pastoral operations were affected by their environment and not as concerned with political or legal stimuli (or a lack of thereof). In both regions it was the natural surroundings that were destined to rule in the establishment of appropriate agricultural techniques. Ross Duncan ends his study of the cattle industry in the Northern Territory between 1863 and 1910 with a firm criticism of the South Australian government, blaming it for not doing more to help the graziers by building better railway and steamship facilities for them and for not establishing better roads and stock routes or doing more to help in the fight against bovine disease.[18] What he is saying, and quite rightly, is that government intervention played a very small role in determining the historical development of this form of agriculture in the Territory. The big ranches that came to life there eventually found a way to carry on by adapting to the elements rather than attaining outside support. In Canada, Max Foran has recently shown that the federal government's homestead policy, its various iterations of the original lease legislation, and its failure to provide lease security before

1913 were all influential in the expansion and contraction of the ranching industry. He also notes that the British embargo on Canadian cattle starting in 1892 and a 27.5 percent ad valorem tariff in the United States placed limits on outside markets. There is no denying these facts.[19] However, what becomes evident here is that the major changes in the Canadian industry – the eventual demise of the great ranches and the rise of a much more sophisticated form of production – were predestined to occur irrespective of government policies and programs. Foran acknowledges that fact. "Large-scale open-range ranching," he reminds us, "may never have been as viable" on the northern Great Plains "as romance would have it . . . Indeed, one is led to wonder if the big cattle companies would have come to the Alberta foothills country in the 1880s had they been aware of the realities of cattle survival on the open range" in such an inhospitable setting.[20] One objective of this study is to illustrate in detail all the reasons why that was so in the Canadian Prairie West and not so in the Northern Territory of Australia.

2

THE SHORT HISTORY
OF THE TEXAS SYSTEM
IN WESTERN CANADA

Immediately following the American Civil War (1861–65) Texan cattle traders searched for new markets for largely feral cattle that had been left to wander the plains during the fighting.[1] Many drove their herds to the "corn belt" of the midwestern states where the cattle were placed on farms to be fattened before the final journey by rail to the packinghouses in Chicago. At the same time soon to be well-known paths, such as the Chisholm and the Goodnight-Loving Trails, were opened to stock "new" rangeland in mining districts of the far north. As more and more Texas cattle reached the Montana ranges they interbred with the "westerns" – mostly British breeds including Hereford, Shorthorn, and Angus – principally from California via Oregon – and then with similar stock that the cattlemen began to import from the eastern United States and from Great Britain.[2]

Starting in the 1870s increasing numbers of cattle were driven into Alberta and Assiniboia to feed Native bands facing starvation with the destruction of the bison herds. The missionary brothers John and David McDougall maintained a few cattle near Morley west of Calgary from the beginning of the decade. In 1877 former whiskey trader H.A. (Fred) Kanouse turned twenty-one cows and a bull loose on the open range near Fort Macleod. Then John Miller arrived from Montana with some twenty-five head, which "he too put out to rustle for themselves."[3] During the spring of 1878 a number of small businessmen including Tom Lynch, who had migrated west from Missouri, and George Emerson, a Canadian who had teamed up with Lynch in Montana, drove in hundreds of horses and cattle. These they sold to men already on the frontier, the majority of them former North-West Mounted Police officers who had obtained a discharge from the force to take up ranching. In 1879 Emerson and Lynch drove in a thousand cattle and horses to start up their own ranch on the north side of the Highwood River west of the town of High River. By 1880 some two hundred mostly small herds were grazing on the free grass between the United States border and the Bow River near the present site of Calgary.[4]

Shortly thereafter the era of the so-called "great ranches" entered full swing. It too developed first in the American West. New grazing corporations, which had been hastily thrown together in Boston, New York, Montreal, Edinburgh, and London, appeared on the Great Plains to invest huge pools of surplus capital. By the late 1870s, thousands of joint stock companies, with hundreds of millions of dollars, descended on Montana, Wyoming, Colorado, New Mexico, and Texas. The directors and shareholders of these corporations felt they could make great sums of money ranching in the West, in part because they were able to operate on unclaimed and therefore free range. Their exuberance helped to induce politically astute men of influence and considerable wealth in eastern Canada to lobby the Conservative government of Sir John A. Macdonald for the right to take up similar ventures in Alberta and Assiniboia. This led to legislation in 1881 allowing individuals or companies to start big livestock grazing operations on the bases of 21-year closed leases of up to 100,000 acres of land at the bargain price of one cent an acre per year. The response was dramatic. A number of the companies leased well over 100,000 acres by using a variety of names and within the next few years 111 of them controlled several million acres of western land.

The ranching corporations on both sides of the border all required cattle, and thus what had been a stream of incoming stock suddenly turned into a flood. In the summer of 1883 Montana rancher Teddy (Blue) Abbott was driving cattle up from Texas. As he rode along he was "hardly ever out of sight of [another] herd." One day he looked over the plains from a small hilltop in the relatively flat country near the Platte River. "I could see seven herds behind us," he remembered. "I knew there were eight herds ahead of us, and I could see the dust from thirteen more of them on the other side of the river."[5] By the end of 1880 the number of cattle in the state of Montana had risen to 555,000 and at the turn of the century to just over 900,000.[6] In southern Alberta and Assiniboia the numbers soared from a modest 9,000 to around 100,000 in the early 1880s, and then to 355,000 by 1901.[7]

The largest of three cattle ranching "blocks" that formed in the Canadian West ran in a north-south direction along the foothills bordering the Rocky Mountains west of Calgary. It included three of the original "Big Four" operations: the owners of the Bar U were from the Eastern Townships in Quebec, and those of the Oxley and Walrond outfits were mainly Britons. The Cochrane ranch owned principally by Senator Matthew Cochrane, also from the Eastern Townships in Quebec, was established in the area directly west of Calgary in 1881, and two years later moved south to the Waterton region near the American border. Another block of ranches took root in Canada after starting up in the United States. This group included ranches owned by brothers Samuel and John Spencer, originally from Ontario; the Conrad brothers, William and John, from Virginia; and William McIntyre from Utah. These outfits occupied the hills of the Milk River Ridge stretching eastward along the American border from the second Cochrane ranch. A third block – including the Canadian Agricultural Coal and Colonization Company, or 76, ranch owned by a British syndicate under Sir John Lister-Kaye; the Turkey Track controlled by English-born Henry Whitesides Cresswell[8] and A.J. (Tony) Day; the Circle Diamond outfit of Coloradans Frank G. Bloom and M.D. Thatcher; and the N Bar N outfit of brothers William and Fredrick Niedringhaus of Missouri – settled in the region running eastward from the second block through the Cypress Hills to the Wood Mountain area in Assiniboia Territory.[9]

In this period the northern Great Plains saw a major influx of people as well as cattle companies. A small number of the newcomers were well-healed owners or managers of the big outfits. Far more, however, were the young men who flowed in to work on the big ranches as cowpunchers. A portion of them were Americans who originally helped to drive in cattle from the south and then stayed on, drawn by the relatively good pay offered by the new outfits competing for their cowboy skills. The famous black cowboy John Ware; the manager and then owner of the Bar U, George Lane; the famous bronco buster Frank Ricks; the one-time

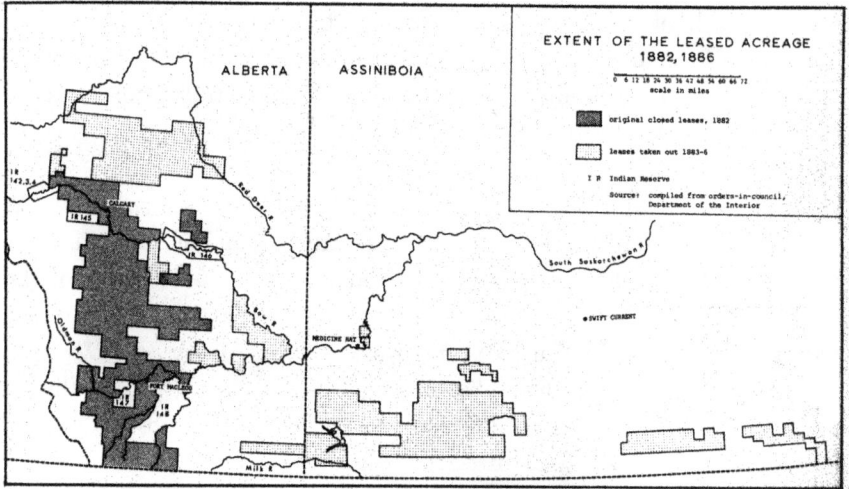

EXTENT OF THE LEASES IN WESTERN CANADA, 1886. SIMON EVANS, "THE PASSING OF A FRONTIER: RANCHING IN THE CANADIAN WEST, 1882–1912," UNPUBLISHED MA THESIS: UNIVERSITY OF CALGARY, 1976, REPRINTED IN DAVID H. BREEN, *THE CANADIAN PRAIRIE WEST AND THE RANCHING FRONTIER* (TORONTO: UNIVERSITY OF TORONTO PRESS, 1983), 46.

foreman of the Bar U, Everett Johnson; the Cochrane ranch cowboys W.D. Kerfoot, Jim Dunlap, and a Mexican known as Ca Sous; and the first Walrond ranch foreman, Jim Patterson, had, like Emerson and Lynch, all learned their trade in the American West.[10] A lot more of the migrants, however, were from eastern Canada and Great Britain. Many of them, were "wannabes" who were hoping to live up to the heroic image of the western frontiersman they had met in a host of American, and one or two Canadian, dime and romantic novels; and they wanted to do so as quickly as humanly possible.[11] After they stepped off the train in the rapidly expanding town of Calgary, they headed to local shops to secure the wide brimmed hat, the boots, the bright shirt and bandanna, and the spurs they needed to play the part of the working cowboy. Some of these young men failed miserably, turning to drink, prostitutes, and general dissipation before heading back home in disgrace. Others, though, signed on with one of the cattle operations and learned to ride, rope, brand, and even handle a six-shooter. Before the late 1870s, according to one rancher, "no one had heard tell of a cowboy" on the northwestern plains, but by 1883 "leather chaps, wide hats, gay handkerchiefs, clanking silver spurs and skin fitting high healed [sic] boots . . . had become an institution."[12]

The period of the "great ranches" did not endure. A combination of factors saw all the corporations terminated in relatively short order. The North Fork ranch near Pincher Creek in southwestern Alberta closed down after only three years; the Stair or 76 ranch did so in 1909 due to depleted finances; the Cochranes lost heavily in their first years and then sold out when higher land prices enabled them to recoup some of their capital in the new century; the Turkey Track and Bloom outfits quit in 1907; the Scottish-owned Matador, which was part of a much bigger ranching empire that stretched across parts of Montana, Texas, and South America, ceased active operations in the Canadian West in the early 1920s; and a thorough investigation of the Walrond ranch's accounts, cattle numbers, and stockholder debt has shown that its liquid position was unsustainable before the dreadful winter of 1906–7 severely reduced what was left of its cattle inventory.[13] All of these vast spreads were to be replaced by much smaller, family-operated units, most of which might more realistically be described as ranch/farms.

There were two important reasons for the failure of the corporation ranches. The most obvious was the beef market. Historians have been inclined to speak of a "beef bonanza" in these years, referring one supposes to a significant period of high prices that netted the western cattle industry great profits and drew many of the capitalists from the East and overseas into the business. This is simply a figment of our collective imagination.[14] Census statistics demonstrate that, after declining precipitously in the mid- and late 1870s, beef prices enjoyed a brief period of recovery from 1880 to 1882 and then dropped year after year through to the turn of the century. They improved only gradually after that and after many of the big ranches had either failed or been too badly crippled financially to endure much longer.[15] As American historian and cattle industry expert James Cox put it, "the magnificent prices, to which we have alluded as making glad the heart of the cattleman in the early 1880s, were succeeded by prices which, while, in some instances, they left a nominal margin of profit, took away the gold-mine appearance and reputation of the trade."[16]

The other reason for the collapse was environmental. Left to fend for themselves on the open range, too many cattle succumbed to predators, including wolves which could prey with ease on cattle spread out across the plains; the mange, a disease that passed from one animal to another as the herds mingled on the open range; and, above all, ferocious winters. The winter of 1886–87 was remembered by many cattlemen as the worst of all time. It caused huge losses on the Great Plains from Canada all the way south to the panhandle of northwestern Texas.[17] Alfred E. Cross, the well-known owner of the A7 ranch in the Porcupine Hills, some seventy miles south of Calgary, acknowledged that "the custom" when the open range system was first used in western Canada was "not to feed almost any cattle." The blizzards of 1886–87 were "the most severe known in the country," he recalled. Cross's cattle "drifted south in the storms with a large number of new cattle on the range." He lost "25 to 50 per cent" of his stock during this time, "principally" the gestating cows essential to herd development and future sales.[18] Journalist L.V. Kelly used his literary talent to depict the devastation more generally: "Clustering in the coulees or huddling in the open, the animals suffered and died in enormous numbers. Some, breast-high in packed and crusted banks" of snow "died as they stood; some sheltered somewhat by bluffs or coulees" but unable to get at the grass through the deep cover of white "starved pitifully, ravenously searching for food until the frost had reached their vitals." In the spring, Kelly remembered, "the bodies of great steers were found . . . heaps of them, with their throats and stomachs punctured and torn by sharp splinters from dried and frozen branches and chunks of wood, which they had swallowed in their anguish." Many of the cattle just lay down in the snow to die. When cowboys found them "buried in the . . . drifts or lying, too weak to get up," they used their six-shooters to put them out of their misery.[19]

Cross believed that "few of the ranchers lost less than 40 per cent" of the animals they had on the open range that winter, "some losing 100, many losing 75 per cent."[20] The Quorn operation to the east of the A7 lost "nearly every hoof." To the northwest Tom Lynch was left with a mere eighty out of his eight hundred stockers. The N Bar N outfit, which had brought six thousand cattle to the Wood Mountain area in 1886, pulled out of Canada in the spring of 1887 trailing a scant two thousand.[21]

After that winter most ranchers realized it was necessary for them to make some modifications to the Texas grazing system. They began putting up a small amount of feed for the weakest animals in their herds – principally the old cows and very young calves – when the weather was at its worst. However, they continued to turn all the rest of their cattle loose on the open range year round. And year after year they suffered financially as a result. The blizzards and extreme temperatures of 1891–92, 1892–93, 1896–97, 1897–98, and 1902–03 also did considerable damage. Finally, the horrendous winter of 1906–7 signalled the end of open range grazing in western Canada, as something like 50 percent of all the cattle in the roaming herds were lost.[22]

The blizzards by themselves are evidence of Nature's destructive power on the northern plains, but it is seldom recognized that two other primarily ecological forces also added significantly to the death toll. Before the cattlemen appeared in this region timber and grey wolves had almost died out, excessively hunted for the fur trade and deprived by the depletion of the bison herds which had traditionally supplied much of their diet.[23] When the ranchers turned their first cattle loose, however, the beasts gained a new food source that was much easier to kill than the wild, wary, and relatively powerful buffalo had been. By the late 1880s wolf numbers were on the rebound, and by the mid-1890s these predators had become one of the stockmen's most formidable enemies.[24] Fuelled by the abundance of raw meat, the wolves grew to an impressive size and sometimes ran in packs that could bring down a full-grown cow. Most of all the beasts were a threat to younger stock.[25] Wolves "have been giving us a hard deal during the last two weeks," David Warnock, the onsite manager of the Walrond ranch, told his general manager, Duncan McEachran, in July 1894. In just "a few nights they killed . . . a number of yearling cattle and calves. . . We found several of the carcasses freshly killed in fact warm and poisoned some of these but the wolves did not touch the bait. We have been doing our best to kill them with the dogs but so far, have only succeeded in killing two full grown ones. The dogs are too light and get a terrible mauling every time they tackle" one of the wild creatures.[26] In an attempt to explain why the cattle count fell far short of expectations in 1897, Warnock suggested that four-legged predators were largely responsible. "Take for instance, the damage" they did "amongst horses," he said. They "killed in less than six months some forty odd head of one and 2 years old colts belonging" to the company.[27] This was about a twelfth of all the well-bred (and relatively valuable) Clydesdales and Shires the ranch owned; Warnock was intimating that similar damage must have been inflicted on the cattle.[28]

The other natural force greatly destructive to open range ranching was the mange, a disease that occurs when parasitic mites attack the hides of both cattle and horses, causing them tremendous discomfort.[29] The mites usually take hold when cattle are penned up in a corral for a substantial period. After the 1886–87 winter the northern Great Plains ranchers put up hay and enclosed their weakest animals through much of the cold season; these creatures became infected and later infected the range herds when turned loose. Outbreaks became increasingly frequent and severe as the years passed. The diseased animals develop huge sores because they rub against trees, posts, buildings, or anything substantial enough to relieve the itch, until their hair drops out and their hide is torn.[30] The disease also stresses the cattle and puts them off their feed so that they lose weight and become susceptible to pneumonia and other ailments. Consequently many of the range animals went into winter in poor shape and succumbed to the cold more readily than they otherwise would have. The only way to treat the mange was to conduct a special roundup and dip the animals in a tank filled with a solution of kerosene and/or sulphur mixed with lime and water.[31] In 1902 a newspaper editor illustrated how difficult it was to deal with the problem in an open range situation. Rancher A, he said, "goes to the expense of putting in a dipping vat and buying dip" and then "dips his cattle in a thorough manner twice, takes them home and says he is all right so far as itch is concerned. The next evening he rounds up his cattle and finds three or more of [his neighbour's] diseased cattle in his herd and two weeks later finds his cattle" more severely contaminated than before he dipped.[32] The mange became so widespread in Canada that the government erected tanks in strategic locations near the border in which to treat animals imported from the United States.[33] In 1904 it declared a huge tract running east of the Rockies well into Assiniboia "an infected place" and ordered that all animals subject to the contagion in that area be isolated and treated.[34] This measure did not sufficiently halt the spread; livestock associations soon began to develop a communal approach to treatment. Dipping was costly, not just because vats, tanks, and corrals needed to be constructed for processing the animals but also because special roundups had to be undertaken. The cattle had to be trailed in over long distances from all directions, and be held in crowded conditions for days at a time waiting to be treated at least twice; they also had to endure the frightening process of being forced by their alien tormentors through the vats of hot, stinking solution.[35] The cattle must all have lost weight during the ordeal, and in their weakened state some unquestionably contracted other illnesses and later died

How thoroughly the great ranchers in Canada adopted the fundamentals of the Texas system in total disregard of the environmental obstacles they faced is demonstrated by an interview Duncan McEachran gave in January 1887 when in Australia in conjunction with his position as Canada's chief inspector of livestock.[36] McEachran does not seem to have been aware that, even as he spoke, the cattle herds on his own and all his neighbours' ranches were being decimated by one of the most devastating winters of all times.[37] Ranches on the northern Great Plains, he said, "date from 1881. . ."

> Since then, large areas in Alberta, lying close to the foothills of the Rocky Mountains, for about 400 miles north, and 100 miles east of the United States boundary line, have been utilized for the breeding and feeding of cattle and horses. These ranches are within sight of perpetual snow, being 5000 ft. above the sea level, but the climate is so modified by the proximity of the Pacific Ocean that herds of cattle and horses can find abundance of food the entire year round. Snowstorms . . . sometimes last for two or three days, during which time from 7 in. to 8 in. of snow will fall; but it is light and powdery, and rarely "pocks." The wind, which prevails almost continuously, is known as the Chinook wind – being of a high temperature, the snow sometimes disappears within a few hours. Ice crusts are scarcely ever seen there. On the contrary, the snow seems to evaporate – for it leaves no slush or mud behind it. Consequently, particularly on the slopes of the foothills facing towards the west, from which these winds generally blow, the cattle have no difficulty in getting at the long thick grass. No shelter of any kind is provided for them anywhere . . . So they are left to care for themselves as they best can, after the manner of the thousands of buffaloes which preceded them on the ground. It is customary in ranche companies to write off 5 per cent for losses; but on well-managed ranches in the Alberta district the percentage of loss is less

than 3 per cent, and I know a company where 1 to 2 per cent represented the [average loss.]

Back in Canada McEachran would in future years consistently send his mainly British stockholders annual dividend cheques based on his estimates of the number and value of his cattle. Ultimately his profit analyses were to prove as unrealistic as his assessment of the environment.[38]

None of the ailments that so severely afflicted the open range business in the Canadian West was nearly as destructive in the region in which that system originated. It was only in the panhandle of the northwestern part of Texas that harsh winter weather was a familiar factor and it almost never struck with the same ferocity there as on the northern Great Plains. Though the Texan ranges too were inhabited with wolves, the lankier, fleet-footed and more powerful Longhorn cattle were much better equipped to protect their young than the more compact and slower Shorthorn-, Angus-, and Hereford-influenced stock on the Canadian ranges. Since the southern cattle were virtually never penned up for any prolonged period, moreover, outbreaks of the mange were almost unknown in the Deep South.[39] The historian is left to explain why the Canadians, many of them hard-nosed businessmen, should have been convinced to invest such large sums of capital on a pastoral approach that had only ever proved successful in a region so dissimilar to their own. The knowledgeable James Cox, who was, to put it mildly, unimpressed with all the so-called "cattle kings" of the corporation era, blamed the expansion of the Texas system generally on a lack of expertise and on greed. "Undue haste to become rich and to find the road to wealth," he wrote, caused "the killing of the goose to secure the golden egg."[40] He pointed out that many of the men who financed the cattle companies were urbanites from the East and Great Britain who knew nothing of ranching or its limitations. Their invasion of the West all up and down the foothills of the Rockies from Texas to Canada ("the British Territories") in the late 1870s and early 1880s, he insisted, had a hysterical quality to it. "There was a wild rush into the range country on the part of people inexperienced in the cattle business but anxious to participate in the profits said to be so easily made by cattle raising there."[41] In this process, he argued, the big ranchers were themselves the cause of poor beef prices between 1883 and 1900. "In the opinion of the most conservative members of the trade, these were the men who broke down the prosperity of the . . . industry of the West and Southwest."[42] They over invested and overstocked the plains and quickly created a great glut of beef on the international market.[43]

Cox's description of the men who underwrote the cattle companies rings true for the Canadian West. While some had agriculturally derived wealth there was in most cases no ranching and very little *direct or first-hand* agricultural involvement. Four of the ranch owners considered to be the elite leaders of the industry were typical. Senator Matthew Cochrane had a 1,100-acre farm in Compton, Quebec, where he raised purebred short-horn cattle, but he made his money primarily through a leather processing and shoe factory that employed some five hundred people and as a founder of the Eastern Townships Bank.[44] Sir John Walrond Walrond was a British member of the upper gentry whose son-in-law was a titled aristocrat. He held a large estate near Exeter in southwest England, but in the tradition of the British landholding classes leased his land to tenant farmers. His two sons, William (who took a close interest in the Canadian venture) and Arthur, were bankers.[45] Lord Lathom of the Oxley was a British aris-tocrat who also leased out his large estates, and his partner, Alexander Staveley Hill, was a high-ranking official in the Conservative govern-ments, respectively, of Lord Salisbury and Arthur Balfour; Sir Hugh Allen from Montreal, who financed the Bar U, made his money as a shipping magnate, railroad contractor, and miller.[46]

Cox placed some blame on the media for convincing numerous such men that they could augment their wealth on the basis of the Texas sys-tem. He pointed out, for instance, that a London newspaper had fuelled unrealistic enthusiasm by explaining "with great care . . . how a yearling" steer "could be purchased" for the incredibly low price of "three or four dollars, fattened" on western ranges at next to nothing "and then sold at about sixty or seventy dollars . . . net." He said that "in order to dem-onstrate the truth of these remarkable figures," the paper had absurdly estimated "that so rich were the pastures . . . that an ordinary steer of three years" could be expected to weigh from "twelve hundred" to "fif-teen hundred pounds" and yield a thousand pounds of marketable meat.[47] Such figuring was "idiotic," he insisted, but its influence was evident from "the tremendous rush of inexperienced investors to the West . . . all de-termined to buy cattle at half or a third current prices," raise them "at a third or fourth the actual cost," and sell "them at figures about double the ordinary quotations for two and three year olds raised in the manner described."[48]

Writing in 1895, Cox had the benefit of hindsight. He had watched the industry suffer as prices declined over the previous decade. He also knew enough about the cattle business to understand how overly simplistic much of the financial reasoning was. He must have known as well that virtually all the media on both sides of the Atlantic embraced it and that four promotional writers in the United States ranked above the rest in terms of the influence their published works yielded:[49] a general in the United States Army, James S. Brisbin;[50] a German aristocrat who speculated in land, Walter, Baron von Richthofen;[51] a surgeon for the Union Pacific Railway, Dr. Hiram Latham;[52] and Joseph McCoy, a town site promoter.[53] They fuelled the passion of other writers and ultimately did much to pique the enthusiasm of Eastern capitalists for ranching on both sides of the Canadian-American border.

All four of these men propagated endless confidence in the Texas system not just in the Deep South but in geographic areas significantly removed from and environmentally unlike that region. In his 1871 pamphlet *Trans-Missouri Stock Raising*, Latham led the way by appealing to his readers on a pseudoscientific level. To maintain a large population of labourers whose products could be sold in the competitive markets of the world, he announced, the United States had to develop an inexpensive and inexhaustible supply of food and clothing. The cheaper the food and clothing, the cheaper and more competitive industrial production would be and thus, by implication, the wealthier and more successful the entire nation. Food must include meat for a well-balanced diet. Therefore it was necessary to use cattle and sheep to convert feed into beef and mutton. The best way to do this was to rely on and expand the grazing approach that was then being so successfully applied in the state of Texas. He argued that there was a never-ending amount of virgin grazing land in the entire Great Plains region and that its potential could easily be tapped. As the land was still unsettled, it could be accessed for little or no cost, and as grazing did not require tilling the soil, the purchase and operation of expensive implements was unnecessary. Moreover, as the animals could largely fend for themselves, few hands were needed to watch over them.

All the media representations propagated the belief that profound neglect could be undertaken with impunity even in the far northern regions of the Great Plains. Brisbin, in a book of 1881 tellingly entitled *The Beef Bonanza or How to Get Rich on the Plains*, quoted what he claimed were the glowing appraisals of ranchers who had grazed cattle in Montana. These he then used to support his opinion that there was "no place in this section of the country . . . where cattle and sheep will not winter safely with no feed but what they will pick up." Showing the flare for hyperbole that so disgusted Cox, he estimated that "all the flocks and herds in the world could find ample pasturage" year round on the "unoccupied plains and the mountain slopes."[54] The boosters produced incredibly optimistic estimates of investment and yield. Within a few years, profits of 100 to 200 percent were to be the norm. The animals themselves would harvest the prairie flora while their owners did little more than watch and rake in the money.[55]

Joseph McCoy wrote in 1874:

> There is an immense belt of country along the Rocky Mountains and extending eastward about four hundred miles, with a length of near two thousand miles which, from its character, climate, and comparatively rainless seasons, is preeminently adapted to sheep husbandry and the breeding of cattle. . . . This vast area is covered with a fine species of grass . . . which is equally nutritious in winter as in summer. Either cattle or sheep not only live well but fatten fast so long as they can get an abundance of Buffalo grass. No matter how cold the air may be, so warm and nutritious is this grass at all seasons of the year, that cattle or sheep do not care for hay or other feed in winter.[56]

What such depictions failed to mention, of course, was that on the northern plains the four main grass varieties – the tall native rough fescue and wheat grasses along with the shorter blue grama and needle and thread – though rich and nutritious during specific seasons, were largely dormant during about eight months of the year when nighttime temperatures tended to drop to near or below freezing and when the grasses were likely to be obscured by snow.[57] To make the case that anyone could make a fortune in this business, von Richthofen laid out simple figures indicating what one man "who does not wish his name thus advertised" had accomplished while a full-time banker in Denver.

In 1878 he bought 320 head of cattle for	$4,000
In 1879 he bought 1,000 head of cattle for	10,000
In 1880 he bought 1,900 head of cattle for	20,000
In 1882 he bought 1,900 head of cattle for	38,500
	$72,500
Horses and ranch	3,500
Total	$76,000
In 1880 he sold steers for	$ 5,500
In 1881 he sold steers for	13,000
In 1882 he sold steers for	27,500
In 1883 he sold steers for	150,000
Total	$196,000[58]

The banker's net profit in the five years, von Richthofen insisted, was $120,000.

The excitement that these writings helped to create induced Canadian ranchers to believe in the open range system and it also persuaded them to invest far more than they should have in their initial livestock herds and ultimately ensured that they got an inferior product. As we have seen, there was a short period of rising prices in the early 1880s. Undoubtedly, the established cattlemen who were efficiently supplying slaughter cattle made some money. However, their relative prosperity helped to set off a veritable frenzy among Old World capitalists to get into the business. Consequently, the cattlemen who made the most money were those prepared to sell the novices breeding stock and one- and two-year-old store or feeder steers that were still in the growing stage for their initial herds. Suddenly, as Cox noted, the "cattle raisers and producers who had been content to . . . risk their lives as well as their capital, with only a prospect of moderate returns . . . suddenly awoke in the spring of 1882 to the fact that their herds were veritable gold mines. Cows and calves had advanced in a comparatively short space of time from eight to ten dollars a head to thirty and thirty-five dollars per head, while youngsters, yearlings and two-year-olds had advanced almost 300 percent in three years."[59] It is an indication of just how much the new investors lost sight of reason that many bought their cattle without even counting them. In 1888 a United States commission was appointed to investigate problems in the beef industry. One of the highly regarded expert witnesses told the members that

> a great deal of money was sent out from the East and from
> Europe to invest in cattle; and, in numbers of cases, cattle
> were bought at very hgh prices and at book account by men
> who did not know what they were doing, they representing
> large capitalists and syndicates. Therfore, . . . in many instan-
> ces where Texas cattle were bought at twenty dollars, they
> paid forty dollars on the book account. The same thing held
> good in Wyoming Territory, . . . the price there being about
> thirty dollars for stock cattle . . . plenty of sales were made . . .
> where cattle were sold at thirty dollars a head, and on book
> account they cost sixty dollars or more.[60]

If some investors failed to count their cattle, they also paid little attention to quality. "Speculators" as well as "ranchmen who wanted [stock] for breeding purposes" went to the American Midwest to find extra supply to feed the demand. "Stimulated by the high prices" they were willing to pay, the cattlemen in "the Mississippi Valley and the great corn belt" allowed themselves to be "virtually 'skimmed' of cows and heifers" many of which were of such poor quality they had been earmarked for the packinghouse.[61]

How many of the Canadian ranchers bought their initial herds on the basis of book value is unknown. Given, however, the difficulty of getting proper counts of relatively wild stock in places such as Montana where the cowboys rounded up thousands at a time for the sales without enclosed pastures or corrals in which to hold them and take stock, one suspects their own books were at best imprecise. It is clear, too, that even if they did count them they lost an unknown percentage after the drives north. These cattle were all immediately turned loose on the Canadian ranges and, because there were no fences to keep them from straying, many at once instinctively headed back towards the home from which they had come on the other side of the border. McEachran sent a man from the Walrond back down to Montana the summer after he brought in his first several thousand head to claim and gather all the returnees he could find. In this he needed the co-operation of the American contributors. "Charles

Raymond is now in Montana looking for our strays," he told T.C. Power, who had sold him the stock. He "reports quite a number on your range at Warm Spring. Will you please instruct" your hired men "to deliver all cattle branded WR to Raymond? He says Mr. Brooks claims six cattle" of ours "which he says were crippled" and therefore dropped out of the drive north and were never branded. Brooks "has no right to do so. At the time I did object to a few cripples" among the cattle originally purchased "but he would not let us" reject them "and they were driven out into the herds" for the trek north. Some could not keep up and therefore "fell out" and were left along the way to be gathered later. "I would be sorry if Mr. Brooks would give us any trouble, in the face of the fact that I paid you for two of your cattle, which we found in the herd after reaching here" last summer.[62] There was, of course, no guarantee that co-operation would be forthcoming. There was also no way to know how many cattle had died on the return trip south or were stolen by one of a number of rustlers operating in the volatile borderlands regions between the Walrond and Warm Springs.[63]

Therefore, even the Canadian ranchers who took the time to try to count their original cattle could not have known exactly how many animals they had actually been able to keep. There is varied evidence, moreover, indicating that the original herds were typical of many in the American northwest and not of the best quality. In 1887 McEachran reprimanded one of his administrators for overselling the breeding stock. The man assured him that the vast majority he had marketed were sub-standard as there were so many that could be described that way in the original herd. "I have no doubt we killed a few . . . that you would not want killed," he said, but most had various flaws including "big bags" or "big jaws" or were "non-breeders," or "cripples," or "cows as old as to be toothless and consequently almost certain to die within the next year or two." You remember, he said, that the original herd "contained a large number of old cows and we understood that one of the benefits the company would derive from the contract" to provide beef to the Indian bands "would be to turn them into money and get the herd cleaned up."[64] One cowpuncher from the Bar U remembered that in the beginning that outfit "in common with other ranching enterprises . . . was compelled to purchase as its foundation stock, cattle of a low and inferior type." Then, due to the random mixing on the open range, it took years "to weed-out" the inferior animals and replace them with "a better type."[65] As this suggests, small improvement seems to have come in the early years as the big operations brought in better breeding animals from the East and overseas. However, the problem of inferior quality would remain an obstacle to efficient production as long as the range remained open and the inferior bulls and poor cows could mix and mingle with those animals and with each other.[66]

Ultimately, it is thus evident that large-scale, open range ranching got off to a very bad start in the Canadian West. Its product was inferior, much more expensive than it should have been, and, ostensibly, in many cases less plentiful than the owners had been led to expect. These factors contributed to the inevitable collapse that was to be all but complete before the end of the first decade of the twentieth century. They exacerbated the fundamental problem – that to leave cattle to fend for themselves year round in a northern environment with its ferocious winter storms, periodically plunging temperatures, predators, and parasites was, to put it mildly, unrealistic. One of the important findings of this study, discussed below, is that the first big ranches in the Northern Territory of Australia actually succumbed even faster than their western Canadian counterparts. At first this seems puzzling in view of the fact that the natural environment there was to prove much more conducive to the Texas grazing approach than in Canada. The explanation is complex but, as will become evident, largely environmental as well.

3

THE SHORTER HISTORY
OF THE TEXAS SYSTEM IN
NORTHERN AUSTRALIA

At the time the Eastern and British corporations were instigating open range grazing in the Canadian West similar companies, almost all owned by Australians, were introducing it to the Northern Territory. Despite the fact that the men who financed the Australian companies had more grazing experience and more realistic ambitions than their counterparts in Canada, and that the open range system was ultimately to prove amenable to the Territorial environment, their operations were destined to fail at a very rapid pace. Many years after the fact, Alfred Giles, who between 1877 and 1879 drove one of the first big livestock herds to the Territory, remembered that in the southern part of the Territory around Alice Springs "few if any of the original lessers of these great pastoral areas of the Finke River and MacDonnell ranges" survived.[1] Indeed, "all went out" in rapid succession "after suffering enormous losses." To verify this, he said, "one should read the evidence given before the 1897 Pastoral Commission by the late A.G. Downer and published in the *South Australian Gazette and Colonial Register* of May 25, 1926."[2] "It shows that" Edward Mead Bagot and Churchill Smith, the first owners of Undoolya station several miles east of Alice Springs, "lost everything" and Andrew Tennant and John Love to whom they sold that station also "lost heavily." Mr. A.M. Woolridge "with others lost 20,000 pounds in Barrow Creek properties" 200 miles north of Alice Springs. F.A. Grant and F.W. Stokes "lost 50,000 pounds in

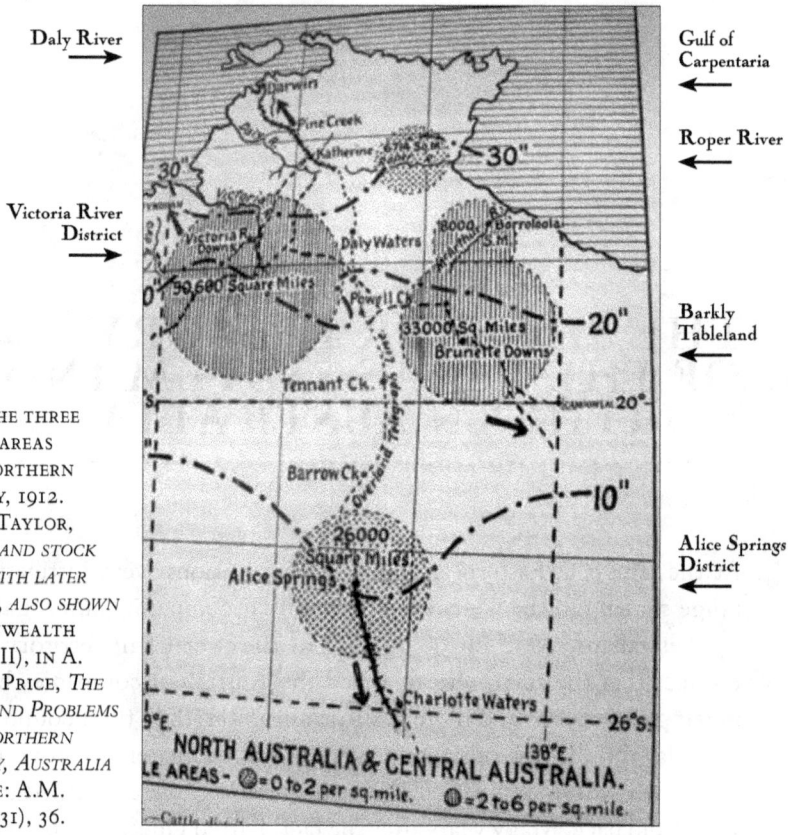

Daly River →

Gulf of Carpentaria ←

Roper River ←

Victoria River District →

Barkly Tableland ←

Alice Springs District ←

MAP OF THE THREE PASTORAL AREAS IN THE NORTHERN TERRITORY, 1912. GRIFFITH TAYLOR, *RAILWAYS AND STOCK ROUTES, WITH LATER ADDITIONS, ALSO SHOWN* (COMMONWEALTH BULLETIN II), IN A. GRENFELL PRICE, *THE HISTORY AND PROBLEMS OF THE NORTHERN TERRITORY, AUSTRALIA* (ADELAIDE: A.M. ACOTT, 1931), 36.

Idracowra" and other ventures on the Finke River south of Alice. "Two young Englishmen, Parker and Walker of Glen Helen" northwest/west of the town "lost everything." Richard Warburton at Horseshoe Bend south of Idracowra "lost heavily," and "the same" applied "to the several early owners of the Crown Point properties south of Horseshoe Bend." The "late Joseph and William Gilbert" also lost a large fortune at Owen Springs in the MacDonnell Range west of Alice Springs.[3] To indicate that the failures were pretty much universal, Giles ended his discussion with the words "and so it goes on." Because he was quoting from the commission report he named properties in the southern pastoral area only. However, he noted that similar losses had been experienced by "scores" of the first pastoralists in the other two grazing districts – the Victoria River area and the Barkly Tableland, both of which were in northern parts of the Territory. The map above shows the three main grazing districts as of 1912.[4]

Giles probably knew as much about Territorial developments generally as anyone. In 1879 he had started the first operating pastoral business at Springvale north of the Daly River near the town of Katherine, and he was often hired by organizations interested in investing in the outback to explore and report on the potential of specific parcels.[5] Unfortunately he did not give an in-depth explanation for the failures he enumerated. The main point here is that one of the reasons the Australian stations declined so rapidly was *not* the same frantic over-estimation of the frontier that afflicted North American investors.

From 1863 to 1911 the Territory was under the administrative control of the state of South Australia. As in Canada, one of the factors that triggered investment was a favourable financial arrangement. Initially pastoral rents had been set at six pence per square mile for the first seven years of a twenty-five-year term and ten shillings per square mile thereafter. With only a few exceptions, potential investors were unwilling to take out leases under those conditions since in the state of South Australia land was available at just two shillings and six pence per square mile per year for an entire twenty-five-year term.[6] In 1881 the regulations were revised to give prospective lessees in the Territory the same deal as in South Australia only with an introductory period of seven years when the charge was just six pence per square mile per year.[7] They were also given three years to stock their land. This helped to set off a wave of new applications. The first stations were, like the great ranches in Canada, relatively speaking very large and in the majority of cases incorporated.

The Territorial environment posed some major challenges to frontier graziers too. The Victoria River district contained the largest of the three pastoral areas. It ran along both sides of the Victoria River with the Daly River to the north and the eastern boundary of West Australia to the west. As mean annual temperatures typically range near 30 degrees Celsius throughout the Territory, the main concern of all cattlemen was (and is) rainfall to sustain both vegetation and animal health. The Victoria River country receives an average of nearly forty inches a year in its northern regions, which is ample. Further south, however, drought is a constant threat, as around fifteen inches is the norm. For stock drinking water, some of the Victoria River district is reasonably well supplied with numerous small lakes or "billabongs" in its undulating terrain that swell in size during the wet season, or "wet," from December through February and fade but do not normally disappear during the long dry season, or "dry," from June through August. In some parts of the district where the grasses are suited to grazing, however, surface water is not what one would describe as plentiful.[8] When asked about the situation on the best-known station – Victoria River Downs – one of the employees stated in 1895 that the company's land was not really "well watered" but that there was "good water on it." He added that "there are . . . many waterholes which could be made good watering places" if dams were constructed.[9] Dams to increase the size of billabongs or to create reservoirs in rivers and streams would undoubtedly have been helpful, but the rough and rocky terrain made carting materials and workers to the appropriate sites difficult and expensive. Most stations eventually drilled for sub-artesian water but the wells varied considerably in depth and in both the quantity and quality of the water.[10] They were also extremely expensive to drill.[11]

In the heavy clay soils of this district there are treeless grasslands, but grasslands with widely spaced eucalyptus shrubs and low trees are more common. Pasture is characterized by several perennial "drought-evading tussock grasses." The commonest of these are Barley Mitchell grass, native panic, blue grasses, feathertop, and Bull Mitchell grass. Normally the spaces between the tussocks also have a fairly dense cover of Flinders grasses and other drought-evading varieties. These mixed species are more nutritious than the Mitchell grass that dominates the Barkly Tableland to the east, and thus the best grazing areas have a "slightly higher carrying capacity" than the latter region.[12] In the Victoria region as in most of the rest of the Territory, cattle tend to do well when new growth grass appears during and immediately following the rainy season but then are liable to stagnate and even lose weight as the grass becomes tall, coarse, and relatively unpalatable.[13]

The Barkly Tableland region runs along the McArthur River in the north and then parallels the west coast of the Gulf of Carpentaria from about 100 miles inland. It extends to the border of the state of Queensland to the southeast. The Alexandria is the largest and probably the best-known cattle station in the region. It is one of only a few corporations in the Northern Territory to endure to modern times under the control of the original owner families. Presumably this is mainly because its first shareholders, Queensland pastoralists Robert, Martin, and William Collins; Sir Thomas McIlwraith; William Forrest; and the proprietor of the *Illustrated London News*, Sir William Ingram, were able to supply the necessary capital to keep it operative through difficult times.[14] The second biggest of the cattle runs was Brunette Downs, which was taken over by New South Wales pastoralist James C. White in 1904 and remained under the control of his extended family until the King ranch of Texas bought it in 1958.[15] Throughout the Tableland the most important grass species for grazing is the tall Mitchell grass, which is hardy with long roots and thus well adapted to dry soils and periods of drought. It predominates over short-lived varieties including Flinders grasses, which tend to come on after the rains. Annual temperatures in the region are about the same as in the Victoria River district. The northern parts receive about thirty inches of rain annually while the southernmost parts receive about twelve inches. Soils are stony or leached and low on phosphorus and other minerals.[16] In its early stages of growth the Mitchell grass is nutritious. However, during the growing season, which is about nineteen weeks in the north and only seven weeks in the south, it also becomes unpalatable as it matures. At that stage cattle graze the more temporary varieties, but as they deplete them they are forced back to the Mitchell grass at which time they might lose weight to the point of morbidity. The Tableland has few sustainable water surfaces. Cattlemen understood that conservation was imperative. Dams across creek beds did not work well because, due to the relatively flat terrain in the region, the waterways are shallow and slow moving and during the long hot "drys" are readily depleted by evaporation.[17] Therefore, sub-artesian wells were needed. However, at the outset cattlemen attempted to operate without them. When drought set in, their herds suffered greatly. Unremitting dry spells occurred in 1883, 1884, and 1889 and conditions were so severe in 1892 and 1893 that "none of the principal watercourses ran" for two and a half years.[18] In 1897 the rains again failed to come; Alexandria Downs lost 5,000 head of cattle and Alroy Downs lost 1,500.[19] At times, moreover, there was sudden torrential rainfall with flash flooding so severe that it could carry off and drown full-grown cattle. And even under normal circumstances, scorching heat during the dry season was a major threat to newborn calves, as the low Eucalyptus trees are too widely spaced to provide adequate shade. Some years many died from exposure.[20]

The southern Alice Springs region is more or less in the centre of the Australian continent. Rainfall is sparse in all parts of this region. From south to north it fluctuates between eight and twelve inches. There is practically no permanent surface water, so here too stock would eventually have to be supplied from sub-artesian bores. The Finke and Palmer Rivers and a multiplicity of creeks – including the McMinn, Maloney's, Five Mile, No 6, and Napplebar – flow through the region, and though they fill to overflowing when the rain comes, often flooding the plains around them, they turn into dry, sandy beds shortly after the rains stop. These rivers and streams feed some fifteen waterholes that normally provide drinking water for longer periods but usually also eventually dry up.[21] The Finke River has nine water holes along its route, though it normally only flows for from a few hours up to a week or two from its headwaters in the midst of the western MacDonnell Mountain Range to the west of Alice.

Due to the sporadic and unreliable nature of the rainfall throughout the year, there is no definite growing season in this region. The bulk of the grazing is done on an assortment of short grasses and broad-leafed herbaceous plants. The grasses generally are the more palatable and nutritious options. Kerosene grass and oat grass are most common after summer precipitation, while broad-leafed varieties such as white and yellow daisy follow wet spells. Initially, particularly in the summer, these species provide good pasturage, but after they are consumed stock are forced to subsist on the less nutritious drought-resisting spiny-leaved tussock-forming grasses loosely referred to as inland spinifex, and on the leaves of Acacia and other shrubs and low trees.[22]

As in the other two regions, corporations predominated among the initial lessees in the Alice Springs area. However, eventually more family operations began to take over there.[23] This seems to be a reflection of the fact that both dry spells and flash floods are somewhat more frequent and less predictable here than in any other parts of the Territory. It thus required a closer hands-on form of management to keep track of the herds and to move them out of harm's way when the rivers overflowed their banks and to drive them to better pastures or to cut out and sell marketable cattle when some grasslands were depleted by incessant heat.[24] Two very well-known properties were settled around Alice Springs well before the big rush for leases in the Northern Territory began and then were

taken over by one family that kept them through to the modern period. In 1872 William J. Gilbert leased the nine hundred square miles of Owen Springs, the first station in the Territory, to the west of the town of Alice Springs and E.M. Bagot leased Undoolya, which covered six hundred square miles to the east of the town. Thereafter the two leases changed hands a number of times before William Hayes, with wife Mary and six children, took over both of them between 1903 and 1908. In the beginning the lessees were dependent on two semi-permanent water sources, the abundant Owen Springs on the Owen Springs station and Emily Gap on Undoolya, which collects water flowing out of the eastern MacDonnell Mountain Range.[25] After they took over the properties the Hayeses drilled and expanded an ever-growing array of wells as and when their financial position permitted.[26]

It is the previous pastoral experience of the owners in all three of the major grazing districts in the Territory that sets them apart from the venture capitalists who headed to western Canada. As we have seen, four out of five of the original partners in Alexandria had been graziers before they headed north. In the Victoria River district, Charles Brown Fisher, an Australian pastoralist originally from London, founded Victoria River Downs, though his partner, Maurice Lyons, was a Melbourne magistrate. Nat Buchanan, co-owner at Wave Hill in the same district, was a famous explorer, drover, and Queensland cattleman.[27] E.M. (Ned) Bagot, the first investor in Undoolya, was a railway contractor, stock and station agent, and pastoralist from Kapunda in South Australia.[28] William Gilbert was also a cattleman from that state. Dr. William James Browne, who leased three runs – Springvale near Katherine on the Katherine River in the far north, Newcastle Waters on the western edge of the Tableland, and Delamere in the Victoria River region – was an English-born Melburnian who had a chain of stations in South Australia when he took out his Territorial leases.[29] Sir Thomas Elder, who purchased the Owen Springs station years before the Hayes family bought it, was a founding partner in Elder, Smith & Co, which over the years built up a grazing conglomerate stretching across the continent. F.A. Grant and F.W. Stokes, who took over Glen Helen and Idracowra in the early 1890s, brought in their stock from their Bendleby station in South Australia.[30]

One reason why pastorally naive venture capitalists of the sort that appeared on the western Canadian frontier were not drawn to the outback was the relative scarcity of print media hyperbole promoting the region in the years preceding and shortly after settlement began. True, there were some rather widely read expressions of hope that this opening land would be productive. However, compared to many enthusiastic descriptions of the northern Great Plains, the media accounts about this region were relatively moderate. Probably those that got the most public attention were the reports of explorer Alexander Forrest. In 1879 Forrest led a party from Perth on the western coast of the state of West Australia through to Katherine. He kept a journal, and extracts from it were published in southern urban newspapers. Along with the party's various tribulations, including having to butcher and eat some of their own horses to avoid starvation, Forrest described in relatively restrained tones some "twenty millions of acres, suitable for pastoral purposes" and even a large area he felt could be utilized "for the growth of sugar, coffee, and rice."[31] Other favourable comments were contained in one or two documents written by officials working for the South Australian government, whom one might expect to have positive views about the land they administered.[32] The country near Delamere station in the Victoria River district "produces herbs and grasses of a most fattening character, similar to many that are found on some of the best cattle stations in Queensland," the Government Resident at Palmerston reported on the basis of very little evidence in 1883.[33] After buying out his partner in 1886, Charles Fisher was forced by financial difficulties to seek shareholders in Britain.[34] Instead of taking this as an ominous sign about the industry in general, the Government Resident gleefully announced "the beginning of a new epoch in Northern Territory pastoral occupation." Up to now "the northern portion of the Territory has been depending almost entirely upon the enterprise and capital" of Australians. "In securing the active co-operation of English investors who possess large city connections, after most careful investigation on their part of the freehold land and leases, the suitability of the soil and climate for stock breeding and fattening and cultivation has received a signal confirmation." What Fisher had done was form the Northern Territory Pastoral Company to take over his holdings, which included the Victoria River Downs station, and raised some 300,000 pounds sterling on the London stock market.[35] In 1889 the company would back out of the arrangement and let the holdings revert to the original mortgagee, Goldsborough, Mort and Company of Adelaide. The shareholders were later to sue Fisher and Goldsborough, Mort in the Court of Chancery in London for fraud.[36] Local Territorial newspapers that were anxious to "boost" business through increased settlement were also inclined to offer optimistic estimates of the Territory's pastoral resources. The "magnificent" land on the Barkly Tableland, the *Northern Territory Times* predicted, "will be the choice of the Territory, for it is second to none for fattening qualities, and growing wool."[37]

However, none of the representations one finds in print exuded the wild enthusiasm that James Cox identified with respect to the North American ranching frontiers. Moreover, while the Australian press displayed admiration for Texan ranchers and their methods it was also prepared to acknowledge their financial challenges. In 1879 the *Brisbane Courier*, citing the *Weekly Drovers' Journal*, stated: "even the highest average prices named for the best cattle" in recent times in Britain "do not exceed 17 s[hillings] 8 [pence] for bullocks and 10 s[hillings] for cows per 100 lb." This, it argued, should "dispel the idea . . . of shipping" live cattle to England from Australia "seeing that, even at the above prices, the Americans do not find the traffic very remunerative."[38] In 1880 the *Northern Star* warned that "the margin in the cattle driving business is now considered so close" in Texas "that buyers hesitate before they close a contract. Profits are estimated by cents, almost, where they were formerly calculated by dollars."[39]

One fact that requires an explanation from anyone attempting to ex-onerate the Australians of over-exuberance is the vastness of their hold-ings. Most of the Territorial stations make the great ranches on the north-ern Great Plains look tiny; and only part of the difference can be explained by disparate carrying capacity of the natural grasslands in the individual regions. Lessees anticipated that the ratio of cattle to area in the two more northern grazing districts in the Northern Territory would be one animal for from every forty to around ninety acres. Initially, the Canadian ranch-ers thought they would be able to run one cow or cow/calf pair or year-ling steer for every ten acres.[40] Thus one might expect the bigger holdings down under to be from four to nine times the size of the Canadian ones, when in fact they tended on average to be from five to nearly ninety times larger. In 1888 the bigger Canadian ranches leased from 10,000 to 300,000 acres and the average amount of land per ranch was about 30,000 acres.[41] At one time the Cochrane and Walrond each held about 300,000 acres, the Oxley 216,640 acres, and Bar U 157,940 acres. The biggest in-vestors in the northern regions of the Northern Territory were Fisher and Lyons. By 1881 they had leased 34,000 *square miles* (21,760,000 acres) for four separate stations and they had also purchased 40,772 acres. Including improvements, their total initial investment was apparently nearly a quar-ter million pounds sterling (about $1,250,000). Dr. William Browne leased 2,848 square miles (1,834,963 acres) for his three stations;[42] John Costello at Lake Nash and the Limmen Bight leased 11,044 square miles (7,068,160acres);[43] the Northern Australia Pastoral Company's Alexandria station covered some 12,243 square miles (7,835,520 acres);[44] the Guthrie family's Avon Downs, to the south of the latter, covered over 2,000 square miles (1,280,000 acres);[45] and to the west and north Brunette Downs, Eva Downs, and Walhallow station had at one stage, under a single own-ership, a total of 10,000 square miles (6,400,000 acres).[46] Around Alice Springs the leases were smaller. However, even there they were many times bigger than the *average* corporation ranches in Canada.[47] J. Gilbert's Owen Springs, for instance, encompassed 1,200 square miles, or 768,000 acres; Undoolya 1,199 square miles, or 767,360 acres;[48] and Idracowra covered a total of 3,034 square miles, or 1,941,760 acres.[49]

Moreover, for many years the Australians never approached grasslands capacity in terms of herd numbers – unlike the Canadians, who, as we will see, severely overgrazed. A survey published after a thorough onsite assessment of the runs in the Barkly region as late as 1923 noted that virtually none of them had yet reached the point of overuse. Newcastle Waters, which could have been running 24,220 head based on the feed its pastures produced, had a mere 8,269 cattle and 780 horses;[50] Anthony Lagoon Cattle Station, covering 1,260 square miles and with an estimated grass carrying capacity of 15,120 head, had 2,196 cattle and 290 horses;[51] Brunette Downs, capable of running 89,060 head, had 20,461 cattle and 742 horses;[52] and Alexandria, which by then had enough land for 160,000 head of cattle, had a mere 42,962.[53] Evidence suggests that in the other two major pastoral regions the tendency was also to undergraze. For instance, in the 1890s the Victoria River Downs station, which had 8,264 square miles of land and which, according to one of its principal participants, had yet to properly develop its waterholes, was running 30,000 cattle and 500 horses when it might have grazed three to six times that many.[54] Undoolya, then under Tennant and Love, leased 1,100 square miles in 1883 for 4,000 cattle when its pastures could have carried at least double that number.[55]

On the basis of such statistics it could be argued that the Northern Territorians simply lost sight of reality when they applied for their leases by laying claim to far more land than they could ever hope to stock. On close examination, however, size appears to reflect practical thinking on the part of the owners rather than unjustified euphoria. Previous grazing experience had taught the principal investors in the Territory that the major potential challenge to their industry in almost any region of the country was aridity and drought. It would be going too far to suggest that all these men had been open range pastoralists before they headed to the new frontier. Many of the stations in the more southern regions of the country were closer to what might be called large mixed farms than ranches. In southern Queensland, New South Wales, and much of South Australia they cultivated fields and harvested grains and most ran more sheep than cattle. However, the majority of operations incorporated a significant grazing component and the owners undoubtedly understood what the greatest natural threat to their industry was continent wide.[56] Above all, these cattlemen knew to be concerned about the possibility that extended periods without rain could cause a lot of the surface water to dry up altogether, leaving thousands of cattle in danger of dying from thirst.[57] The more land they held, they reckoned, the more natural supplies of water they were likely to find and the less likely this dire possibility. As they took over their new leases, their personnel scoured every inch of them for each and every river, creek, and billabong. Jeannie Gunn recalled, "We breakfasted at the Springs, surrounded by the soft forest beauty; ate our dinner . . . and spent the afternoon looking for a lost water-hole. . . . All we knew was that it was there . . . somewhere in that corner of the run – a deep permanent hole." It took "long wanderings and futile excursions up gullies and by-ways" to locate it.[58] In 1890 one of the founding partners in the Alexandria run told the Government Resident that "we started out in 1882 with 2,000 cattle principally breeders," then we "bought 2,000 more. The cattle have increased moderately well, our herds now numbering over 10,000 head." However: "we found the country very indifferently watered, in fact there was not a drop of permanent water on any part of the 10,000 square miles we originally held. We have spent considerable sums of money in conserving water, partly in making dams and partly, and to greater advantage, by sinking wells; but the cost of labour is so excessive that we have been unable to make" these "improvements keep pace with the increase in our stock." The man confessed he lived in constant fear. "We are well aware that we are running a tremendous risk, and in any exceptionally dry season may lose a large proportion of our stock."[59]

There was good reason for such caution. At times, despite it, some stations lost heavily when the rains did not come. "At many of the" depleted "waterholes quantities of dead cattle are lying rotting on the banks and polluting what little water there is to such an extent as to make it unserviceable for both man and beast," a newspaper article announced in 1883.[60] Along with their own past history, such occurrences convinced pastoralists that they could not be confident about the success of their industry in the Northern Territory until sufficient water supplies were secured. The media stoked this conviction. "No surface water between Renner Springs and Anthony's Lagoon" on the Barkly Tableland, the *Northern Territory Times* noted in 1894, continuing: "Boring party at Brunette [Downs] struck unlimited water in No. 1 and No. 2 bore at 180 ft., but sinking continued to 250 ft. Now boring in No. 3." The amount of water found in this last well was expected to indicate much about "the future of the pastoral industry. It is generally conceded that given a plentiful supply . . . the . . . tableland will develop into one of the finest and richest pastoral areas to be found in the Commonwealth." [61]

The pastoralists who ventured into the Northern Territory in the late nineteenth century were actually trying to minimize their risks by leasing larger tracts of land than they needed to support the number of cattle they brought in to stock them. They believed that the more land they had, the greater chance of finding a pool or two or three of fresh drinking water hidden here and there that might save their stock when the hot Australian sun scorched the land and the rains failed them. Obviously they were not always successful, but given the climatic setting of their new hinterland they had the right approach. True, this did not prevent the first round of them from going quickly out of business, but it certainly made their position somewhat less precarious. As we will now see, the widespread failure of the first round of leaseholders in the Northern Territory was the result of a lot of other rather complex and largely insurmountable challenges.

4

THE OUTBACK FRONTIER

Alfred Giles noted in later years that "the failures of the leaders" in the Northern Territory became "the successes of the followers."[1] What he meant was that once the pioneering pastoralists were gone, those who took over their properties were able to use what they had learned and what they had invested to rebuild the grazing industry on a secure footing. That they would also continue to rely on the Texas grazing approach confirms that the problem in the earliest period was not that that system was out of step with climate and ecology. The more germane explanation is that challenges that the graziers encountered in the initial phase of settlement were insurmountable. This chapter argues that it was those "start-up" challenges that destined them to fall away one by one even more rapidly than their counterparts in western Canada.

In 1895 a commission was appointed by the South Australian government to examine why the industry had not managed to gain a secure footing in the Territory. While gathering information the commissioners interviewed one of the principal players from the Victoria River Downs station.[2] When a member asked him why the industry had struggled so he listed six basic factors. Each was either directly or indirectly related to an obstacle the cattlemen had encountered in the process of setting up their businesses. The first was the "very heavy expense that had to be incurred in taking stock to the stations"; the second, "the distance from market, and the difficulty in securing buyers for the surplus stock"; third, "the extensive staff that had to be kept up to protect the stock from blacks"; fourth, "the high rate of wages"; fifth, "the expense of carriage of stores";

and sixth, a bovine disease that had attacked the incoming herds.[3] While all of these issues impacted the Canadian cattle industry too in its initial stage, only one did so as severely.

Before viewing each of these important factors in detail we need to recognize that there were two that the man from Victoria River Downs did not mention and that were also considerably more problematic in the Territory than on the northern Great Plains. The first was the station owners' lack of familiarity with the land at the time when they chose the parcels they were going to lease. Virtually all frontiers are, almost by definition, remote, with the concomitant reality that the people who first invest in them cannot have a thorough understanding of all their basic attributes. The Australians had a reasonably good grasp of the climate in much of their country and they understood pastoral conditions and requirements in their home state. However, the Northern Territory was very distant from their businesses in southern Queensland, New South Wales, or South Australia and difficult to access. There was no rail transportation in and, as the Alexander Forrest expedition made all too clear, travel to the interior by horse was an extremely difficult and arduous undertaking. For that reason the first station owners had to do some educated guessing when it came time to deciding where to locate. Many thus chose some or all their lands in areas where ecological circumstances were simply inappropriate for grazing purposes. Tropical Australia is the largest of these areas. It is in what is known as the "top end" of the Territory – the northern tip, above the area around the Daly River on the west side and the Roper River on the east. This region has lots of rainfall and fairly abundant natural drinking water. However, deficiencies of phosphates, nitrogen, and various metals in the soil inhibit the nutritional value of the vegetation. Moreover, heavy tropical rainforests overwhelm the native grasses in much of the area. In places that are not heavily treed, the grass is nutritious during the initial spring growing season but then grows too high, developing faster than in any other part of the Territory. The initial herds the cattlemen brought in could not come close to keeping it grazed down as it shot up to over four feet in height. At that stage digestion became not just difficult but impossible. In the midst of abundance, the animals would literally starve – in many cases, to death.[4]

The first two well-known failures in the top end were Glencoe station and Springvale. The owners took out their leases before the 1881 legislation was passed, but they may well have got a special deal by negotiating with the government.[5] Whatever the case, the new regulations would have been available to both stations from 1881 on. Roderick Travers and Albert William Sergison started Glencoe on the Adelaide River east of Palmerston in 1877.[6] Sergison had visited and explored parts of the Territory around the Katherine, Adelaide, and Daly Rivers as a government employee and had extolled its potential as an agricultural region.[7] The partners seem to have believed his written claims that one could make a healthy profit on a fast turnover. They started stocking the station with eight thousand cattle in 1879.[8] The next year two wealthy businessmen from Melbourne, Charles Fisher and Maurice Lyons, bought the station with visions of making it the headquarters for a Northern Territory empire.[9] In 1881 they hired Nat Buchanan to drive another twenty thousand cattle in from Queensland. Fisher and Lyons then took out leases to start up Gerowie and Marrakai Stations further upstream. Disaster followed. Glencoe "was prettily situated on the banks of a wide lagoon . . . tall bamboos" lined "the banks of the stream" and "nice-looking open black soil flats" underlay what appeared to be lush grasslands. However, as one pioneer put it, "one can't judge a book by its cover, and though the first cattle delivered there . . . did fairly well – probably because they had the pick of the sparse top feed" – those that arrived later "died in the hundreds soon after delivery."[10] In 1883 the partners moved their headquarters and much of their stock to their Victoria River Downs lease.[11] The two men did not recover from their early losses, however. Within a few years they were forced to seek investors in England and then to give up control of their holdings to Goldsborough, Mort and Company of Melbourne. In 1886 an assessor for the law firm representing the latter company reported that all the country bordering the Adelaide River on the east side and stretching some thirty miles inland is "worthless for pastoral purposes, being only swamps with rushes" and very coarse grass. He advised "the abandonment" of this and other portions of the lease, as "there is no advantage in paying rent however small for country not likely to be utilized for many years."[12] The firm accepted this advice.

Springvale was located 200 miles south of Palmerston on the banks of the Katherine River a few miles north of the Daly River system, and as such also in the top end. After reaching the lease with the first cattle and sheep in 1879, Alfred Giles stayed on to run it and the two other

Northern Territory properties owned by Dr. Browne. Browne appears also to have been influenced by Sergison's writing. Losses were severe at Springvale and eventually its stock had to be moved to Browne's other stations – Delamere and Newcastle Waters. By 1886 Browne was in financial trouble and by May 1887 he was forced to abandon all three runs.[13] Giles remained at Springvale until 1894 running cattle, horses, and sheep but on a much-reduced scale. George McKeddie, a Darwin merchant, purchased the operation in 1896. However, thereafter it was never revived as an active station and eventually the government turned it into a heritage site. Delamere and Newcastle, in better localities, were eventually taken over by bona fide cattlemen and operated into the modern era.[14]

There were numerous other failures in the top end.[15] Many of the first pastoralists who leased outside this area discovered that, within otherwise good pastoral regions, there were also substantial pockets of land that were marginal or worse due to factors, or combinations of them, that included very rugged terrain, thin soils, insufficient water, and/or rank grass.[16] In central Australia and the Tableland, sand plains with spinifex that is too sparse for pasture are scattered here and there, particularly in the southern extremities.[17] And all the land along the coastal regions running from 50 to 150 miles inland in the Victoria River and most of the Tableland districts is unsuited to grazing for basically the same reasons as those found in the top end – the soil is mineral deficient and for a substantial time of the year the vegetation is too coarse for the cattle to digest.[18] In the early 1880s, John Costello started his first massive station near the mouth of the Roper and Limmen Rivers, which flow into the Gulf of Carpentaria on the far eastern side of the top end. He was forced to move inland and south to Lake Nash on the Tableland near the Queensland border after only a few years mainly because of the poor quality of the grasslands. As we will see, he never recovered from his early losses.

From the late 1880s, having now had time to observe the peculiarities of the land, men who took over any of the original leases after the first round of pastoralists had left gave up the worst parts of them. In his 1893 annual report, the Government Resident pointed to a process of decline in area leased and stocked that had started some six years earlier. "On looking at past records I find that in the year 1888 the revenue from our pastoral lands reached the highest figure, viz., 26,371 pounds. The following year there was a slight decrease, and since the year 1890 there has been a falling off at the rate of between 4,000 and 5,000 pounds annually, until last year, when the decrease was 2,622 pounds."[19] This, he surmised was "chiefly due to the fact that lessees are retaining only the best of the country." It was also because station owners who increased their holdings in the better areas were able to take advantage of the provisions of the 1881 legislation that allowed the first seven years of all new leases at 6 pence per square mile. Still the total leased area continued to fall. During 1892 and 1893 some 36,000 square miles were given up and fresh leases taken out comprising only 29,380 square miles. The Government Resident believed this was a very bad deal for the state of South Australia. "The result is that the annual revenue derived from all our pastoral lands, at the present time, amounts to the miserable sum of 9,000 pounds; and when it is considered that 5,000 pounds is being expended" from the public purse "in assisting the exportation of stock, that a large portion of the moneys voted for police protection and mail services, is for the benefit of pastoralists, and that 2,710 pounds has been expended during the last two years in boring operations" it is evident "that the industry does not exhibit a very satisfactory state of things."[20]

The Canadian ranchers would also have been better off had they been more familiar with the geographic location to which they were transferring large amounts of their wealth in the later nineteenth century. They did, however, have a slight advantage over the Australians, which would ultimately help them survive a little longer. They were able to get a somewhat better view of the land before they leased it and, therefore, to pick out the best (or least bad) portions of it. Even before the completion of the Canadian Pacific Railway through to Calgary in 1883, men who were interested in investing were able to make their way to the opening frontier by travelling along the St. Lawrence River from Montreal to Kingston via the Grand Truck Railway, then by steamer across the Great Lakes to Chicago, by rail from Chicago to St. Paul, Minnesota, and by steamer again up the Missouri River to Fort Benton, Montana. From there they could ride horseback the last few hundred miles north to Calgary.[21] It was a fairly demanding trip but nothing compared to what it would have been from southern regions of Australia to the outback of the Northern Territory. From 1883 on, of course, the Canadian Pacific Railway gave much more rapid and relatively convenient access to the Canadian West to anyone who wanted it. Thus the majority of the cattlemen managed to locate in the high country of the foothills, the Milk River Ridge, or the Cypress Hills where the rough fescue was the most lush and where evergreen and aspen trees, cut banks, and steep hillsides offered animals some protection.[22] This obviously did not save the stock from dying in droves, particularly in the winter, but it helped more of the ranches to survive longer than would otherwise have been the case.

Though the Victoria River Downs representative did not list the cost of poorly chosen land as one of his six issues when addressing the commission in 1895, he clearly understood that it was a factor. Speaking of his own station's coastal regions he said that "when the south-east monsoon blows" these regions are "excessively dry, and . . . there is no pasturage . . . whatever. About, November, thunderstorms come up, and from then to February you have some 70 in[ches] of rain, with intense heat. This brings up a flush of grass, which is only useful for cattle" when it is "very young." After that it rises "above the backs of the cattle" and "you can hardly see through it when riding."[23]

The other significant factor this man did not list was the capital that too many Australians wasted trying to get into the sheep industry. In the beginning there was great optimism about the potential of the opening north for a viable wool and mutton trade. In 1881 a reporter chatted with the manager of the Glencoe station and questioned the wisdom of running sheep considering the coarseness of the grass. The manager assured him that "when the country gets well stocked . . . both cattle and sheep will thrive well" because "in time . . . in every country the feed becomes finer and richer for being eaten off."[24] Reasoning of that sort persisted even as the years passed and the industry failed to materialize. "When I stop to think and compare" the "miles of well-watered country, in the Victoria River district . . . with other parts of Australia," a newspaper editor mused some two decades later, "I feel it to be a thousand pities that" the people in those other parts "were not blessed with this magnificent country – or, I should rather say, that the Territory is not blessed with the presence of a few of these struggling settlers to its own and their advantage . . . This is admittedly the best pastoral country in the Territory for all classes of stock, and I predict that some day these plains will be covered with hundreds of thousands of sheep."[25]

Virtually everywhere pastoralists tried sheep, however, they abandoned them, and in the great majority of cases they did so after a very short period. During the 1880s, Austral Downs on the Queensland border carried 19,000 sheep and 1,400 head of mixed cattle and in 1884 Milne River station, Louisa Downs, and Austral Downs also on the Tableland were making "extensive improvements for sheep."[26] All four stations continued in the business for only a few years.[27] In 1885 the Government Resident in Palmerston announced enthusiastically that Victoria River Downs was about to start up a large sheep component. In 1893 he noted "with regret" that Goldsbrough, Mort and Company, which had taken over the station by that time, had "decided to relinquish sheep-breeding and that the flock has been sold."[28] The one station that kept sheep "successfully" for decades was Avon Downs on the Barkly. It finally sold out in 1919.[29]

Stations gave various reasons for giving up. The small animals were relatively slow moving and comparatively weak, and predation was high. After speaking of the industry in 1895 a manager at Victoria River Downs stated that Native depredations were "one of the great causes of loss and failure."[30] In the early years animal predators were bad in some regions too. "Stock of all sorts do remarkably well and increase rapidly," Sergeant Major W.G. Stretton reported from the Borroloola police headquarters in 1890, "except sheep, which are so harassed by dingoes and eagles during lambing time that very few lambs can be saved."[31] The dingoes must have been particularly troublesome. Many years later researchers at the Fortescue River recorded that many of the beasts learned to hunt and kill sheep very quickly and were actually slaughtering them for sport.[32]

Flooding also at times greatly reduced the flocks. Throughout the Northern Territory the sheep were often victims of flash flooding. In one incident reported by a frontiersman's biographer, "the wide, swift overflow of the rivers swept to death many of the stock on the low, flooded flats and, in other places, trapped them on the . . . long islands" that "became inundated as the rapidly rising waters rose to abnormal heights."[33] Anywhere that drinking water was scarce, moreover, sheep were less able to cope than larger grazing stock. At most, sheep can graze three to five miles from a water source. Once the grass got eaten down in a wider radius than that by the somewhat more mobile cattle they would lose weight and often die either of thirst or malnutrition.[34] Heat and unpalatable grass also presented huge challenges. When the sheep Alfred Giles brought to Springvale proved not viable he stocked Delamere and Newcastle Waters and lost heavily on those stations too. After Dr. Browne sold out in 1887, Giles reported all the setbacks he had encountered at the three stations.

> For fattening and healthy condition of the sheep we found the wet season preferable. After the first heavy rains the grass grew so rapidly that we could put three flocks at the one camp . . . The sheep kept the grass fed down within an area of three miles, but outside that area the grass grew coarse to a height of from 6–10 feet that was like a boundary fence. At the end of the wet season this grass "forest" had to be burnt off. The trouble was, however, that as soon as the first new crop was eaten off it never grew a second time until the next wet season. This necessitated shifting the flocks about every fortnight or three weeks . . . As the dry seaon extended, so did the grass disappear and the sheep lost condition they had gained in the wet season . . . All varieties of grasses produced seed detrimental to wool, but some, such as the spear and black grass, were simply deadly. The latter, especially, was so penetrating that its seeds would work their way gradually through to the bowels of the sheep and many died from that cause. We tried one lambing in the dry season, just before the wet set in, but the result was most disappointing. The lambs were small and miserable, the ewes were poor and had no milk and deserted their lambs. We next tried lambing in the wet season, which is the hot season, but here we had a fresh and unexpeccted set-back, for while the ewes were in fine condition with plenty of milk and the lambs strong and healthy, the terrible heat of the sun scorched the young lambs' backs so serioulsy that the tender wool was shed and the skin simply shrivelled and wrinkled up and scores of the young lambs died.[35]

The peak year for sheep numbers in the Territory was 1891 when there were just over 99,000. By 1898 the total had dwindled to just over 64,000 and by 1910, when there were over half a million cattle, there were only 55,000 sheep.[36]

The amount of money stations lost (or wasted) investing in the smaller, more fragile animals cannot be estimated in any very realistic way, but there is no question that few could afford this in the earliest period when they were facing numerous other costs. Running sheep was expensive compared to running cattle. It was necessary to hire a large labour force to herd and protect them, to build huts for both men and sheep, and to erect numerous fenced yards or corrals. It was also essential to buy a wool press and other equipment for shearing. One or two exceptions aside, ranchers in the Canadian West largely avoided the industry. Sheep were originally banned there because it was felt they grazed the grass so low to the ground that they would kill it, and, presumably, also to avoid the range wars that had broken out between sheep men and cattlemen south of the border.[37]

Of the six factors the man from Victoria River Downs did pinpoint when listing the problems in the early industry, the one that was more costly by the greatest amount in Australia than in Canada was trailing in the initial herds. Most of the cattle for the more northern parts of the Northern Territory came from Queensland to the east. In the late 1870s and early 1880s the cattle business in that state was concentrated mostly in the far southern regions and, therefore, even when supplying the Barkly Tableland the stock had to be driven nearly a thousand miles. For the Victoria River area the distances could be more than twice that. A percentage of the cattle were also brought into these areas from New South Wales to the south of Queensland, in which case the distances were even greater. The region around Alice Springs was supplied principally from South Australia. The cattle normally came from the far southern parts of that state as well and, therefore, it might be necessary to drive them some eight hundred to well over twelve hundred miles. In all areas a diverse assortment of obstacles stood in the way. Alfred Giles put it in heroic terms when reflecting back on the entire process. A general account of the movement of stock to the frontier, he said, would be "a history of . . . pioneers, drovers and their attendants who doggedly determined to get there, in the face of almost insufferable obstacles. Alternately blocked by floods, droughts, impassable scrubs [thick bush], hostile savages, sickness and death," these men "ever kept their faces towards their objective, in some cases thousands of miles from their starting point."[38]

For their own nearly two-year trek from South Australia to Springvale, Giles and his brother Arthur engaged a huge contingent of men, stock

MEN SCOOPING WATER FROM DRY STREAM BED. NATIONAL LIBRARY OF AUSTRALIA, CANBERRA, PIC-AN557686-V, GEORGE HAMILTON, ARTWORK, 1840.

horses, drays, wagons, and saddlery and they carted in stores at the exorbitant price of "30 pounds and 45 pounds a ton from Port Augusta" on the southwest coast of South Australia.[39] The crew carried "ploughs and scoops so to trench" dry riverbeds when there was no other way to get water. They even hauled along their own "well sinking party" and "iron troughs" to find and contain the precious liquid when all else failed. When they reached Leighs Creek, one of Dr. Browne's properties just south of the Northern Territory border, they encountered "great difficulties and setbacks as the whole country was in a deplorable dry state" and there was "a total absence of feed." The cattle must have suffered tremendously during that period and Giles had to buy "chaff" for the draught and stock horses at thirty-five shillings per bag.[40] On the other side of the border the drovers "encountered . . . a perilous 105 miles waterless stage" in which they were forced to rely on their scoops to save themselves and their stock and then monsoonal rains and the treacherous, overflowing waters of Newcastle River.[41]

How many cattle perished on that trip is not known, but evidently the numbers lost on all the cattle drives in the early years were enormous. "Twenty seven thousand head . . . left Moodie and Richmond Downs and other N[ew] S[south] Wales properties for the . . . stations in 1879 and until 1883 the 18,000 odd that arrived safely . . . were constantly on the road and being delivered."[42] In 1880 Nat Buchanan brought in the 20,000 head of mixed cattle for Glencoe in five lots of 4,000. Buchanan had to divide them into ten separate groups of around 2,000 and to employ seventy men all told "for five months."[43] Crocodiles in the northern rivers frequently stampeded the cattle, and when one deliriously thirsty bunch of cattle arrived at the mouth of the Robinson River in the northern part of the Territory they "rushed" into the water only to discover that it was undrinkable due to the salt content. The animals panicked and "there was a rather bad smash. Some went mad and got beyond control. A few were steered to fresh water further upstream, and others reached it by themselves and were picked up later by drovers; but a great number were lost." Near Katherine, "early storms had swollen the Elsey River" and when a bunch of cattle reached it the head stockman neglected to chase "a few coachers" across first to encourage the others to follow. When the herd leaders thus got well out into the stream they lost their nerve and turned back. "The weight and crush of the mob [i.e., the herd] behind smothered and drowned seventy of them."[44]

The expense of cartage, as the man testifying before the 1895 commission noted, was also enormously onerous, and this continued to be the case when it came to bringing in provisions after the original herds were in because transportation systems were so poor. True, the Australian cattlemen, like the Canadians, needed only limited supplies once they reached their leases. However, what they did need cost them dearly. They did not fence the open range either, but they too required small enclosed paddocks around their home place to keep their working horses accessible and to hold bullocks for short periods after the musters to ready them for the long drive to market. Many stations also built short line fences of barbed wire to help them direct their herds to gathering corrals during the mustering process. And, of course, all the pioneers needed assorted outbuildings for various purposes. Typically these included "a large store, blacksmith's shop, harness-house, beef house, kitchen, cellar, cart shed, milking and horse yards, [and] stone tank" for watering stock. The buildings were not luxurious.[45] Most were constructed of galvanized iron sheeting and wood or stone found locally.[46]

However, all the construction materials and equipment, whether iron for roofing or barbed wire and nails for fences or stoves for cooking, had to be carted overland via the cattle trails or shipped to Darwin from southern centres such as Brisbane, Sydney, or Melbourne and then hauled thousands of miles to the stations. In response to Giles's request to put up fifteen or twenty miles of fence at Springvale in 1886, Browne pleaded that "with cartage at present prices," this "would ruin the Bank of England."

> My outlay up to the present time is most alarming. I really cannot make any improvements that can possibly be done without. When you first wrote about [the first] . . . seven miles or so of fencing I did not like to say no to it but now hearing from you as to the cost and seeing the great deficit account . . . [and seeing] the urgent necessity for diminished outlay every where especially in the N. Territory where I fear already it will take some time even with a successful increase of stock to represent it, I must ask you to review all your operation and see if you can by any means reduce the present outlay and as to fencing to keep cattle in bounds we must consider as quite beyond our means at present. In the old days of our cattle business we never created fences on our . . . runs to keep them from straying but trusted our stockmen. I must ask you to do now as you remember we did then and make no improvements nor incur any outlay that you can possibly do without until the stations are at least paying working expenses.[47]

Browne was running desperately short of capital at this time. He ended his lecture with the words "so if you have bought wire for this fence please sell it again."

It was only after they had built basic infrastructure to house themselves and their personnel and to exercise limited control over their stock that the Australians could think of boring water wells in strategic locations on their leases. Some of them drilled one or two, or as in the case of Alexandria a few, of what in later years would become a whole network of watering facilities throughout their runs. This was a most expensive undertaking and cartage was a big part of the cost because very bulky drilling equipment had to be brought in along with men and provisions, usually from Brisbane on Queensland's east coast. As we will see, the financial charges could well prove to be the final and insurmountable blow to solvency.

For the first Canadian ranchers neither trailing in the cattle nor hauling in materials and supplies was nearly as challenging as it was for the Australian pastoralists. Most of the first Canadian cattle came from Montana and, by walking them north via the level plains to the east of the foothills during the comparatively mild summer months, the drovers normally escaped climatic extremes. Along the way, moreover, they were never short of water. Ample drinking water for men and beasts was provided by the Musselshell, Missouri, and Marias Rivers and Cutbank, French, Lodge, and Sun Creeks in Montana and by the Milk, Old Man, South Saskatchewan, Bow, and Highwood Rivers and too many streams to enumerate on the Canadian side. Moreover, the distances the first Canadian cattlemen had to cover were small in comparison to those faced by the first Northern Territorians. The Canadians purchased most of their stock from brokers either at Fort Benton or Warm Springs, Montana, both of which were under 100 miles south of the international border. Since most of the Canadian ranches were no more than twice that distance on the other side, few had to trail their herds more than 400 to 500 miles. At eight to ten miles a day the journey could be made in weeks rather than months or years. One or two notable exceptions aside, it was usually accomplished without incident.[48] Once they got their herds to their leases the Canadian cattlemen needed basic infrastructure too, but the railway made it possible to bring in all other goods and services efficiently and at a relatively reasonable cost.[49]

Another expense named by the man from Victoria River Downs that was greater in Australian than in Canada in the earliest period was wages for the stockmen. It does seem doubtful that the Territorial cattlemen had to hire more men relative to the number of stock they were running, since after the 1886–87 winter the Canadians had to take on extra staff to put up feed for their weaker and more vulnerable animals and then to feed it to them during inclement weather.[50] However, account books kept by Goldsborough, Mort and Company, now in the National University Archives in Canberra, and by the Walrond ranch, now in the Glenbow Archives in Calgary, illustrate that the Australians did pay more per man. In 1909 the top stockman at Victoria River Downs, R. Townsend, was receiving more than 41 pounds a month, which was equivalent to about 205 dollars and in 1910 he got a raise to 61 pounds or 305 dollars. His counterpart on the Walrond ranch was paid from 150 to 200 dollars a month in the same period. The average wage on the Victoria River Downs station for regular rank-and-file stockmen and station hands was between 6 pounds and 15 pounds a month for an average of about 14½ pounds or 72 dollars. The regular cowboys on the Walrond ranch got 35 to 40 dollars a month.[51] One important reason for the difference was that the population in the Northern Territory was so much smaller than that in western Canada. When pastoralists began the movement to their respective frontiers, the numbers of non-Natives in the opening lands on both continents was, of course, very small. But in southern Alberta and Saskatchewan the newcomer population expanded more quickly with and after the arrival of the cattle, growing to one hundred thousand by the end of the first decade of the twentieth century. In the Northern Territory there were still fewer than eight thousand new settlers when South Australia took control in 1911.[52] This reflected the difference in accessibility and, one suspects, also to some extent, in the amount of literature extolling the respective frontiers.

The man from Victoria River Downs seems to have been correct in intimating that the other reason for relatively higher wages in the Northern Territory was related to Aboriginal hostility and predation. In a later chapter this factor will be examined in considerable detail.[53] Here, let it suffice to say that racial conflict was a much greater problem for the northern Australians than for the western Canadians. In the Northern Territory Natives roamed the wilds more or less freely, and in the early years many deeply resented the intrusion into their lands of white Anglo invaders, not the least because the intruders often depleted the natural water supplies with their thirsty stock, basically kidnapped Aboriginal women for their sexual pleasure, and in many cases violently wiped out Native communities that resisted them.[54] In Alberta and Assiniboia, by contrast, the North-West Mounted Police placed the Indians on reserves and restricted their movements, mostly to stop them from interrupting settlement. This did not prevent racial violence but it does seem to have moderated it a good deal.[55]

The sixth and final major cost described by the interviewee to the commissioners which was more burdensome in Australia than Canada in the earliest frontier period was contagion. Some diseases such as the mange and blackleg that plagued other frontiers did not pose a great threat in the Territory. Both these diseases commonly develop when animals are penned up and share a common feed for a relatively extended period. But in the Territory the cattle were pretty much all left to wander the open range throughout the year. Outbreaks of pleuropneumonia occurred when the cattle were under stress, as when being driven over long distances, but once the animals were settled into their new surroundings these became less common. In time some cattlemen began to use an inoculant to prevent it.[56] They would take live viruses from the lungs of a diseased animal, store them in a beer bottle kept cool in a wet bag, and then saturate a piece of wool with the viruses and insert it in the animals' tail "just above the switch."[57] Far more burdensome than any of these diseases in the minds of most of the early pastoralists was "Texas tick fever," or redwater disease. The babesia bacteria carried by the common cattle tick, *boophilus microplus*, causes babesiosis and anaplasmosis, both of which are a form of redwater. These diseases were fatal in about 80 percent of cases.[58] One theory is that redwater first reached the continent carried by ticks in Brahman cattle imported from India to Darwin in 1872. It then spread south and east into the Barkly Tableland as more cattle were brought to the top end.[59] The first major epidemic in the Territory seems to have occurred at Glencoe station "about the years 1880–81." Shortly after a mob was trailed in from Queensland, a large percentage of the cattle died. Later a man with the last name Lawrie bought "a number of [Glencoe] cattle to take to Port Darwin," probably for slaughter. A considerable portion of these animals died en route. "Subsequent arrivals at Glencoe experienced a like mortality."[60] In 1885 J.H. Gordon was driving some three thousand cattle from Cloncurry in Queensland to Wave Hill. Between the Elsey and the Katherine Rivers the disease broke out in the mob and many of the animals became sick. "It was thought that some poisonous plant was the cause, and all haste was made to the Katherine; but in a few days about twelve hundred head had died."[61] A year or so later Alfred Giles brought one hundred fifty head of cattle to Springvale from Newcastle Waters and then headed them north, ostensibly to market in Palmerston. Nearly half died before they got there.[62] At first it was believed the infestations were almost all in the northern droving route through the Roper, Elsey, and King River regions. However, it was soon discovered that flare-ups were occurring from time to time "all over the Northern Territory." Stock "may be healthy on the runs," one experienced cattleman noted, "but as soon as they are moved they are liable to get it."[63] According to the Government Resident this had become a serious setback to the entire northern industry by 1888 because lessees "will not run the risk of the ruinous loss which may attend the attempt to stock new country."[64] Some years later a scientific expedition observed: "all parts of the Northern Territory which are capable of maintaining ticks . . . are affected more or less."[65] In 1896 the governments of South Australia, New South Wales, and Queensland banned the importation of infected cattle from all parts of the Territory until they were dipped twice in a solution consisting of arsenic, caustic soda, Stockholm tar, tallow, and water. This was to kill the tick that carried the disease. The process was a difficult and drawn out affair very much like the mange treatment in Canada. In 1907 a concrete tank was constructed at Anthony's Lagoon near the Queensland/Tableland border and in 1908, 16,556 head were dipped there.[66]

Disease losses from redwater became considerably less severe as time passed. The cattle were no longer subject to the stress of the long and arduous treks inward and had had enough time in the Territory to develop some natural immunity. After the turn of the twentieth century science was to play a significant role in controlling the disease worldwide.[67] On the northern Great Plains of North America, redwater did not cause major damage even before that because the Texas tick was unable to survive either the cold winter weather or the dry inland atmosphere. Arguably the mange was significantly more expensive in Canada than redwater was in Australia, but it did not become a substantial problem until near the turn of the century – some fifteen to twenty years after most of the great ranches had come into existence. It did not take a toll early and, therefore, cannot be considered a start-up cost. Some frightening outbreaks of blackleg did occur on the northern plains.[68] It was, however, only the small numbers of Canadian cattle that were penned up in the winter that were at risk. Furthermore, a vaccination for blackleg became available in 1895 and it seems to have been used quite widely.[69] Pleuropneumonia also struck Canadian cattle but it does not appear to have been any more destructive on the northern Great Plains than in the outback.[70]

One other major impediment to the Australian industry that the witness pinpointed in 1895, the lack of markets, was also greatest in the earliest frontier period. Another was predation by Anglo-European humans (which he did not mention). However, both were approximately equally problematic to ranching in western Canada and will, for that reason, be examined in a later chapter. How all the main costs of starting business in the Northern Territory combined with a few more commonplace ones to bring about the fall of the first round of pastoralists is clearly seen in John Costello's struggle and ultimate failure to establish a vast grazing empire on the eastern side of the Territory in the 1880s. Costello first tried to launch his cattle enterprise at his Valley of the Springs station on the Limmen Bight River along the coast of the Gulf of Carpentaria extending as far north as the Roper River. His difficulties began as soon as he gathered his herd in Queensland and started the journey to the lease. "The first night it took nearly all hands to keep the mob on camp. Over one thousand seven hundred beasts, all in the wild and restless state, demand some holding in the dark."[71] After travelling some distance the cattle grew accustomed to the ordeal and they settled down. But soon the drovers encountered other problems. "Although the route was on the coastal fall, which, in normal seasons, gets rather too much rain, yet on this occasion the whole area was suffering, more or less, from the dry weather," which put the stock under considerable stress.[72] When Costello and his men reached Burketown in the northern part of the state, they discovered that it had only one store "and from this, large quantities of rations would have to be bought."[73] The carriers had Costello at their mercy and they demanded "special inducements" to haul the provisions to the new station. Finally, he was able to hire an outfit for the astounding price of seventy-five pounds sterling a ton. "It was a case of take it or leave it, so far as the staggering prices were concerned. Men were scarce, also very independent, and rendered inferior service. The cost of stocking new country under these conditions was formidable in the extreme."[74] To make matters worse, half or so of the high-priced supplies were eventually lost on the long trek to the station headquarters, ostensibly because the wagon used to haul them broke down in the rough terrain.[75] The journey was also very costly in terms of the pounds of live beef lost. Much of the country consisted of "heavy sand, covered with a dense, low non-edible scrub. Here and there, patches of ti-tree flats growing a sour, wiry grass of little nutriment." The daily ordeal of "rough, dry feed had a decidedly weakening effect on the stock and they fell away in condition as time wore on."[76] Inevitably pleuropneumonia struck the emaciated animals.[77] After he finally got them to Valley of the Springs, Costello watched his numbers dwindle because of ticks and redwater disease, hostile Aborigines, Anglo gold prospectors, and, most of all, the coarse, mineral-deficient grasses in the coastal region.[78] Finally in 1890, after malaria and other diseases, white ants, and bush fires had also plagued him, his men, and his family, he realized he had not chosen his rangeland well.[79] In 1890 he decided to move the entire operation some four hundred miles south to the Lake Nash area on the Barkly Tableland.

At the new lease the grass was somewhat finer and a little easier for the cattle to digest, but Costello soon found himself struggling with severe flooding caused by heavy seasonal rains. He realized, however, that the greatest threat was the tendency of his natural water sources to dry up. He tried expensive "overshot dams" in the rivers and creeks. These were valuable, and at times no doubt saved the stock, but "the periodic droughts would see them all dry."[80] He was finally forced to bring in a big boring outfit from Brisbane to drill for water. He knew this was extremely expensive and it was risky since there was no guarantee that water would be found.

> The drilling machinery was erected . . . and . . . operations were commenced. But it took several hundred feet of . . . sinking before . . . [water] was struck, and it was of a remarkable and somewhat inky appearance, giving a strange, unpleasant odour. Sinking was continued, the unsatisfactory fluid cased off and, at last, an abundant and unexhaustible [sic] supply of good, clear water was obtained.
>
> It was what is termed sub-artesian, and had to be equipped with a powerful and expensive pumping plant. This consisted of an eight horsepower steam engine, heavy walking beam,

with it accessories, as well as inner casting, rods and pump and when these were in fullest operation, the capability of the bore was thoroughly tested.

No impression could be made on the wonderful underground reservoir, though the engine and pump worked day and night without ceasing for a moment. Another bore was put down on an excellent piece of country . . . with a similar successful result.

These cased wells had an immense capacity for watering stock and countless numbers [of cattle] could obtain sufficient drink. Thus . . . the permanence of the water supply was secured — never again would the station be absolutely dried out.[81]

The bores required Costello to invest, as well, in windmills or engines and huge earth storage tanks and troughs. Unfortunately "the high price of material and . . . carriage, coupled with wages and many other charges, all in the aggregate, involved a payment which strained" Costello's finances "to the utmost limit."[82] He found himself running a large overdraft, and a short time after the well water became available his bank manager arrived with a legal document authorizing seizure of the Lake Nash station.[83]

One of the facts this case helps to demonstrate is that many of the big stations in the Territory were in very rough shape before the international depression that started in America in the early 1890s, quickly spread to Europe and other countries including Australia, and kept the price of beef declining worldwide through to the end of the decade.[84] Costello's finances — like those of Charles Fisher, Maurice Lyons, and William J. Browne — were in a precarious state before that widespread financial decline took hold. Nat Buchanan kept Wave Hill going in the 1880s and made it into the early 1890s by selling "a few lots" of cattle "in the Darwin markets, and . . . a few to the Kimberly goldfields." When the depression began he was already staggering "under an ever-increasing overdraft and interest burden." He finally surrendered Wave Hill to his brother, William F. Buchanan, in 1894.[85] "So, like many another pioneer of the interior," he dropped out after making "the track easy for others to prosper."[86] E.A. Macpherson of Corella Downs on the Playford River told the Government Resident in 1890 that he was "one of the pioneers from New South Wales who, nine years ago undertook the hazardous and expensive task of stocking the Northern pastoral blocks." I have, he said, "spent near 26,000 pounds, without yet a return" and many are in a similar situation. This business as a whole "is acknowledged on all sides to be a failure." Faced with "enormous expenditure year after year without profit I do not see how the present state of things can continue." We need "some substantial assistance from the Government" to develop markets and to help with the cost of sinking new bores.[87]

It seems evident, then, that at this early stage the big ranches in the Northern Territory were generally in a weaker position financially than those in the Canadian West. To say this is not to suggest that all the latter were immune to enormous losses in the first years. Indeed, in one or two cases their operational deficits were enormous. Senator Matthew Cochrane purchased his first cattle – 6,634 head – in Montana in 1881 and hired the men he needed to trail them north.[88] The drive, bigger by far than any that had previously brought stock to Alberta, soon proved disastrous. It was late in the fall season when the cattle arrived and the trail-weary beasts were wiped out in droves by a severe early winter storm. The second big drive, conducted the next fall, had a similar result. Cochrane decided the weather was too extreme around Calgary, and he took out a new lease and moved his cattle operation some 125 miles south to the Waterton area near the American border. He then transferred the Bow River lease to the British American Ranch Company, got a special permit from his friends in the federal government, and brought in over seven thousand sheep from Montana and Wyoming. Hundreds of these animals died in prairie fires and one particularly severe blizzard.[89] Later, Cochrane's sons disclosed that the first years in the West had cost the family something like $400,000.[90] Some other operations that were unfortunate enough to mis-time their arrival in the West lost so much before they had a chance to properly settle that they had to almost immediately give up the fight. The N Bar N outfit arrived in the Wood Mountain area in the summer of 1886 with several thousand cattle. After the horrendous blizzards that struck that winter only a small remnant of the herd remained alive. In the spring the ranch closed its Canadian venture for good. The Turkey Track ranch brought its initial herds into Assiniboia just in time to collide with the notorious winter of 1906–7.[91] It too pulled out of Canada the following spring. On the whole, however, most of the first Canadian ranches had somewhat more staying power than their Australian counterparts, largely because their initial challenges were not quite as severe. For them the process of decline had just begun when Fisher and Lyon, Costello, Browne, Buchanan, and many of the pioneers in the Northern Territory were on their last legs. Much of the rest of this investigation will attempt to explain why the tables would turn – why the big, open range cattle stations were able to re-establish and find ways to carry on in the three pastoral regions of the Northern Territory while the Canadian corporations would disappear for good.

5

THE SOCIAL ENVIRONMENT

Notwithstanding their differences in everything from climate and ecology to the size of their leases and their start-up costs, the big cattle operations in these two new hinterlands were strikingly similar in important respects. Along with the open range approach, the most obvious attribute they shared was the craft of the cowboy. As the industry unfolded in both places their respective labour forces developed almost identical skills simply because the jobs they had to perform were essentially the same. Where the range was "huge, and fenceless . . . the year's mustering and branding" was "no simple task" on either end of the globe. Cattle were "scattered through a couple of thousand square miles of scrub and open timbered country," and therefore each section needed to be "gone over again and again" during the summer season, each mob, or herd, "travelled to the nearest yard and branded."[1] Every cowboy or stockman had his work to attend to, "but every one's work was concerned with cattle."[2] The men who tended the stock were predominantly young, and they were all able to spend a considerable part of their life riding the vast ranges. They could handle a rope, work on calves with branding iron and knife, and, while glued to the back of a rugged and fast moving horse, cut out semiferal steers "culling each mob of its prime bullocks" and then droving or trailing them off to market.[3]

The following description of a day's activities during muster in the Tableland region indicates a communal effort just like that utilized by ranchers on the North American continent. The trail boss

ROUNDUP CREW, COCHRANE AREA ALBERTA, CA. 1890. GLENBOW ARCHIVES, CALGARY, NA-2084-66.

gave his orders for strategic gathering of the far scattered mobs. Some of the party sent out to the right, others to the left, a few more up and down the various creeks and all in due time concentrating with their mustered stock to a certain cattle camp where the "cutting out" or drafting on horses, would take place. With the exception of the small horse paddock at the homestead, there were practically no fences. . . . So it might be that attending the musterings of "Lake Nash" there would be stockmen from other stations far and near – from "Headingly," "Austral Downs," "Avon Downs," and "Rocklands"– all taking the opportunity to collect their wandered cattle. After the midday lunch, the active work of "cutting out" would commence. Special horses were kept solely for this purpose. They were animals, frequently, possessing exceptional adaptability for the work. These steeds, cat-like in their activity, would wheel around as on a pivot, baulking all efforts of the drafted beast to return to the mob. An unusually wild and speedy young bullock would frequently test the camp horse's cleverness at every point – turning, twisting, propping – sometimes charging, but the horse, like lightning, meeting and countering every move, till at last the defeated steer joined the small drafted mob.[4]

When that part of the process was completed it was time for "the drive to the branding yards and there the breaking away of scores of big calves, the chasing, rounding up and final yarding at sundown."

At that point Territorial practices diverged slightly from those used in North America. Once the calves were corralled with their mothers, it was usual in Canada and throughout the American plains for cowboys to rope them from horseback and hold them by wrapping or "dallying" the rope around the saddle horn. Men on foot would then wrestle the young animals to the ground and perform the necessary operation(s):

> The scene is one of the greatest confusion. The ropers, spurring and checking the fierce little horses, drag the calves up so quickly that a dozen men can hardly hold them; the men with the irons, blackened with soot, run to and fro; the calf-wrestlers, grimy with blood, dust, and sweat, work like beavers; while with the voice of a stentor the tallyman shouts out the number and sex of each calf. The dust rises in clouds, and the shouts, cheers, curses, and laughter of the men unite with the lowing of the cows and the frantic bleating of the roped calves to make a perfect babel.[5]

The Australian stockmen did not normally rope from the saddle.[6] When gathering the cattle they carried a stock whip instead of a "lasso," or "lariat," which was longer than the heavier, more compact "quirt" the early Texan cowboys had carried. The stockmen would crack their whip over the heads of the cattle as they rode along behind them to encourage them to keep moving. When they had the cattle penned up they would use one of two methods to treat the calves: either a man would simply walk among them, cast a rope over their heads one at a time and with the help

CHARLIE RUSSELL PAINTING OF MEN ROPING CATTLE ON THE OPEN RANGE. "THE HERD QUITTER," (WIKIMEDIA COMMONS, HTTP://COMMONS.WIKIMEDIA.ORG/WIKI/ FILE:HERDQUIT.JPG).

of a couple of his fellow stockmen, throw them to the ground;[7] or the men would chase several calves into a long narrow log chute or "race" they had previously constructed and operate on them through the rails.[8]

There were some trivial differences of dress as well. For instance, down under riders wore the traditional Australian "cabbage-tree" hat instead of the somewhat broader rimmed cowboy hat or sombrero and, often, knee-high English-style riding boots rather than what was known as the cowboy boot in North America.[9]

The open range system not only made *nearly* all the same skills of the cowboy and conventions of the range necessary in these two regions, it also helped to provide for the development of a similar way of life. It enabled a rugged, largely masculine culture and fostered a rather cavalier attitude among ranchers, station managers, and stock hands towards the law and what were considered civilized standards of behaviour. In making that point, this chapter will signal what is not widely recognized – that this was economically destructive, primarily because it subjected the roaming cattle to the constant depredations of thieves.[10] It would be difficult to determine in which country rustling, or as the Australians called it, "duffing," was the more destructive, because in the frontier setting so much that was illegal went undetected and unrecorded.

Four circumstances were key to allowing an unruly lifestyle to take hold in the two regions: the relative weakness of legal authority, gender imbalance, the coming together of disparate racial-cultural groups, and unfenced ranges.[11] All of these were, to a considerable degree, man-made, or at least man-controlled, and in that sense, a reflection of social rather than what might be called natural forces. An examination of their impact thus allows the historian to illustrate the importance of the social environment in moulding human conduct on the frontier. Ever since Henry Reynolds in 1981 provided evidence of Anglo brutality towards Australian Aborigines, frontier scholars have tended to argue about whether or not it happened rather than explaining it.[12] The present chapter indirectly supports the Reynolds side in the course of shedding light on why the bloodletting was widespread, but it also indicates that brazen racism and cold-heartedness were only part of the story. The frontier encouraged people to violate so-called legal and moral "standards" in numerous ways. Consequently, the expansion of what James Belich has termed the "Anglo-world" was bound to be a relatively unruly affair almost everywhere during the early settlement period, with or without racial strife.[13]

To say as much is not to insist that western Canadian and northern Australian societies were *necessarily* less law abiding and orderly than any specific other societies. Nor is it to suggest that one of them was less so than the other. It is merely to indicate that a large percentage of the people had a tendency to ignore legal rules and traditional moral values, and that can, to a significant extent, be attributed to social forces associated with the frontier. The first of the above-mentioned circumstances – the weakness of legal authority – was primarily the product of a sparse population base. When the number of people inhabiting remote areas was still comparatively small, tax revenues were meagre and governments were loath to invest much in them financially. For that reason, they tended to call on a handful of under-equipped lawmen to exercise some control over huge tracts of land while at the same time fulfilling numerous other functions besides keeping the peace. In Alberta and Assiniboia, on average about 500 men patrolled nearly 500,000 square miles for most of the period between 1874 and 1914, while at the same time constructing their own living facilities, hauling firewood, feeding and caring for their mounts, protecting the civilian population from prairie fires and winter blizzards, and providing state services normally offered by specialized agencies in more mature societies. These included delivering mail, collecting weather data, and providing medical aid.

While Australia's Northern Territory was under the administrative control of South Australia, the government seems constantly to have been aware of the need to keep costs down. One result was that from 1874 to 1910 the entire 515,733 square miles of the Territory had a police force that at its peak numbered a mere 48 men.[14] True, the official non-Native population was never more than a fraction of that of western Canada. Still the Northern Territory police, like their counterparts on the northern Great Plains, had a substantial Native population to contend with and also hundreds of thousands of widely scattered cattle, horses, and sheep to try to protect from human predation. As sheep numbers dropped from 100,000 to half that number from the late 1880s onward, cattle numbers rose from 200,000 to well over 600,000, and horses from 8,000 to 24,500.[15] The South Australian censuses of 1891 and 1901 *estimated* that there were 21,000 and 23,000 Aborigines respectively in the Northern Territory. They said nothing of the offspring of Native–non-Native unions.[16]

The supervisors at the major police headquarters at Palmerston (later Port Darwin) and Borroloola, on the McArthur River about thirty miles inland from the Gulf of Carpentaria, commonly lamented the dearth of good men as well as deficiencies of everything from magistrates to jails and weapons.[17] "It is quite impossible" for us to do our work "efficiently unless there is a reinforcement of another constable and a couple of extra [Native] trackers," the chief at Borroloola wrote in 1888. He then complained bitterly about the general state of his unit's weaponry. It was "most unfair to constables stationed here where not only the . . . [Natives], but some of the white population were ready to take life without compunction, to palm off upon them any sort of old and indifferent firearms. Two mails ago I sent my revolver to Palmerston, asking that I might have a reliable one returned in place of it, and I was surprised to find . . . that instead of a good revolver arriving I was allotted one of those already at the station." All of these guns "except one" were "useless" and the one that was not useless was "most unreliable as it frequently misses fire." He claimed that on a recent patrol he had actually been obliged to borrow a revolver from one of the other men in order to defend himself.[18]

The Australian "troopers" were also required to perform a great number of duties over and above keeping order and defending the law.[19] In the beginning they too built and maintained their own stations, living quarters, and stockyards and saw to the care and feeding of their mounts; and as time passed they manned a bewildering assortment of official positions. They regularly served as clerks of the courts; bailiffs and assistant bailiffs; clerks of the licensing bench; registrars of births, deaths, and marriages; registrars of dogs; commissioners for affidavits; labour bureau agents; insurers of miner's rights; fisheries inspectors; insurers of Aboriginal rations; brand inspectors; stock inspectors; slaughterhouse inspectors; inspectors of public houses; Rabbit Act inspectors;[20] public vaccinators; jailers; Crown lands rangers; electoral registrars; and destitute department officers. William R. Wilson concludes that police force members' lives were uneventful and even tedious for much of the time.[21] That may well have been because they were too often preoccupied with routine administrative duties to patrol the cattle ranges or track down criminals. Time and again, local residents accused them of acting more like civil bureaucrats than police officers. "Can you inform me if the Police Force of the Northern Territory do any duty at all?" one asked. "Here we are with five or six great hulking fellows lolling about, doing nothing, and day after day the inhabitants are losing their property without the slightest check being attempted."[22]

Gender imbalance was a fact of life in both of these frontier communities. On the northern Great Plains of North America, single young men, most of whom worked on the cattle ranches, outnumbered women in general by a ratio of around two to one and they spent the vast majority of their time without any female company.[23] As such they were subject to what Professor Belich calls "crew culture." They could work hard and co-operate closely when on the job but, equally, they drank heavily and tended to be excessive and raucous in their recreation.[24] As a Montanan put it, "when paid their habit was to immediately ride off" to the nearest town or city "and spend all they had on drinking and gambling and having a right good time. They returned after every dollar had been squandered and started piling up for the next orgy."[25] "Crew culture," according to Belich, also inspired them to assume the right to make their own decisions about which of society's rules were and were not to be obeyed.[26] In simplistic terms, when single young men greatly outnumber the married (or marrying) type in any society they are inclined to establish a culture based on the satisfaction of basic animal urges. They compete with each other on the most fundamental levels and they seek sexual satisfaction and unrestrained entertainment in various forms of nightlife. That, and certainly the weakness of enforcement, gave the young frontiersmen the tendency to ignore virtually any regulations respecting alcohol. In western Canada liquor was prohibited except by special permit until 1892. Sam Steele, the commanding police officer at Calgary, went through the motions of trying to impose this but he had no illusions about how successful he was. "The officers and men hated this detestable duty," he said, because it

> gave them much trouble and gleams of unpopularity. We soon learned that compulsion will not make people sober. . . . The prohibition law made more drunkards than if there had been an open bar and free drinks at every street corner. Liquor was brought in . . . by every conceivable trick. Egg shells were emptied of their contents and alcohol substituted; tin imitations of the Holy Bible were filled with intoxicants and sold on the trains; metal kegs filled with alcohol came concealed in the centre of barrels of kerosene, and mince-meat soaked in brandy and peaches prepared in the same manner were common.[27]

Young male North-West Mounted Policemen were known to drink heavily in those days. The diary of Sergeant S.J. Clarke, now in the Glenbow Archives in Calgary, provides glimpses of drunken members becoming unruly at social gatherings or getting into brawls with the locals or entertaining a lady of the night at headquarters.[28] On the Northern Territory frontier, gender ratios were even further out of balance than on the Great Plains. Males outnumber females "34 to 1 according to [the] last census," one of the police chiefs noted in 1883.[29] This changed over the years, but slowly. In 1910 there were still more than seven times as many males among the colonists as females.[30] These men too tended to be a rugged lot. "The population of the" Victoria River "district consists of station managers, cattle duffers, horse thieves, wild and woolly stockmen, and outlaws," a visitor commented. "A man is almost out of the pale of the law" here "and it may well be called 'NO Man's Land.' Unless [the] offence is murder the authorities will not trouble to look for him; and he may remain for years wandering about the country."[31] Not surprisingly, single young male Australians were every bit as indulgent as their North American counterparts. George Byng Scott, the Government Resident during the 1870s, believed that an excessive lifestyle was simply part of the local culture from the beginning, even in his own bureaucratic workforce at Darwin. "I soon learned that I had undertaken a task that was not easily to be managed," he later remembered; "I found that many" of these men "were quick to drink and that they considered their only mission in life was to 'eat, drink and be merry,' do no work and plunder the Government whenever they had the chance of so doing." This attitude, he believed, permeated society: "there were about 1700 Europeans in the Territory" at that time "and drinking and gambling was carried on to a considerable extent."[32] Canadian entrepreneurs produced a portion of their own liquor in illegal stills. Fred Ings tells of the time when a keg of home brew was found near the cook tent during a roundup, saying, "That was a wild and hilarious branding and calves that year wore their brands at all angles."[33] Because the northern Australian frontier lacked a rapid transportation connection to existing metropoles it was in a sense more isolated than those in western North America. Consequently, the Australians seem to have relied on an even higher percentage of home-grown liquor, which they generally referred to as "sly grog." It flowed throughout the Territory from the remotest of the gold camps, which had sprung to life with the arrival of Chinese miners starting in 1874, to the far reaches of the cattle stations. In 1889 a settler urged the magistrate stationed at Borroloola "to let the constable in charge of the police . . . know [about] the illicit trade [that is] being carried on, and the injuries the settlers are sustaining" as a result. The trade "is gradually getting worse," he warned, "instead of better."[34]

Opium use also proliferated in Australia. There the Chinese were by far the largest non-Native ethnic group throughout the frontier period, and the tendency of white commentators was to blame this on them.[35] Reports of opium circulating through their enclaves appeared in numerous newspaper articles and in at least one rather scathing government document.[36] Cattle station managers also turned to opium to build up their labour force. Because there were so few Europeans, the stations badly needed cheap Aboriginal labour to work their herds and maintain their infrastructure. The drug was used rather universally to attract them. I "refused to give it to the blacks for a long time," one northern Queensland manager claimed. Unfortunately "my best boys left me and were employed by my neighbors who gave them opium regularly in spite of my repeated letters to them begging them to desist from the practice on the commonsense plea that if the blacks knew they could not get . . . [it] the craving would cease." He stated that he now felt compelled to take up the practice of providing opium himself.[37] The drug appeared on both sides of the western Canadian/American border.[38] However, its availability and impact do not seem to have been great, possibly because geographically its principal land of origin, China, was more distant.

On both frontiers, consumption of intoxicants went hand-in-glove with gambling. Casinos operated in the larger urban centres of western Canada offering poker and roulette, and, informally, individuals were inclined to lay bets with one another on everything from blackjack to horse racing.[39] What was reputed to be the "greatest blackjack game ever played" on the Canadian plains took place in the late 1890s in High River between two men named Iken and Todd. After the game, Iken was forced to turn over land that Todd later sold for forty thousand dollars.[40] Rightly or wrongly, Chinese entrepreneurs were blamed for much of the illicit Northern Territory betting business. As gold mining began to wind down in the 1880s and 1890s many Chinese settlers established market gardens and engaged in various forms of honest commerce.[41] However, according to local lore at least, some made their living by setting up covert rooms wherever they could in which the traditional Chinese game of fan-tan was played. One thing seems clear – all newcomer races participated. "Under the laws here, which they laugh at," the gamers "flourish amazingly, and the low-lived ruffians and swindlers can be seen lying about all day, doing no honest work for a living, smoking opium, and fattening on the spoils of their victims," a local resident fumed. "Lotteries are carried on openly, and Europeans patronize them" too, "notwithstanding the fact that the odds against getting the smallest prize are fully 14 to 1."[42] Some feared that gambling was destroying an entire generation and severely hurting the local economy. "The youth – and in many instances those who hold high positions," the same person insisted, were "fostering, aiding, and abetting a most monstrous system of swindling the unwary victims out of their hard earned money." The writer was sure "that many have lost money, which ought to have been paid to their storekeeper, their boot maker, and their laundress, in defraying what they term 'debts of honour.'"[43]

One illegal pastime single young men in the Territory engaged in even more, relative to population size, than their North American counterparts was the hiring of sex workers.[44] To be sure, the sex trade thrived in the latter region too. In North America, prostitutes quickly recognized the high demand for their services in a predominantly male society and scores of them "followed the trail herds." They came out West from centres such as Omaha, Chicago, and St. Paul and, as Char Smith's work indicates, they tended to move back and forth across the international border as they saw fit.[45] Many travelled regularly between Miles City, Great Falls, Lethbridge, and Calgary to meet the cowboys arriving with the annual supply of slaughter cattle for shipment to Eastern markets. Their business flourished and some of the madams who conducted it flourished as well.[46] Lizzie House operated a series of extravagant bordellos in Calgary with furnishings that are supposed to have equalled those of the best houses in the East.[47] Carrie McLean, better known as "Cowboy Jack," started her career as a prostitute in Montana and then moved on to operate her own establishments north of the line. In Lethbridge, Alberta, she had "an imposing two-story house with a horse trough in front where drunken cowboys frequently dumped their frolicking pals."[48]

The trade was even more deeply ingrained in Australia, at least relative to the population, mainly because newcomer women were even scarcer there, relative to the overall population.[49] Quite a number of the first prostitutes came from China on the heels of the gold miners, and from Japan to service Japanese pearl divers who arrived on the shores of the Northern Territory in the 1880s.[50] Some white women also got into the business, but by far the greatest supply of sex providers eventually came from local Aboriginal groups. The existence of Native prostitution did not, of course, make Australia extraordinary. In both Alberta and across the line in Montana, individual tribes set up teepees near urban centres specifically for that purpose.[51] One official estimated, however, that "in the settled districts" of northern Australia the "greater portion of the aboriginal women" had been drawn into the business.[52] "Since their association with European and other nations, besides their own savage habits they have acquired vices and contracted diseases imported by the colonists previously quite unknown to them." On both continents, Native male entrepreneurs played a central role in bringing the two cultures together. One northern Great Plains cattleman remembered that "one old fellow offered me his wife, for twenty-two dollars . . . not to keep . . . just a temporary arrangement . . . Most of the Indian tribes was doing a regular business of that kind with the white men, and some of them, especially the Crows and Sioux, had got so low they would offer you their wives. But the way they did it in most of the camps," they had women who were "just like sporting women among the whites."[53] If newspaper accounts can be accepted, the immense demand in the Northern Territory encouraged both Natives and whites to turn the business into the crudest of human auctions. At one event, which was apparently held each year, Aboriginal groups "from the Adelaide and Alligator rivers" appeared on the outskirts of Palmerston. The following morning the men would do what they could "to vend their merchandise." They would display it "in lots of twenty and thirty" and when "a European" stopped they would offer the "old women . . . at sixpence" and others at "one and two shillings." They demanded the highest amounts "for quite young children under ten years of age."[54] Of course, individual European men directly engaged Native females, as well. In Australia they tended to do so by getting them addicted to intoxicants. The Inspector of Police in Palmerston opined that female Aborigines would "do anything for grog"; and that prostitution "is so greatly on the increase can only be attributed to the leniency with which . . . it is viewed and treated by the magistrates."[55]

Native sex providers who stayed temporarily with individual men for some form of payment were not always exploited on either continent. They could, in fact, attain a degree of power, as they were able to make certain demands for their services, which they could withdraw. They were also able to bring income, often in the form of food or supplies, to their kinship groups.[56] However, in Australia many European men took Aboriginal women from the local population by the force of their firearms and, in essence, enslaved them. Male Aborigines did not take this lightly, and time after time bloodshed ensued. In his book *Frontier Justice*, Tony Roberts explains that a Native man was likely to follow a white man who had stolen his mate, spear him, and take her back.[57] What the white men learned to do, therefore, was simply to shoot the male beforehand. Many of the Native Australian women were, like their North American counterparts, eventually abandoned when European women became available.[58] "A very large number of the white population of this town keep a black lubra" [Aboriginal woman], the Deputy Protector of Aborigines reported in 1884. "Nearly everyone coming from Queensland has a young black girl with them and in some instances they have been turned adrift to get back to the place from where they were taken the best way they can."[59]

A Palmerston resident pointed to one of the consequences of Native-newcomer fraternization that does not seem to have been prevalent in the North American West – infanticide. "The lubras almost invariably destroy their half-caste offspring." He claimed to know for sure of five newborn babies that had been murdered by "their mothers and other female relatives."[60] In 1883 the Acting Government Resident asserted in his annual report that "the almost total absence of half-caste children" strongly suggested that "the progeny" of inter-racial fraternization was being "put aside as soon as born."[61] Ann McGrath explains that this was, to a degree, because mixed-race children "posed a problem for Aboriginal communities, who interpreted the strange hue" of their skin "as signifying deformity or evil spirits that could harm their world."[62] It may well be that extraction methods used to take Aboriginal females from their kinship groups also made many of these children less acceptable to both Europeans and Natives than they were in North America.[63] Scholars Silvia Van Kirk[64] and Jennifer Brown[65] have demonstrated that, in the Canadian West, Indian women originally agreed to mixed marriages during the century of the fur trade prior to 1870, in part because there were certain important strategic and/or material advantages to be gained. These women became real partners to their white husbands, who depended on them in order to adapt to life in the wilderness and to forge much-needed commercial links with local tribes. The pattern was much the same in the United States, and a tradition of union based on some degree of mutual esteem was established. Only a little too optimistically, Montana rancher E.C. "Teddy Blue" Abbott once recalled that "every white man I ever knew that was married to an Indian . . . thought the world of them."[66] These women may generally not have been as prized as white women later on but, exceptions aside, during the early frontier period they were considered, and they considered themselves, respectable. Therefore, mixed-race children, though they unquestionably faced prejudices, could be integrated into Indian communities or educated and assimilated into the white world, or else they settled on the land in cultural enclaves to live both a ranching and hunting-and-gathering existence.[67] In Australia, on the other hand, the huge gender imbalance created a greater sense of urgency from the beginning for the attainment of sex-providers and, torn by force or addiction from their home society, these women lived with little status or power. Consequently, "half-caste" children in general were more likely to be seen as a symbol of disgrace. How widespread this practice of infanticide was has been debated of late.[68] However, in 1911 there was a total of only 58 "half-castes" in the Territory and 3,310 whites and Asians.[69] Eventually most became part of the pastoral proletariat on the cattle stations, living and working in the region where they had been born. Others lived in a semi-settled condition in the bush, accepted neither by whites nor blacks.[70]

As stated above, the taking of Aboriginal women was an important reason for numerous attacks on colonists. Undoubtedly the fact that in Australia, as in both Canada and the United States, white society took up the practice of institutionalizing Native children for the purpose of assimilation also *eventually* provoked resentment.[71] That Aborigines were concerned as well about incursions into their homeland is evinced by the fact that some of them began assailing the newcomers well before any significant numbers of them had actually settled in the Northern Territory and committed these egregious acts.[72] One of the first attacks occurred in 1870. Arthur Ashwin, who helped drive stock north from South Australia that year, later remembered that at one point when he and the other drovers were resting on the trail an Aboriginal man walked into their midst. Ashwin was leery and tried to keep an eye on him. However, when he was tying his horse to some bushes the man smashed his club down on the skull of John Milner, the brother of the expedition's leader, so hard that he died instantly, one of his eyes popping out of his head.[73]

Whatever the reason, incidents of this sort occurred over and over again. In 1892 the *Northern Territory Times and Gazette* reported that Aborigines murdered W.S. Scott, the manager of Willeroo station in the Victoria River district. Scott had left the station to gather cattle. He had stopped to eat at McClure Creek, on the Victoria road, at which time a number of "blacks came up in a mob" and began chasing his horses away. Scott sent Rollo, his stock hand, out after the horses. When

Rollo returned to the camp, he found Scott's lifeless body with several spears stuck in it. There was also a gash in Scott's forehead, thought to be a "tomahawk" wound.[74] The newspapers obviously did nothing to cool animosities when relating such incidents. In 1905 the *Northern Territory Times and Gazette* recounted that an Alligator River Native, Tommy, had "suddenly picked up a rifle and fired two shots" into a white worker named Frost on Victoria River Downs.[75] Frost did not die outright, the report noted, but "lingered on in his agony until the following night – for the most part of this time lying in the solitary camp wounded and alone except for the presence" of a dead Native child whom Tommy had also supposedly killed. After the shootings, Tommy "coolly saddled and mounted a horse, and taking with him a rifle and a plentiful supply of ammunition, deliberately rode out" to find two white workers named Edwards and Benning. When he found them, he shot Edwards "killing him instantly" and then set off in pursuit of the fleeing Benning. "An exciting chase ensued" during which "the black murderer . . . fired six or seven shots at the flying whiteman." Luckily for Benning, he "had the better horse," and managed to get away.[76]

Aborigines were apparently every bit as antagonistic towards the Chinese as they were towards Europeans. Possibly animosity originally developed when the Asians first came to the Northern Territory and monopolized some of the waterholes for panning gold.[77] Some contemporaries also believed that Chinese men did what they could to get Native women dependent on narcotics and into prostitution.[78] Many attacks were dramatically reported in the newspapers. On 10 June 1882, a party of Aborigines overwhelmed four Chinese travelling in a horse-drawn dray on "the main road between Rum Jungle and the Banyan." They first killed the driver and one of the passengers by hitting them over the head with "waddys."[79] Then they chased down the other two Chinese as they made a run for it and "knocked" them "about their heads and faces" nearly cutting them "to pieces."[80] Aboriginal groups were also hostile towards fellow countrymen who worked on the cattle runs. Managers on the runs often brought in indigenous stock hands and labourers from distant regions, hoping to make it less convenient for them to return to their people or to plot with them to attack the stations. Local Aboriginal groups saw the outsiders as enemy collaborators and, when occasions presented themselves, they took their revenge. One night some of the Natives enticed two of the workers from the Springvale run to accompany them on a journey. The next morning the manager, Alfred Giles, organized a search party and tracked them down. He was "horrified to find" his workers "lying dead in a deserted camp of the wild blacks. Both had been speared and their heads battered in while they were asleep."[81]

Roberts concludes that in the region of the Northern Territory adjacent to the Gulf of Carpentaria inter-racial violence was perpetrated far more by whites than blacks.[82] In 1883 the Acting Government Resident, G.R. McMinn, offered the same view when speaking of the entire Territory, writing, "It is a well known fact" that the Natives "are not always the first aggressors."[83] Interestingly, however, very little was written in the police or Government Resident reports or in the *Northern Territory Times* about this or the appalling way in which Aborigines were treated generally.[84] But when Natives committed homicides, the police often went to considerable trouble and expense to track them down.[85] The punishments were usually life in prison or execution. On occasion, to make a point, officials took the supposed transgressors to the place where their crimes had been committed and executed them "in the presence of their different tribes."[86] The most effective deterrent, however, was quasi-vigilante summary justice in which settlers banded together with or without the police to travel into the areas where violence against whites had taken place and massacre any Natives, often including women and children, that could be found. In 1881 Duncan Campbell, the head stockman of Elsey station, died after being speared. Enraged white settlers indiscriminately took revenge, decimating the local Yangman and Mangari people.[87] A resident in the Alice Springs area described an event which indicates that genocide was an acceptable objective to many colonists. "We made a tidy mob . . . about twenty all told," he said, "eight or nine cattlemen, some of the chaps from the Overland Telegraph [Company] an' a mob of police. The 'nigs' . . . poor devils . . . [We] rounded 'em up on that razorback hill over there . . . We ran a cordon round the hill an' peppered 'em" with bullets "until there wasn't a 'nig' showing . . . there must have been 150 or 170 of 'em on that hill and I reckon that few of 'em got away . . . But what could we do? We had to live up here. That was the trouble of it."[88] Gordon Buchanan also expressed support for vigilante justice when recounting his family's history on the Wave Hill station in the Victoria River district.[89] In 1890 the *Adelaide Register* commented: "Many of the actions which were taken against the blacks were . . . taken with the object of exterminating them, and especially the men. If a squatter kept cattle, and there were blacks on his run, either the blacks or the cattle had to go."[90] The involvement of the police in the episode near Alice Springs, along with the many indiscretions of officer William Henry Willshire, who was tried for murdering two Aborigines at the Tempe Downs station, is evidence that the overall weakness of legal authority in the Territory gave even the men designated to enforce the law a sense of release from traditional legal proscriptions.[91] Here they were, they believed, in extraordinarily nasty circumstances that required extraordinary measures.[92] Paul Foelsche, the commanding officer at Port Essington, evidently felt this way: "I wish the government would authorize me to deal out summarily punishment to these tribes," he wrote in 1880 after hearing rumours that some local Aborigines had killed two white squatters, cooked them over a fire, and eaten them.[93]

Given the much smaller newcomer population in Australia, the level of racial violence appears disproportionately high even compared to that in the American West, where it was considerable. In western Canada, the most celebrated Indian killing was the infamous Cypress Hills massacre of 1873, in which a number of American "wolfers," Canadian traders and Metis, shot up an Assiniboine camp, killing at least twenty men, women, and children.[94] Thereafter, the North-West Mounted Police were able to reduce this type of violence by settling indigenous tribes on reserves where they were separated from settler communities.[95] In a 2004 article, Andrew Graybill argues that the police do not deserve the praise some historians have heaped on them for taking a humane or civilized approach. Their objective was to cut the Native people off from their traditional food staple, the bison, thereby preventing them "from interfering with the white migration and the establishment" of Euro-Canadian "military and political authority." Ultimately this subjected the Cree and Blackfoot to the same life of poverty and starvation that many of the American Indians faced.[96] A very recent study, *Clearing the Plains; Disease, Politics of Starvation and the Loss of Aboriginal Life* by James Daschuk, as its title suggests, takes that argument to some of its logical conclusions.[97]

It might be pointed out too that even after the establishment of the reserve system in Alberta and Assiniboia, racial conflict did at times result in bloodshed. In 1896 Almighty Voice, a Cree, shot Sergeant Colebrooke of the Mounties. He then killed another four policemen before being captured after a long manhunt and executed.[98] On 10 February 1897 Charcoal, a member of the Blood tribe, was hanged for shooting Sergeant A.B. Wild of the North-West Mounted Police. Charcoal had previously murdered a fellow tribesman and shot and severely wounded a white farm agent.[99] At the Blackfoot reserve east of Calgary, in 1894, a tribesman killed a white official who had denied his dying son an extra ration of meat. "A posse" of infuriated and trigger-happy citizens led by some police tracked the man down and cornered him on a hillside. After his arm was shot nearly off, the police ordered that he be taken alive. Nonetheless, an overzealous volunteer fired one last round, killing the man instantly.[100]

It is thus evident that Native–non-Native violence happened all too often in these early societies. While this speaks to the influence of the frontier environment, we (and Australian scholars in particular) should be mindful that, in one important respect, it was also an Old World phenomenon. Many people of Anglo descent were firm believers in a social Darwinist philosophy, which in its most basic form insisted that the strong and intelligent in human society were meant to flourish and prosper and the mentally and physically less capable to falter and die out. This they considered a natural, providentially ordained, evolutionary process by which the entire human species had, and would continue to be, improved.[101] The social Darwinist philosophy was enlisted in particular in the fight against humane intervention on behalf of the poor in Great Britain. Ultimately, however, it lost much of its appeal in domestic affairs as compassionate members of the rising middle classes saw to the passing of more and more legislation to control working conditions in factories and mines, and to build schools for ordinary people and prisons and asylums aimed at rehabilitation. But eventually men like Walter Bagehot recast social Darwinism as a pillar of imperialism.[102] Essentially, they insisted that it was the strong races, i.e. the British, who were destined to achieve greatness at the expense of backward and feeble races. Over and over again, leaders from various walks of life advanced this theory in print and in speech. On 31 March 1897 Colonial Secretary Joseph Chamberlain, an avowed champion of imperialism, voiced it with much acclaim when speaking to the Royal Colonial Institute. By colonizing people in the far corners of the globe, he said, "we are fulfilling what I believe to be our national mission, and we are finding scope for the exercise of those faculties and qualities which have made of us a great governing race." Unmistakably, he was prepared to accept the death and destruction of local populations in this process. "No doubt, in the first instance, when . . . conquests have been made, there has been bloodshed, there has been loss of life" among indigenous peoples, "but it must be remembered that that is the condition of the mission we have to fulfill. It seems to me that the tendency of the time is to throw all power into the hands of the greater empires, the minor kingdoms – those which are non-progressive – seem to be destined to fall into a secondary and subordinate place." Chamberlain's objective was to rule the world basically at any cost. "No empire," he said, must "ever surpass" us "in area, in population, in wealth, or in the diversity of . . . resources."[103]

As British, Australian, Canadian, and American Anglos set about the task of colonization in the outback of Australia or the opening ranges on the northern Great Plains, they felt they had a sacred mission to "carry the flag of Empire into the unknown open spaces" of remote lands.[104] This allowed them to be contemptuous of local populations and devoid of empathy. People like Mary Inderwick on the North Fork ranch near Pincher Creek, Alberta, could with clear conscience argue that the sooner the "backward" tribes with which she had come in contact became extinct the better it would be for them and for humanity.[105] Similarly, in a letter to the *Northern Territory Times*, a concerned Australian could assert that Aboriginal peoples "must move before the tide of civilization, or . . . even, as every man will crush a snake under his heel, so must the hand of every man be raised against . . . inhuman monsters, whose cowardly and murderous nature renders them unfit to live."[106] The frontier changed the racism many people of European descent carried with them primarily in the sense that it gave them evidence that they felt confirmed their presumptions of superiority.[107]

Of course, frontier conflict was not always racial in nature. European men who lived and worked on the ranches and stations commonly carried revolvers and/or rifles and sometimes they turned them against each other. However, they were less likely to do so in Australia than in the Canadian West.[108] The reason for this is simply that the European population was much smaller there and spread out so thinly across the huge expanse of the Territory's pastoral regions.[109] On the northern Great Plains, cowboy-instigated gun violence often erupted when crew culture got out of hand – that is, when armed young men, their passions fuelled with copious amounts of liquor, competed in bars, often for women, whom they greatly outnumbered. Sometimes this form of violence transcended national borders. One night a group of British, Canadian, and American cowboys working in Alberta rode into a Montana tavern. "After the boys had several drinks they proceeded to shoot up the saloon."[110] Canadian historians have tended to ignore this type of disorder in their communities. However, if one looks closely one finds numerous incidents of it. "Blazing away with a pistol, whenever a man gets drunk, whether it be in the hands of a policeman or a citizen is getting monotonous," a reporter in Fort Macleod, Alberta, complained in 1886.[111] Canadian barroom shoot-outs could at times be as bloody as any in Montana or Wyoming or Texas. In the summer of 1900 David Warnock, the onsite manager of the Walrond ranch, told his boss about an episode involving their cowhand Tom Miles. Miles was thought to be dead "from the effects of his wound" and some "Pincher Creek men" had "been killed."[112] Five or so months later Warnock reported, "Miles is back looking very well and quite recovered . . . He made a narrow escape of sharing Morden and Carr's fate, the bullet missing his spine by less than one inch."[113]

Inebriated young Australians seldom gathered together in large numbers, and they mostly avoided this type of bloodshed.[114] It speaks to the overarching influence of the social environment, however, that in the uncommon instances when they did gather in fairly large numbers, the results could be about the same. Borroloola was the gateway between the north end of the Northern Territory and Queensland to the east. When law enforcement was still very weak, men heading one way or the other sometimes "flocked in" and the transient population skyrocketed. The town could then become "quite as wild and lawless" as any raw frontier community. During the day "respectable inhabitants had to watch drunken men practicing with rifle and revolver . . . in the township streets." At night the occasional "drunken brawl ended in a free fight. Knives were drawn, shots exchanged, sometimes without much danger, at other times with the loss of a life or two."[115]

If the Australians were less likely to get involved in gun violence than their North American counterparts, they did not lag behind them in arguably the most rampant crime, and for the pastoral operations the most damaging. That was cattle and horse rustling. It proliferated because, along with the inadequacies of legal deterrent, the young stock hands had a habit of blowing their wages on alcohol and sex and were constantly tempted by literally thousands of poorly supervised herds that regularly wandered miles from their home range. To many men who considered turning to crime, it was doubly tempting that a substantial number of the animals, including newborn calves and colts and the stock of careless owners, were unbranded. Much has been written about the waves of rustling that struck the Montana grazing industry in the 1880s and 1890s and of the vigilante organization known as "Stuart's stranglers" that formed under the leadership of rancher Granville Stuart and, both with and without support of a sheriff or two, either shot any thieves it found or hanged them from the nearest cottonwood tree.[116] Much less well known is that the rustling problem might have been even worse in Assiniboia and Alberta, as rustlers fearful of vigilante justice commonly migrated north where due process of the law in the hands of the North-West Mounted Police was much less efficient. "Cattle and horse stealing are the crimes I believe to be most prevalent, and they are most difficult to detect," reported Police Superintendent Sanders just after the turn of the century. He knew that a whole list of men – white, Native, and other – had just recently been prosecuted for the crime. Julius Young of Cardston had been sentenced to four years for stealing horses; Fred Brouillette had been charged with stealing a horse from a member of the Peigan Tribe; Joe Vare had been convicted for stealing a colt; Hugh Brewer, of the Blood Tribe, had been sentenced to three years in jail for stealing horses from the Brown ranch; and "a halfbreed Indian who stole four horses from a Blood named Chief Moon, and who had taken these animals to the Cochrane ranch where he had a job hauling logs, was given two years" in jail.[117] The most famous of the men who worked back and forth across the international border were in the Dutch Henry gang. In 1900 Henry and his cohorts joined forces with the rival Nelson-Jones gang and set up headquarters in Assiniboia.[118] Together they were a formidable force. In June 1900 the *Macleod Gazette* reported that Jones and Nelson alone had "stolen over 300 head of horses and thousands of cattle from the northern [Montana] ranges all of which" had been "driven into Canada and disposed of."[119]

The ranges in northern Australia were as open as those in North America and the cattle and horses, a percentage there too unmarked, roamed just as freely.[120] Consequently, "duffing" became a major problem. In 1886 an editorial in the *Northern Territory Times* held out hope that at

CANADIAN COWBOY WITH SIX-SHOOTER. TOM GRAHAM ON HORSE, HIGH RIVER AREA, ALBERTA, [CA. 1893]. GLENBOW ARCHIVES, CALGARY, NA-237-20.

last something was being done to deal with the criminal element near the town of Katherine. Policemen had finally been sent there, it stated, "and not before they were wanted. It is to be hoped they will check the cattle killing and horse stealing scoundrels."[121] All over the Territory the crime continued to proliferate, however, and the police themselves commonly acknowledged their inability to control it with the limited resources at their disposal. "There are a number of horse and cattle stealers . . . camped on the border of Queensland and this colony," the chief at Borroloola reported in 1888, "and I have no doubt that they will now start" operating "on a larger scale as they have no other means of living."[122] The chief knew that Aborigines undertook a large percentage of the duffing in the Northern Territory.[123] He insisted, however, that white perpetrators were themselves a bane to the cattle industry. "To successfully cope with the savage blacks of this district" as well as the "savage and lawless whites" it would be necessary, he said, to bring in another constable as soon as possible as he, himself, had to see to the imposition of customs duties and, therefore, was usually confined to the town. He also wanted a magistrate appointed within or near the town. Since he had come to Borroloola he had "had very little assistance except from the Native trackers," and he had "been placed in a most unsatisfactory position . . . there being no magistrate nearer than the Limmen Bight" some 150 miles to the north. Less than a year later the succeeding chief at the same station insisted that the road between the two centres "is now generally used by the reputed horse and cattle stealers, and I believe it is selected by them because the police stations are a great distance from each other."[124]

While some of the white Australian duffers likely also started out as stock hands and then were tempted into a life of crime, others apparently were criminals from the beginning. In 1896 a frustrated squatter at Auvergne station on the Victoria River described such men in intricate detail. In his mind they were wandering vagabonds who emerged first with the gold fields. They considered legal sanctions largely irrelevant, and they tended to play loosely with all forms of other people's property. "A few years ago" when gold was discovered in Kimberly, Western Australia, "men went there from every quarter, and got there either by fair or by foul means; several got there . . . by coming to this station and stealing from 60 to 100 head of horses." Now, however, Wandi Goldfield in the Northern Territory was apparently more productive and "many of these horse-stealing and cattle killing scoundrels" were reappearing.[125] Three had recently come to his station claiming to be destitute and hungry. He felt sorry for them and gave them supplies, including a large amount of beef. After they slipped away without warning he decided to follow them. "The first night they camped eight miles from the station at a large lagoon and here willfully and wantonly shot a young bullock for no other motive . . . than to see the poor brute drop dead." Further along their trail the man found the lifeless body of a second animal. The duffers had taken "about 100 lbs. of beef" from it, "salted" the meat "on some green branches close by and left . . . about 700 lbs, to rot in the sun." The squatter used the occasion to take the standard swipe at the police for their inability to protect the cattle herds. "These sorts of criminal actions do not occur where there is police protection provided. All that we want now is for the Government to decline to take our rents and then we will know that they completely ignore our existence." He also suggested the need for vigilante justice. If proper protection "be denied me," he fumed, "then I certainly think the least the Government can do is to give the law-abiding subject full permission to deal with these horse stealing scoundrels and cattle killing assassins the way he thinks best."[126]

For those thieves who wanted, sooner or later, to market their takings, the unmarked cattle were no doubt the safest ones to steal. However, some of the Australian criminals learned to use what cattlemen in the Canadian and American West dubbed the "running iron." It was a short branding iron with a curved end on it that could be heated over a fire and then used to alter existing brands. In 1896 a Northern Territory outlaw named Jack Monaghan working near Turn Off was known to have changed the brand W22 on some horses belonging to William Osmond of Elsey Cattle Station to M33. Another man named Jim Campbell "got into trouble" for "altering the Victoria Downs cattle brand G10 to his brand (diamond eighty eight)."[127] The degree of sophistication such men developed in their illegal activities reflected the fact that they had become, in essence, professional criminals. Their "conviction . . . is very desirable," one of the police supervisors noted, "as they will not work."[128] Some ranchers on both ends of the world built up their herds principally by pilfering their neighbours' cattle. On the American Great Plains this crime also sometimes crossed the international border. Newspaper reporter Leroy V. Kelly wrote that in August 1901 a Montana roundup "came over picking up strays, and one cow with the "WW" brand of William Wallace of Montana seemed very loath to leave Canadian herds and territory." It escaped "from the American cowboys" and "dashed madly back into the ranks of the Canadian stock, where she found her calf just as widely, but more blindly, searching for her." When the police investigated they discovered "that the cow also carried the "2PD" brand of a Canadian rancher named Henry Marshall." Wallace was arrested, tried, and fined seventy-five dollars and costs.[129] Among the Northern Territory duffers, Martin Fleming, for one, was supposed to have accumulated several hundred head this way for his cattle station on the Daly River.[130]

There can be little doubt that Native depredations of the livestock herds was more costly to the first Australian graziers than to the Canadians. At one point the interviewee before the 1895 commission referred to this problem directly: the Natives "have been a very heavy cost to us.

With blacks it is not only what they kill, but they run your stock about," which causes stress and carcass shrinkage. "When I was at the Victoria Downs I came upon a camp a few days' old with between thirty and forty blacks' ovens . . . That meant that the number of blacks in the camp was about 100, and there were the remains of eight head of cattle that they had slaughtered a few days before."[131] He pointed out that this kind of slaughter often went on under the nose of the settlers. The camp he spoke of, he said, was only four miles from Gordon's Creek station. Reports of destruction came from all parts of the Territory. On the far eastern side along the coast of Carpentaria, a stockowner noted: "all through the wet season, the cattle were constantly attacked and killed. Down towards the coast, the salt water tribes made frequent successful raids, whilst the mountain blacks took heavy toll in the . . . valleys. A great number of the stock speared were eaten, many died from wounds, and some appeared to have been slaughtered for sport and devilment." The writer believed that "the worst trouble was with the small mobs of cattle which the natives cut off from the main herd. These little lots, scared to madness . . . would rush, floundering through the endless bog and slush. As they went on they got ever more and more split up and constantly attacked by fresh tribes." Even the few that survived were often lost, as they "would be scattered, so far as to be practically impossible to muster again."[132] Natives also killed cattle during the open range period in Canada as the animals wandered across lands that had once been occupied by their natural food staple, the buffalo. In the 1890s one ranch manager reported that "about twenty Blood Indians" were "under arrest for killing" a neighbour's cattle "to procure tongues for the Sun Dance."[133] Years later another told one of the police commanders that he had caught some Peigan Indians corralling one of his steers. "Had I not been short-handed," he said, "I would have sent for you and had the whole gang arrested. To allow these Indians to camp" out "for weeks at a time without . . . men to oversee them is I think a strong temptation to commit depredations on cattle and something will have to be done.[134] However, for the most part the damage was small – one or two cattle here and there. The Mounties not only did an efficient job of keeping the Indians on the reserves, they also quickly extinguished any attempts by white ranchers to exaggerate the costs or to take the law into their own hands. In the early 1880s George and Edward Maunsell put 103 cattle on the range on the Milk River Ridge. A half dozen or so other ranchers followed suit. Within thirty days all but 56 of the Maunsells' cattle and a similarly large percentage of their neighbours' had disappeared. As soon as they became aware of their losses, they went to the local police. Indian Commissioner E. Dewdney, backed by Colonel James F. Macleod, the commanding officer at Fort Macleod, told them in no uncertain terms that attacks by ranchers on Indians would not be tolerated. Much of the loss of livestock, Dewdney told them, was undoubtedly due to cattle wandering back to Montana and of rustling by whites. "Can we shoot any Indians we find killing" our stock, one of the ranchers asked. Dewdney replied, "If you do you'll probably hang."[135] From that point on Native predation on the herds was mentioned from time to time in the police reports and the local newspapers, but the losses were normally light.[136]

How much cattle rustling added to the financial difficulties the cattlemen struggled with cannot be estimated. Widespread failure within the industry on both continents enables us to say one thing for sure, however – the cattlemen could ill-afford it. The evidence of livestock theft, like all the other forms of misconduct presented in this chapter, is, admittedly, anecdotal. It has to be. In expansive, under-policed communities where legal redress was often unattainable, a couple of hungry, out-of-work stock hands could, without witnesses, butcher a steer; or one man could siphon off a few calves from another man's herd and incorporate them into his own. Therefore, documents such as court records just do not tell anything like the whole story.[137] The historian is left with impressions gained from the newspapers, the existing correspondence of police and others, and the reminiscences of some of the people who experienced frontier life first hand. What these kinds of sources evince about the societies examined here is that they were anything but orderly and law abiding. Single young men found their own ways to deal with a shortage of nighttime entertainment facilities and a dearth of sexual partners, and, generally speaking, they broke laws with relative impunity when it suited their purposes. A disproportionate number of women were drawn into prostitution, illegal liquor circulated regularly through the land, gambling proliferated, and assault and murder were anything but rare. In that sociocultural setting it is not surprising that livestock commonly disappeared from the ranges without a trace. The fact that all the above forms of disorder and violence transpired in ranching societies in different hemispheres at precisely the same moment in their historical development illustrates the hand of environmental forces over and above climate, ecology, and region. More than anything else, what encouraged people to evade or distort the conventions and rules of behaviour that had evolved over time in the worlds from which they had come was the frontier itself.

6

PRODUCING "FATS": THE CANADIAN WEST

The future would gradually bring a more orderly culture to both of these regions as law enforcement agencies improved, gender ratios became more balanced, and families rather than single young men increasingly set societal norms and values. In the meantime, there were two other substantial challenges western Canadian and northern Australian pastoralists faced in common. Both derived to a significant degree, if not totally, from New World circumstances. One fundamental challenge was overcoming the barriers to the production and marketing of high-quality finished beef in a geographically remote, open range setting. The other challenge involved compensating for the ranchers' own failures in pasture management. This chapter will illuminate the situation in Alberta and Assiniboia, and the next chapter, that in the Northern Territory.

The Canadian ranchers, on the whole, started out with inferior stock and then attempted to clean it up by selling the worst of it for meat. They also worked slowly over time to upgrade the overall quality of their herds by bringing in well-bred bulls and cows via the Canadian Pacific Railway from the East and overseas. Upgrading the herds proved daunting, however, because the range on both sides of the Canadian-American border was quite saturated with inferior scrub bulls. Some of these seem to have originated as calves that were missed during the roundups and were never subjected to the knife. Many, however, were, as James Cox pointed out, simply poor-quality animals that the corporations imported from the American Midwest during the period when they were most euphoric

POORLY FINISHED RANGE CATTLE, HAND HILLS, ALBERTA, PRE-1908. GLENBOW
ARCHIVES, CALGARY, NA-3929-8.

about the future of western ranching and clamoured to find stock. "A
very large number of bulls that, under ordinary circumstances would have
been" culled out of the herds in the Mississippi Valley and butchered, had
been "preserved and shipped to these Western ranges" where they fetched
the high prices of prime breeding stock.[1]

The other thing that damaged beef herd quality in western Canada
as time went on was the tendency of the ranchers to augment their herds
by purchasing unsuitable stock from dairy farmers in the East. As their
livestock numbers declined due to severe winters, wolves, and the mange,
the cattlemen became desperate to find ways to recoup. They discovered
that there were large numbers of relatively cheap one- and two-year-
old steers and heifers that the dairymen in the more eastern provinces of
Manitoba and Ontario produced in the process of keeping their cows bred
and lactating. These, the western ranchers purchased in large numbers and
shipped to the frontier by rail. They then grazed them on their ranges,
hoping to bolster their sales as yearlings would mature and, they hoped,
be ready for the slaughter market in significantly less time than their newborn calves. The integration of the dairy breeds illustrates the naivety of
some of the owners. Holsteins, Jerseys, and Guernseys, or crosses thereof,

POORLY FINISHED RANGE CATTLE, MILK RIVER AREA, ALBERTA, 1904. GLENBOW
ARCHIVES, CALGARY, NA-3914-5.

tend to have a stringy, less well-rounded and fleshy body than beef breeds
such as Angus and Hereford and they do not fatten up well. On the slaughter market they tended to grade about the same as the other rougher cattle.
Moreover, while the males were normally relieved of their propagatory
organs before the ranchers purchased them, the females usually came with
their ovaries intact and few of the ranchers bothered to remove them. The
low qualities of these cattle also diluted the quality of the herds.

Consequently, the western ranchers not only dug into their company
purses to cover extra expenses, they also failed to attain the desired recompense. When it came time for them to put their "fats" up for sale, the
brokers discounted the rougher sorts, usually marketing the beef locally rather than trying to compete for the more discriminating palates of
Europe. The two photographs above are typical of those found in the
images of early range animals in the Glenbow Archives in Calgary. The
motley cattle are generally on the thin side with a sinewy, "shelly" carcass
and a slight, rather boney rump. The spotted colouring of many reflects
dairy bloodlines.

The other obstacle for the western ranchers when trying to produce
quality beef was their own distinctly cavalier attitude towards pasture

management. On the northern Great Plains the growing season is short – basically four months – and it has become clear that the only way to get the best production out of it, particularly when attempting to graze year round, is to practise a sophisticated form of grasslands conservation. This technique, often called "rest rotational grazing," is hands on and refined, and requires substantial infrastructure, particularly extensive networks of fences and mechanical watering systems. It is, in short, more or less the antithesis of the profound neglect approach. Ranchers who practise it fence their ranges into a multiplicity of relatively small pastures and then *rotate* their cattle every few to several days from one pasture to the next so that the leafy matter on the grasses is never eaten off by more than about two-thirds. "Grazing or browsing too much of the leafy material, the collector of solar energy, will wear the plant down and reduce its ability to store energy in its roots." This keeps it "dependent on surface water" and unable to access "deeper, more abundant supplies."[2] During the summer months rains sometimes fall infrequently on the Great Plains and, with limited moisture, overgrazed plants suffer.[3]

Under the rest rotational system, each fenced-in pasture is given a number of rest periods over the course of any one season and then is allowed to replenish for an entire year every several seasons.[4] The other important management approach cattlemen are utilizing along with it is known as "time-controlled grazing." The purpose is specifically to enhance the dominant grass species that nature selected for the area long before European pastoralists appeared. Rough fescue is dominant among these species on the northern plains. When the land is good to it, the rough fescue returns the favour as it produces substantial "litter" that contributes organic matter to the soil and enhances moisture retention and infiltration.[5] Moreover, its long roots help to conduct moisture down into the subsoil. Its growth cycle begins early in the spring and is complete by early summer. Rough fescue is particularly ideal for winter grazing. It cures on the stem and retains its food value after the summer months, and its long, stiff leaves will stand through even deep coverings of snow.[6] Efficient ranchers who graze cattle year round keep their stock off their winter pastures in the spring and summer to maintain it in the healthiest possible condition. On many ranches, lowland fields are grazed early in the growing season (early June to late July) since the other tall species there – wheat grass – matures early and loses its nutritional value if not eaten down at that time. The drier upland ranges are kept free of livestock until the dormant period from August on, when the rough fescue can be used to best advantage. These practices allow the regrowth that plants require for rebuilding roots

Many modern ranchers have been particularly determined to find ways to protect their grass in delicate riparian areas – that is, those along and around natural water sources. Left on their own, cattle will inhabit these areas almost exclusively in the warmer months. There the stock finds the thickest stands of grass and can readily access water. The problem is that as the animals crowd in along the water's edge they eat the grass down to nothing and trample it into the mud. They also kill off woody vegetation (saplings and bushes), the roots of which help to maintain bank stability along rivers and streams. Once the grass in one riparian area is depleted to the point where grazing becomes impossible, the animals move on to another area inflicting similar damage on it. Eventually all the prime grasslands on a particular ranch may be affected. If, after time, the animals can no longer find good grazing by a water source they will move some distance away from one, making the trek back to it when thirsty. This will cause them to "walk off" much of the nutrition they take on from grazing and, therefore, to fail to gain weight properly. To protect riparian areas, ranchers place a tank some distance from a natural water source and pump the water to it. Usually the animals prefer to drink from such a facility rather than wading into a stream, lake, or slough. The tank is moved from time to time to prevent damage to the grass around it. Particularly conscientious operators also fence off their natural water source to ensure that their cattle stay well back from its edges.

Refining management techniques can improve productivity on any particular grasslands area as much as three-fold.[7] Those ranchers who practise these methods on the better western ranges expect to graze at a rate of about twenty acres per mature steer or cow calf unit per year. Many of them are aware that, in using a rest rotational approach, they are emulating the grazing habits of the buffalo, which fed off the plains and foothills in the millions before the arrival of Europeans.[8] These animals constantly moved around during each season and thus avoided overtaxing or despoiling particular grazing spots. Normally they also inhabited the lower plains in the warmer months and then migrated to the shelter of upland hills and forests during the cold winter period, giving the grasses in each area several months of rest every year.[9]

The frontier cattlemen used none of these techniques. They did not attempt to control herd movements much further than to try to keep the animals on their leased and/or freehold terrain, and they did nothing to protect the banks and flood plains of their rivers, creeks, and lakes.[10] Cattle do not instinctively follow the migration patterns of the buffalo, so some of the early cattlemen drove their stock down onto the plains in the spring and then back up into the protection of the heavily forested hills as winter was setting in. However, cattle lack the heavy fur around the head the buffalo are endowed with, and so, when the colder winds started to blow out of the northwest, they would instinctively turn their backs to it and then move in the direction it was blowing. Before the range was fenced, therefore, numbers of them would end up on the plains in winter. During the summertime, on the other hand, as riparian areas on the lower pastures became eaten down, some of the cattle would roam back up into the high country seeking better pickings around the streams, sloughs, and lakes there. The net result was that throughout virtually any year domestic animals could be found grazing high and low, and none of the grasslands was afforded time to recoup.

Given their carelessness with respect to grasslands conservation, it became increasingly easy for the ranchers on the northern plains to overgraze, as once stunted, natural grasslands become less and less productive. Pasture mismanagement generally should be seen as a frontier circumstance in the sense that, to some degree at least, it related to the ranchers' ignorance of conditions in their new land; and it occurred throughout the entire North American West.[11] In 1888 an expert testifying to the commission investigating the collapse of beef prices in the United States argued that "the present state of the cattle markets . . . [is] due" in the main "to the overproduction, especially of grass-fed cattle, the marketing of immature animals, which are too thin for the block" and the flooding of the market by "ranchers of the West and Southwest, who herd thousands of . . . inferior cattle upon public lands or lands of little value." The "overproduction of range cattle, has greatly overcrowded the . . . range country, and has, consequently, lessened the quantity of grass and impaired its nutritive quality."[12] The truth is, wrote James Cox, "the feed" in past years has been eaten down "clear to the ground, so that now,

Hereford cattle on lush grasslands, Domburg ranch, southern Alberta, 1892. Glenbow Archives, NA-1940-12.

Roundup crew on lush grasslands, High River area Alberta, 1892. Glenbow Archives, NA-2294-26.

instead of raising such cattle as we did ten years ago, we are producing half-starved, ill-shaped beasts, that do not carry flesh or make weights as beef steers, even when fully matured."[13] Speaking of the impact of the infamous winter of 1906-7, well-known Calgary newspaper reporter L.V. Kelly wrote that on the Canadian side of the border "prairie fires and crowded ranges took the grass off and left little for winter rustling – in fact, in some districts the range was so overstocked that cattle went into winter in very poor condition, even hay being insufficient to strengthen them against the cold." Scarcity "of food, poor condition, and exceptional storms, snow and cold, demanded a fearful toll from the range stock and depleted the herds of the Province by about half."[14]

The two photographs above of land that was clearly not mistreated illustrate what the pastures in the foothills of Alberta would have been like when cattle first appeared on them in the early 1880s. "In some places," Duncan McEachran, the general manager of the Walrond, observed, the grass "was so thick and so long as to impede the progress of horse drawn wagons."[15] The photographs below, taken on ranches from various localities where cattle were pastured extensively, are strong confirmation that grassland abuse was widespread.

The rough fescue and wheat grass have been more or less completely obliterated, and even the shorter indigenous varieties – needle and thread and blue grama, which, respectively, can reach heights of from thirty to forty-five centimeters – have been severely eaten down.

The net carcass yields of the cattle the Walrond outfit's cowboys delivered to the Blood and Peigan Indian agencies in the 1890s provide one of the best and clearest pieces of historical evidence available of the decline in Canadian grass-fed beef resulting from depleted grasslands. In the fall, winter, and spring of 1894 through 1898 the ranch clerk kept meticulous accounts of the dressed weights of these animals.[16] The accounts demonstrate not only that the weights were consistently low but that the drop in the wintertime was always great, and that the average per animal worsened with time. A mature, fully finished grass-fed steer carcass could be expected to yield more than 900 pounds. In the fall of 1894 the August steers at the Blood agency weighed 744 pounds, those for October weighed 808 pounds, those for February 672 pounds, and April 600 pounds. In the same period the cow carcass weights, which one would expect to be around 720 pounds, dropped from 622 pounds to 518

Riparian destruction, Beynon area, Alberta, 1900. The more or less complete destruction of a riparian pasture. Glenbow Archives, NC-43-136.

Bar U ranch cowboys, southern Alberta, 1901. Glenbow Archives, NA-1035-1.

COWBOYS ON ROUNDUP, WEST OF OKOTOKS, ALBERTA, 1892. GLENBOW ARCHIVES, NA-2084-50.

CATTLE ROUNDUP AT STAND OFF, ALBERTA, CA. 1907. GLENBOW ARCHIVES, NA-100-30.

CATTLE ON RANGE, SOUTHERN ALBERTA, CA. EARLY 1900S. GLENBOW ARCHIVES, NA-4035-199.

COW AND CALF
ON PASTURE, NEAR
BEYNON, ALBERTA,
CA. 1900. GLENBOW
ARCHIVES, NC-43-332.

pounds. In November 1896 the onsite manager told Duncan McEachran that "after working over the range John," the cattle foreman, "thinks we will need all the beef" we have "to fill the Piegan [*sic*] contract. A great many of the cows are not fat enough to make beef in January and February and numbers of them will not hold their condition this winter. Stags [i.e., very rough steers] too are not in the condition they ought to be."[17] In April 1897, at which point the long winter season was coming to an end and spring about to set in, his prediction proved true. The animals "are very light now, and it seems a pity to sacrifice them in that way. They could bring far more money three or four months hence."[18] At that time the dressed weights of the steers had dropped from 764 pounds net the previous November to 583 pounds; and the weight of the cows had declined from 647 pounds to 472 pounds. The following winter the Blood weights declined precipitously once again. In September 1897 the steers weighed 647 pounds and in April 498 pounds; and the cows dropped from 575 pounds to 425 pounds.[19]

It is seldom recognized how much slaughter cattle carcasses of a small size reduced total ranch income. At six cents per pound, steers averaging 900 pounds net were worth $54.00. The Walrond ranch could sell a thousand slaughter steers a year. If properly finished it could expect them to bring in a total of $54,000.00.[20] However, poorly or unfinished steers such as those the ranch sold in April 1898 were worth only $29.88. The difference was more than $24.00 a head. The overall difference for the ranch in any given year might be as high as $24,000.00 on steers alone. This was some $7,000.00 more than the ranch was spending to run the entire operation for a full twelve months.[21] The fact that the numbers consistently show carcass weights for both genders clearly trending downward over a relatively long period suggests that the Walrond company was slowly (or perhaps not so slowly) going bankrupt.

As revealed in the photographs of the grasslands in other parts of the high country where cattle were pastured, the Walrond inability to fatten the cattle properly must not have been uncommon. The legacy of pasture abuse in southern Alberta and Assiniboia has cast a long shadow. Even today the native foothills fescue, which "once occupied about 3.8 million acres in southwestern Alberta," is abundant on only "about 16.8 percent of the original grassland landscape."[22] In the later nineteenth and early twentieth centuries, moreover, the ranchers' propensity to send light cattle off to market reflected the same financial circumstances that had led to pasture abuse and depletion. Mounting financial pressures made it difficult, indeed impossible, for them to allow their cattle enough time on the ranges to reach full maturity. The theory of open range grazing called for the marketing of fat cattle – both steers and heifers – at from four to five years of age. Yet everywhere on the western plains, including the Walrond lease, the tendency was to send them off when they were as young as three years of age. Thus, for instance, L.V. Kelly noted that in 1896 "a large number of three-year-old steers were tempted off the range . . . leaving a void in the ranks of the prime four-year-olds for the next year"[23] Had the ranches been able to hold the cattle longer, it might have allowed them to at least reach maximum bone growth and thus to net a more acceptable carcass weight even without the optimal amount of flesh and fat. What underlay their inability to do so was a chronic cash shortage.

As we have seen, all the ranchers on the northern plains had found it necessary from the spring of 1887 to spend money they had not budgeted for on hay, greenfeed, and labour to get their weaker and more vulnerable cattle through the long winter months. On top of that, from 1896 when the government effectively cancelled their leases to accommodate hordes of incoming homesteaders and squatters, most of the big outfits in Canada had suddenly found themselves having to purchase land they needed to continue to operate. Thus, for instance, around the turn of the century the Bar U purchased close to 19,000 acres of deeded land, the Cochrane 65,000 acres, and the Walrond 38,126 acres. To get the necessary capital many took on mortgages or lines of credit from the banks, or they used any monies they still had left from selling shares to those investors who had believed all the hype about the enormous bounties the frontier would ultimately bring. Either way this strained their cash reserves. It left them obliged to service loans and pay interest, or it forced them to make out annual cheques for shareholder dividends.

The latter part of the above statement requires an explanation. The Walrond example is instructive in that regard too. From its inception in 1883 until it ended active operations in 1907, the ranch's economic performance was anything but impressive, and yet year after year – after paying all its bills for labour, feed, and custom work and setting aside capital for land purchases – the general manager, McEachran, returned a 5 percent dividend to the shareholders.[24] He felt compelled to do this because he realized that, should his shareholders decide that their investment was a bad one, they might well liquidate their holdings. And since that was the ranch's only source of capital this could ultimately shut the business down. In other words, McEachran treated the shareholders' investment capital exactly as one would an operating loan at the bank. Dividends, which are supposed to be a return on profits, he paid without considering whether the company was making money, simply to maintain his financing. The truth of this assertion is evinced in the fact that while he was approving the dividend payments year after year his marketable cattle inventory, the Walrond's only source of income, actually declined in numbers and value.

There can be little doubt, moreover, that McEachran was aware of this. What usually induced him and his onsite manager to look closely at the ranch's herd size was any particularly severe winter that they feared had exacted a heavy toll. After the first really bad winter – that of 1886–87 – McEachran "rode industriously over the range, in all places where . . . [cattle] were said to be lying dead" and he convinced himself that the loss was not heavy. "I am justified in believing," he asserted, "that not even 2/3 of these were ours."[25] Unfortunately, later, after the spring roundup, he discovered that he was wrong. "It is a fact," he said, "that we are short of cattle – to a larger extent than the carcasses would represent."[26] He estimated that 18 percent of the pregnant cows and heifers had died. This figure fits with the number of calves branded that year, which was down by about 24 percent from the previous year and, incredibly, by more than 40 percent from the year before that.[27] McEachran calculated that losses of steers, bulls, and "adult she stock" (dry cows) were about 5 percent. His only consolation was that almost "every other Ranche [company]" was "in the same position" as the Walrond. Indeed, "many" were "even worse off."[28]

During the 1888 spring round up the Walrond cowboys conducted a "rough count" of all the cattle. There were *roughly* 8,225 cows, steers, and heifers plus about 1,380 newborn calves (9,605 overall).[29] In 1891 the ranch did a precise count during the fall roundup. There were 10,433 cattle including newborn calves. Thus for a short period the herd may have grown a little. However, the next several winters were severe and quite a lot of cattle were lost on many of the foothills operations.[30] To make matters worse, in 1893 wolves began to prey more heavily than ever before on the calf crop.[31] No counts were done, but in these later years McEachran figured in an overall annual death rate of 5 percent.[32] In 1895 he began to bolster his inventory by purchasing yearling and two-year-old steers, or "doggies," from Ontario to fatten on grass along with the progeny of his breeding stock.[33] With those included he calculated that by the end of 1897 he should have more than 12,000 animals.[34] This would have comprised the cows, steers, heifers, and breeding bulls and all the calves from the previous spring and summer that had been weaned and separated from their mother as well as the doggies. When McEachran asked his men how many cattle they thought there actually were, he was unquestionably perturbed by the answer. John Lamar, the cattle foreman, had been told to get as accurate an estimate as possible during the previous fall roundup.[35] Whether he conducted a thorough count is unclear, but he was a veteran cattleman from the United States and he must have been accustomed to gauging herd numbers. He figured there were only about 9,000 head. After speaking at length with Lamar, the onsite manager David Warnock told McEachran he felt the cattle foreman was not erring on the low side. In other words he believed that 9,000 might well be high.[36]

Even with the Ontario cattle, therefore, the herd had almost certainly deteriorated again. The next thorough count was done in 1901. The ranch papers do not show the actual figures, but Warnock and McEachran were clearly shocked by what they found. The former felt obligated to come up with an explanation of why the numbers were not higher. Interestingly, he wrote two letters to his superior. In the first he simply admitted the deficiency. He did not send that letter. Instead he wrote a second one in which he tried to soften the blow. "I am enclosing a memo," he wrote, "showing number and classification of cattle on [the] books, and number and classification counted. You will notice that there is a considerable shortage in the number counted principally in cows and aged steers." He also noted, "the calf brand was very disappointing" for 1901, "only totaling 1000." The one glimmer of hope he could offer was that a large number of cattle may have evaded the roundup crews when the tally was taken.[37] On that ground he claimed that it was safe to add 10 percent to the steer count. We should note, this was merely a guess and based on a strong need for self-rationalization and, even if it were true, Warnock was far from comfortable with the overall numbers. The upshot, he said, is that "we are short principally in cows ranging from six to ten years old." This, he argued, was a product of circumstances that predated his appointment as the onsite manager. "I think" it "is largely due to the ravages of wolves in the early 1890s . . . In /93/94/95 and 6 wolves caused us heavy losses in horses, and I am afraid they did much more damage among cattle than we suspected. The winters of 95 and 96 too were severe, and the loss among breeding stock may have been heavier than we realized."

The final count that we know of had to be conducted when the ranch sold off its entire herd after the immense losses of the 1906–7 winter. There are no figures for the count in the Walrond papers. However, the sales contract with Patrick Burns is in that collection.[38] The cattle brought $26.00 a head with calves thrown in for free. McEachran decided to use the proceeds from the sale to pay back the shareholders as much of their original investment as possible. After settling the ranch's bills, totalling at most $15,000.00, he was able to send them a mere $36,748.89.[39] This means that there could not have been more than some 2,000 animals left in the entire herd. The ranch was broke.[40] After the repayment it still owed its investors more than $208,000.00, and all it had left for assets was 38,126 acres of land for which it had recently paid $2.28 an acre, or about $89,000.[41]

The severe winter of 1906–7 was the final deathblow for the Walrond ranch, but it is apparent that McEachran had struggled unsuccessfully to maintain the resources of the operation over the course of the twenty-five or so years preceding that event. The fact that he paid dividends year after year indicates that he felt it impossible to come clean with his shareholders for fear of losing their capital. People who go into a particular venture anticipating great rewards are liable to sour very quickly if their expectations are not fulfilled. We are not sure exactly what McEachran had told the interested parties when he initially put together the financing for the Walrond operation, but we have seen that he was prepared to be very imaginative to make the ranch investment look as attractive as possible. This, and the fact that he had almost certainly read all the promotional literature, strongly suggests that he had made grand promises. We know too that after the Walrond met with early reversals and the value of the shares had to be reduced, some of the shareholders expressed the desire to pull out because "the returns for the years past" had not "been what was expected."[42] Under that kind of threat there can be little doubt that the general manager felt enormous pressure to pay out annual returns even while evidence suggested that his inventory (and profits) were dwindling.

There is no doubt that other companies were struggling either to pay dividends or to service substantial loans. The Powder River Cattle Company of Wyoming brought four big herds of 2,500 head into southern Alberta in 1886 after its manager, the irrepressible dreamer Morton Frewen, had run it nearly into the ground attempting to woo investors with large dividend payments.[43] By 1889 its herd numbers were down to 5,800 and the company sold out. At the same time Sir John Lister Kaye and the Canadian Agricultural Coal and Colonization Company, financed by British investors, was acquiring land along the railway from Crane Lake, Assiniboia, to Namaka near Calgary. Kaye bought the Powder River's headquarters and its cattle. He got into trouble and dissolved the company in 1895. The company that re-emerged from its ashes was the Canada Land & Ranche Company, which, like its predecessor, was commonly known as the 76 or Stair ranch. Basically, on the evidence of shareholder dividends, it was rumoured to have done well.[44] That the ranch failed in 1909 because of depleted financial resources strongly suggests that its returns were no more a true reflection of its profitability than were the returns paid to the Walrond's investors.[45]

Among the companies that faltered under traditional rather than shareholder debt was the Bar U outfit, some twenty miles north of the Walrond. The owner, George Lane, was deeply leveraged for most of his life as a Canadian rancher and particularly so after his partner, the cattle-buying firm of Gordon, Ironside and Fares, abandoned him in 1919.[46] When he died in 1925 the banks took all his land and cattle. High financing charges, like so many other financial obstacles, seem to have been common throughout the Great Plains. In 1890 a Select Committee of the United States Senate investigating the fall in beef prices during the years 1888 and 1889 interviewed Philip D. Armour of the giant beef packing company that bore his name. He cited two factors in the decline: "overproduction" which indicated the overstocking noted above, and "over-marketing" by which he meant "many engaged in the business" had been compelled "to prematurely market their cattle" because "incorporated companies and wealthy individuals" needed to bring in money "to meet the payment of guarantee dividends or of interests and mortgages."[47]

In 1909 the Canadian Veterinary General, J.G. Rutherford, was pointing the finger at overstocking and overproduction when he asked rhetorically, "Is it matter for wonder" that our western cattle "arrive in British lairages . . . gaunt and shrunken . . . looking more like stockers than beeves, that our Scottish friends think we have no feed, or that I should declare" the western grazing business "as sinfully wasteful."[48] He also recognized that the immense distance the western cattle had to travel to reach densely populated overseas markets exacerbated these deficiencies. At this stage refrigerated conveyance for dead meat was available but it had not yet been perfected and was far from reliable.[49] Thus in the late 1890s, many of the bigger Canadian outfits looking for an outlet beyond the domestic market had begun sending their live cattle by rail and ocean liner directly to sales rings in London, Edinburgh, Liverpool, and Glasgow.[50] Most of these operations found that, whatever they gained in price, they lost because of the wear and tear on the cattle from the long trip by land and sea. Relatively feral three- and four-year-old animals that had been loose on the open range basically since birth found the gathering process on their home ranges traumatizing enough. Then the sound of whips whizzing over their heads and screams of handlers when they were being loaded onto trains for the overland trip to Montreal terrified them, and crowded conditions on very noisy railway cars did nothing to ease their anxiety. The Canadian Pacific Railway stopped the trains at various intervals to give the stock rest as well as feed and water. However, that entailed more handling, whips, and screams and probably relieved the stress only minimally. On the ocean voyage between Montreal and Britain the cattle were subject to a good deal more anguish. A first-hand report by a man who was employed on one of the ships in 1889 dramatically substantiates this. On the boat the man was put in charge of twenty-five head of cattle in six pens. His duties included feeding and watering them and poking them with a stick to keep enough of them standing that no more than two in each pen could lie down at one time. Presumably this was to cut down on seasickness. In the beginning everything went well. "The first three days out were passed in routine duty beneath a cloudless sky and over the most beautiful, the smoothest sea that I have ever sailed." Then calamity struck – soon after breakfast on the fourth morning:

> I had barely finished my round of dealing out hay and
> water when suddenly a mighty gust of wind struck the boat.
> My cattle were on the upper deck and I realized the full force of

the hurricane, as its battering rams punched our ribs. Quicker than I can write it, another broadside struck us. Black clouds instantly blotted out the sun. The sky grew as dark as night. All hands were called on deck. Coming up from the southwest, we could see a hideous mountain of storm rolling towards us, bounding at us, and the dense, frowning clouds split by blinding forks of lightening [sic]. In a moment the storm stood like a towering wall of death before us. The treacherous seas reared and bucked and pranced like a mad monster. The winds raved and tore and shook the boat as if it had been a toy, heaving her high on the crest of a frantic wave. Back we sank, with a swift and sickening lunge, into the valley of the waters, and the sea that had reared now pounced down upon our deck and broke with the thunder of a million guns.

I have seen animals panic-stricken in a billow of flame: but never before had I witnessed a scene such as this. Never do I want to see another one like it. My heart wept for the poor brutes as they caught the spirit of the coming disaster and bellowed and moaned in frightful distress . . . Another wave, almost scaling the sky, it appeared, washed up and fell to pieces on our deck, crashing through all barriers. To save my own life I climbed in the hold and waited for the storm to die away.[51]

By the time the storm abated three men and seventy-nine cattle were dead. This was obviously an unusually difficult crossing. However, the north Atlantic is susceptible to high winds and towering waves under normal circumstances, particularly in the fall of the year when most of the cattle were being shipped, and the animals often suffered from seasickness and stress and lost substantial amounts of weight.[52] In the words of one Great Plains rancher, "Cattle cannot be sent five thousand miles by land and sea without such a shrinkage that the profit on the transaction is destroyed."[53]

Many of the cattle from the western United States that were sold in Chicago auction rings were purchased by farmers from the corn states – Illinois, Iowa, Kansas, Missouri, and Nebraska – who then finished them properly on excess supplies of corn before sending them to Europe.

Canadian ranchers were well aware that those cattle were doing much better in British sales rings than their own. This was because they not only were bigger and fatter before they left American shores but also because the extra coat of "hard fat" resulting from grain finishing held up better during the voyage. "Our friends in the United States long ago realized the folly of shipping to Europe" live steers "direct from the range" and "soft off grass," the Veterinary General noted in his 1909 report. "Their range cattle are brought to the Middle West, dehorned, if this has not been earlier done, fed for at least sixty days on a ration comprising a liberal allowance of grain, then sent to market . . . carefully inspected and culled. Those deemed fit for export are then taken to the seaboard by fast trains . . . As a result of these superior methods, United States cattle, even when from the Western ranges, arrive in Britain in much better condition than Canadian cattle and, of course, command correspondingly higher prices."[54]

The Canadian ranchers were restrained from selling their cattle in the United States by the ad valorem import duty of 27½ percent, and, before homesteaders fully occupied the farmlands in the West, there was not a vast and very productive agricultural region anywhere in their own country where their animals could be finished on cheap feed grains.[55] Therefore they were forced to continue sending them to Old World sales rings where, in their under-finished and emaciated state, they were severely discounted. "From abroad the supplies of stock consisted of 700 cattle from Canada which were a moderate lot," said a typical British media report. "Some of these were taken for keep," to be finished by British farmers, "the rougher description meeting the worst trade of the season, entailing heavy losses for the exporters."[56] Similar media coverage stated: "the Canadian cattle were a middling and ordinary quality receiving over the whole 56 s[hillings] to 62 s[hillings]" per hundred weight while the grain finished cattle "received 60 s[hillings] to 63 s[hillings]" per hundred weight;[57] "foreign supplies for the week comprised 1,083 Canadians . . . nearly half of which were bought for feeding purposes." Well-fattened cattle "met a better demand."[58] This situation was made worse by the British pleuropneumonia embargo on Canadian stock in 1892. It completely negated the demand for feeders by stipulating that any cattle imported from Canada had to be slaughtered at point of debarkation.[59]

In the final analysis, it seems beyond dispute that large-scale open range ranching in western Canada was doomed from the first. The great operations were unable to overcome the natural environmental challenges associated with grass fattening, all of which were exacerbated by the frontier environmental deficiencies of poor breeding, inadequate grasslands management, geographic isolation, and financial pressures at least in part resulting from the attempt to start an industry in an unfamiliar land where it had not existed before. The following chapter will demonstrate that in northern Australia, where the nearly identical basic open range approach the Canadians were using would endure to the modern era, the first pastoralists faced all the same obstacles.

7

PRODUCING "FATS": THE NORTHERN TERRITORY

Station owners and managers in the Northern Territory also hoped in the beginning that they would be able to market slaughter steers. This idea died slowly. At the opening of the twentieth century, industry observers were aware that in Texas grass fattening had become a thing of the past, and some still felt that its continuance in their own country's grazing lands was simply evidence of the superiority of their natural resources. In 1904 the premier of South Australia, who supposedly had a "good knowledge of the pastoral country of America," asserted that "the best cattle country in the world was the Northern Territory," and that "Texas was not in it [competitive] with the Victoria River" district as "during the last few years" cattle that had been "born, bred, and grazed" in the latter district had been "sent down" to the slaughter markets "rolling fat by tens of thousands." Texan cattle, on the other hand, "nearly all" had to be "topped off with maize in . . . Missouri and Illinois before they were killed."[1]

Had the premier really been familiar with the beef industry in the Territory he would have known that in fact few "rolling fat" cattle had ever been sold out of any of the three grazing areas. Throughout the 1880s and 1890s many of the stations had attempted to market beef by meeting local demand – particularly in Palmerston and/or the goldfields.[2] Because the number of people in the Territory was so small, however, the trade was never brisk. About the largest number of slaughter cattle Alfred Giles at Springvale ever sold in one lot were the fifty he sent to Palmerston in

July 1882.[3] The rest of the sales he recorded were even smaller. Though he was thus not making what would seem heavy demands on his supply herds, which numbered in the thousands at three separate runs, his dressed yields were very much like those the Canadian ranchers were getting. On 4 November 1882 he wrote that he was sending twenty head to a butcher named Ping Que. "They are all good," he noted, "and will run" 700 pounds dressed.[4] When asked for more some ten days later he sent a man to search Delamere for another forty. This he believed "will exhaust my stock of salable cattle." Later the same month, however, he managed to get the butcher to take more, which he estimated would weigh "about" 600 to 700 pounds.[5] "Cattle at Delamere doing very well but not fattening so quickly as I thought they would," he once wrote in his diary.[6]

Lightweight carcasses such as the above, and, indeed, far worse, were a problem for the stations throughout the Territory, and when some tried in the 1890s to gain customers beyond the local markets this proved extremely costly. Before being forced out of the cattle business in the 1880s, Fisher and Lyons had begun shipping to the Dutch East Indies, principally from their holdings at Glencoe and other stations in the top end. In September 1890 Goldsbrough, Mort and Company, having taken over the Fisher and Lyons's leases, sent their man Hildebrand William Havelock Stevens to negotiate with the South Australia Government for support to run a regular monthly beef transport service to Asian states.[7] On 18 July 1891 Stevens signed an agreement with the government giving him an annual subsidy of 5,000 pounds to conduct the trade. Thus was born the Cattle Export Service. In hopes that access to the populous Asian cities could bring huge rewards, the board of Goldsbrough, Mort and Company proved willing to put a sizeable amount of their own capital into the venture. Within days it approved a loan of 30,000 pounds to help Stevens design and build a new steamer, the Darwin, specifically for transporting live cattle.[8] The board also advanced Stevens 500 pounds to upgrade the holding pens and loading facilities at the Port Darwin wharves.

The Darwin made its first voyage from Southampton on 13 February 1892. Unfortunately for the industry, from the beginning the trade was virtually always conducted at a loss. There were a lot of obstacles – from changing exchange rates in Singapore to redwater disease, which eventually got the Australian cattle prohibited in Batavia and Java.[9] However, the most persistent roadblock was the difficulty of finding enough good fat cattle in the Territory to bring a reasonable return. Even after he transferred all the cattle from the Glencoe region to the better pastures of Victoria River Downs, Stevens found it impossible to pull out adequate numbers of properly finished animals from his grazing herds. His contract with the government required him to take stock from other stations too, and he would have been happy to comply. However, even when he combed the entire Victoria River and western Tablelands regions, he was usually (and maybe always) unable to find satisfactory supply. The dressed weights of the cattle shipped to the Asian markets whose sales were recorded in the Goldsbrough, Mort and Company papers, now preserved at Canberra, were all incredibly low for so-called slaughter carcasses. The weights also varied considerably from shipment to shipment. "You will find that the average weight of bullocks killed" in Singapore "in December [1892] was only 430 lbs.," a company representative reported, while for the previous three months "it was 480 lbs." This, he pointed out, resulted in "a serious reduction" in the amount of money the cattle brought in of "about $900."[10] He also noted that a hundred bullocks at Batavia in September 1892 "gave an average weight of *515 lbs.*" and "*100 bullocks* in January gave an average weight of *425 lbs.*" "If the *100 January bullocks* had weighed as much as those in September," he said, "we should have realized – taking the average gross price obtained as 9¾ cents per lb. – $5,115.00" in total "– or say *$14.25* per head more" when all the other costs were figured in.[11]

In 1893, before the prohibitions regarding redwater were announced, Stevens contracted to supply 750,000 pounds of beef to the Dutch military in Java through an agent in Batavia. The agent offered the potentially rewarding price of 8 pounds sterling a head. Unfortunately, however, the dressed weights of the cattle, expected to be around a very modest 600 pounds, in fact averaged less than 400 pounds, and the agent buying by the head and selling by the pound could not make ends meet. Ostensibly, Goldsbrough, Mort and Company was unable to collect a lot of the money he owed them. Considering that a net yield of 900 pounds would not have been extraordinary for a properly finished carcass, the best of the sales the company seems to have made in the early 1890s were worse than poor; they suggest an altogether dysfunctional business.[12] In later deliveries there may have been some improvement. The company sent 104 cattle to Singapore in May 1893, for instance, that averaged

502.48 pounds.[13] However, that sort of yield was obviously still far below what should have been considered acceptable.

While records are not complete, evidence suggests, moreover, that small carcasses remained a problem for the company from that point until the end. Both Stevens and then in 1897 his replacement, Thomas Maldrum, must have known that supplying unfinished, low-yielding stock was uneconomic but they were under pressure to fulfill their company's contracts and just did not have access to the kind of cattle that was desired. In October 1897 Maldrum wrote to A.M. Watson, the manager at Victoria River Downs, with strict orders to find cattle no matter how poorly finished so that the company could fulfill its obligations. "My instructions from Head Office are to get the necessary cattle from V.R.D. even if light by weight, both for shipment and local consumption," he wrote. He actually pleaded with the manager not to let him down. "Only on your good self could I rely," he said, "with the assistance of our drovers, for this to be done." He also indicated that other sources of slaughter cattle had all but completely dried up. "Either through drought, or outside purchases" the entire Tablelands area had been "denuded," leaving the company dependent on its own station "for almost every hoof." It is indicative of the pressure Maldrum was feeling that he closed his letter with: "I can only trust to your sending" the drovers "back not empty handed."[14] Apparently he had made an attempt shortly before this to find suitable stock on the station and failed. "Returned today, no bullocks Victoria Downs . . . too poor, Cattle in bad state for grass and water," a drover had informed him by telegram.[15] He had sent this telegram on to the Melbourne office, only to be told to get the cattle no matter what. Watson must have supplied the necessary cattle. However, that did not relieve the pressure for long. At the end of November Maldrum found himself pleading once again for supply. "Owing to the long spell of dry weather, you will not be able to get a mob of prime fats, but I want you to lift as good as you can find," he told his drover, Joseph Davis. I am "writing to Mr. Watson explaining our practical necessities for the ship and local market, and asking him to do his best in giving you as good a lot as he can."[16]

In December 1897 the government determined that it was not getting value for its money and withdrew £5,000 subsidy. That pretty much ended attempts to penetrate the Asian market. Shortly thereafter the board of Goldsbrough, Mort and Company decided to close down its export business because "with the prohibition of the import of meat into Batavia" there was "no prospect of running . . . at any profit."[17] Along with Alfred Giles's expectations regarding the beef he sold, this episode prompts one to doubt if any significant number of cattle marketed from the Northern Territory in these years yielded well. The man questioned before the beef commission in 1895 certainly did not think so. He testified that at the time when attempts were being made to access the markets in Singapore and Batavia "small cattle" was the greatest obstacle.[18] Cattle throughout the Territory are "very light," he said, "a great deal lighter than they should be. It is very hard to get bullocks over 7 cwt. to ship. The average . . . is seldom over that when they go on board."

The truth is that the Victoria River Downs was unable to grow and fatten its cattle as quickly as H.W.H. Stevens had originally expected when he accepted the local and overseas orders – and considering the station claimed some 30,000 head in its vast herds,[19] and that he could call on other producers as well, supplying the 250 to 300 animals he needed each month should not have been a problem if they had access to decent pasturage year round.[20] Clearly they did not. "Nutritional problems in cattle," which became "most evident towards the end of the dry season," were an annual concern in both the Victoria River and Tablelands districts.[21] Since such problems also occurred during dry periods after any substantial rains in the Alice Springs region, it is evident that it was quite difficult for stations anywhere in the Northern Territory to get their animals fat and keep them in that condition. Moreover, any stock the Australians did send off to market must also have lost weight they could not afford to lose from their boney frames due to shrinkage. They had first to be trailed at least a few hundred miles from their home station to the Palmerston–Pine Creek Railway (completed in 1888), and then "trucked" the 240 kilometres north to Port Darwin. Those heading to Asia were then landed, reloaded, and "retrucked" for the short trip to the jetty where they were herded aboard the steamer.[22] The overseas portion of the journey was shorter and presumably somewhat less arduous than that from Montreal to Britain, but it would have taken a toll in flesh nonetheless.

Though not exacerbated by overgrazing, the environmental obstacles Territorial producers encountered trying to produce fats quite directly mirrored those the ranchers faced in western Canada, where seasonally diminished pasturelands and shrinkage were also barriers to efficient production and advantageous sales. When a member of the 1895 beef commission asked the man from Victoria River to explain why he thought Territorial cattle were so light, he introduced two other factors, both of which were also germane on the northern Great Plains of North America. "One," he said was that "people are . . . in too great a hurry to realise" a return on their investment and consequently they "send their bullocks in" when "they are too young."[23] In other words, their need to pay their bills was pressuring them to market their cattle before they had had enough time to fill out properly. Extremely high startup costs, augmented by interest payments on loans and overdrafts with which men like Costello at Lake Nash and Buchanan at Wave Hill grappled, certainly caused cash deficits. Some stations may also have been paying "guaranteed" dividends, though one doubts this was widespread since the experienced Australian owners and managers had a realistic enough understanding of their business not to make the wild promises to their investors that the North Americans made. The second reason the Victoria River man gave for light stock was that the stations "do not pay enough attention to breeding." They "breed from all sorts of bulls" running loose on the open range.[24] This testimony is borne out by the 1923 survey of Tablelands cattle stations mentioned in chapter 3. "The breeding of beef cattle . . . throughout the Northern Territory needs greatly improving," it stated. "The standard of the herds must be raised very much higher if cattle for beef export purposes" are "going to compete successfully with" those from "other countries of the world."[25] Presumably, most of the more experienced Australian pastoralists brought reasonably high-quality cattle north in their initial herds. There is no evidence of the kind of panic buying of poor breeding stock that underlay the development of the industry on the northern Great Plains. However, inevitably, disadvantageous crossbreeding and, indeed, inbreeding, occurred on all open range pastures and a percentage of young bull calves, not all of which were of desirable quality, also managed to avoid the knife.[26]

The Northern Territory cattlemen could not solve the problem of low carcass yields by adopting grain finishing any more than the first ranchers in Canada could. This was because, as will become clear in a future chapter, their environment was not, and never would be, suitable to arable agriculture.[27] Eventually after the failure of the Cattle Export Service, most of the stations concentrated instead on accessing the markets of southern Australia where populations, particularly in and around Sydney, Melbourne, and Adelaide, were denser and ultimately the demand for beef much greater than in central or northern areas.[28] They had only one way to reach these markets – by retracing the steps of the men who had driven their stock in via one of the long, hard overland routes. Eventually they had to almost entirely give up the idea of producing slaughter cattle. A few stations began sending bunches of what were described as both "store and fat bullocks" south from the southeastern Tablelands in the 1880s.[29] If any of these cattle actually started out with much flesh on their bones, they tended to lose it during the journey, and it soon became clear that they were almost all being bought up by grain farmers from arable parts of southern Queensland or New South Wales or even South Australia.[30] Severe drought in Queensland from 1897 to 1902 emptied the pastoral areas of that state of range stock and this brought a greater de-mand than ever for Territorial feeders. The impact was felt in all three of the grazing districts. By 1906, Alexandria, Brunette Downs, Rockland's Pastoral Company, Cresswell Downs, and Austral Downs were all sending from six hundred to one thousand head at a time down from the eastern Tableland.[31] By then it had become commonplace for more distant runs such as Gordon Downs or Wave Hill from the Victoria River area to walk their cattle more than eighteen hundred miles to the market. There were four main routes: from northern Victoria River and Tableland districts to Borroloola to the west of the Bay of Carpentaria to Burketown in north-western Queensland and south from there to the sales ring in Charleville, Queensland; easterly through Newcastle Waters across the mid-Tableland region, along the Georgina River into Queensland at Lake Nash and then south to Charleville; along the old Overland Telegraph Company line from central Australia south to Charlotte Waters in South Australia and then on to the railhead at Oodnadatta for the sales ring in Adelaide; and from the western Tableland region to Birdsville in southwest Queensland and along the so-called "Birdsville track" to the rail yards at Hergott Springs in South Australia and then Adelaide.[32] Charleville, where the famous stockman and broker Sidney Kidman dominated the ring, was the biggest sales centre countrywide. Kidman sent lots of the cattle by rail directly to individual farmers in the southern states or to the auction in one of the other centres.[33]

The following report of a trip led by William Phillips, droving for William F. Buchanan of Wave Hill, is one of the best and most detailed depictions available of the entire arduous journey from the more distant north. An editor commented that "one of the most striking features" of the journey was "the number of other drovers" who were "'on the track,' over a route which a few years ago was one of the most lonesome on the continent."[34] Showing the same high respect for the Australian stockmen that North Americans tended to feel for the iconic cowboy, the report described Phillips as "an unostentatious man, with no bush swagger" who "doesn't go round boasting of his droving feats." But if you simply "ask him how he fared" on this thirty-two-weeks excursion "he will just tell you a plain, unvarnished tale of his principal movements."

The stockmen at Wave Hill mustered some 7,750 cattle all told for the trip and Phillips and his men started out with 1,250 in their group. They set out on April 4 for Burketown in the first stage and then, after taking on provisions, headed for Burrandilla, a feeding station Buchanan owned some twenty miles from Charleville.

> By the point compass Charleville is southeast of Wave Hill. However, Phillips went northwest for the first 300 miles. He followed the waters of the Northern Territory down to the coast . . . The party crossed the watersheds of the Daly River and Katherine River, and touched the overland telegraph line at the head of the King River, and then . . . [followed] the watershed to the Roper River. The party zigzagged the rivers as much as possible for water. At times water was very scarce. Phillips rode 75 miles a day in search of water. A mob of 1230 head of cattle and 30 horses on a dry, sandy, spinifex . . . need a good drink occasionally. The party set out . . . with 30 horses, but these were increased to 43 head by purchase en route.

> The Roper is not an easy river to cross, for its banks are very steep, and there are only two fordable places in its course – McKenzie's bar and the Roper bar. Moreover, the river is full of alligators, with insatiable appetites. So the plan is to . . . cross when the tide is out. When the tide is up the water

is salt, and alligators are plentiful. At low water the stock can drink and cross without affording a meal to the reptiles. These are important matters to the drover, for his aim is to deliver with as low a percentage of loss as possible . . .

How unpopulated all this country is may be seen from the fact that the droving party proceeded 600 miles before they struck the first store. Aboriginals are plentiful, and not too tame. If unmolested, and if no gins [young girls] are enticed to the droving camps, the blacks are tractable: but if . . . [otherwise] then they show fight. If treated up to their standard of fairness they are friendly enough; they will give information about the country and where to get water. When you strike two stores in 1400 miles, and practically all the people you see are armed aboriginals in the nude, and as wild as the country they haunt, then their assistance is much more appreciated than their opposition. Phillips and his party carried arms and ammunition, ready to be used at a moment's notice . . . There are no tracks or routes from Wave Hill to the Queensland . . . and although the country from the Katherine River to Borroloola, on the McArthur River, was bad, he says that the country from Borroloola to Burketown is the worst bit of droving country in Australia. Leaving Borroloola there was a 40 mile stage absolutely destitute of water. The country was sandy desert, with spinifex or cypress pine and paperbarked-tree scrub. Some of the rivers between Borroloola and Burketown were very dry; drought for two years had prevailed where drought of such length was never previously known . . .

They arrived at Burketown on August 4, and thus were 18 weeks travelling 1150 miles with their mob of cattle, which was excellent work considering the nature of the country. On some of the ranges dividing the watersheds the drovers tied up their horses and let the cattle string down the sides as leisurely as they pleased for safety sake. Even then a few were maimed and lost. Along that route . . . was an 80 mile stretch of storm-strewn country, where the packhorses had great difficulty in picking their way. Trees 2ft through at the butt were snapped like carrots. Evidently a whirlwind, tornado, or some other blast from the air furnace had swept along some little while previously. . . The party had travelled nearly 1800 miles, passed three post offices, and seen four white women . . . The party left Burketown on August 6 . . . and they then met open Downs country for the first time; a great relief from the sand and spinifex country that they had passed. Even then there were only 2½ per cent, of losses of cattle; some died through eating poison bush, and others were lamed when crossing the ranges. After leaving Burketown the mob crossed the Leichhardt River, 40 miles out, got on to the Landsborough River and followed it up 80 miles. On these rivers there are only crocodiles, comparatively tame creatures not like their salt-water compeers, the alligators, that are veritable tigers when men or beasts are about. From the Landsborough they crossed on to the Cloncurry, struck Conobie station; got onto roads and tracks, and generally trod on the skirts of civilization. Crossed the Cloncurry on to Eastern Creek, through Dalgonally station with its large herd of Shorthorns. Here it was necessary to carry firewood in the pack bags, to last two nights. Instead of wild, trackless country, where you had to "trust in the Lord, and keep your powder dry," you now had to keep to the stock routes, and seeing that at Kyuna on the Diamantina, upwards of 70,000 head of cattle had passed this year between January 1 and September 13, the feed was none too good. Most of those cattle came from the Northern Territory and Gulf country.

Leaving Kynuna the Phillips party covered a 45 mile dry stage and feed was very scarce; the preceding mobs left more hoof prints than herbage behind them. The stock routes are one mile wide, but unless rain falls frequently they powder up. Rain now fell three days and three nights, as it knows how to fall in Queensland. The routes were now boggy, and travelling was slow; however, Winton was reached after . . .

27 weeks on the road from Burketown. Moreover, the losses were only 1½ percent from Burketown. On they went from Winton through Vindex to Evesham. Here the heaviest losses were suffered; three inches of rain had fallen, and there was no feed, the routes were boggy, and nine bullocks and five horses succumbed. They pulled themselves to pieces in the bog . . . From there on to Burrandilla 12 in. of rain fell; they had to swim the Thompson, but the rains gave feed and water so the cattle . . . were all right, so only discomfort and not loss was experienced by the drovers to the end of the journey.

Thus a droving party of eight set out with 1250 head of bullocks on a 2100 miles trip, which they covered in 32 weeks with a loss of only 50 head. This is claimed to be for the distance travelled, the number of cattle taken and delivered, a record for Australia. Mr. C. H. Buchanan, taking delivery . . . for Mr. W. F. Buchanan on November 21, 1906, wrote: . . . "I was very well pleased with the condition of the cattle, and the evident way they were handled during that long trip. It was a credit to . . . [the drover]; his losses were only nominal . . . Mr. Phillips . . . thoroughly understands droving cattle through all difficulties that a drover has to meet in such outlandish trips.

Phillips felt he had done a good job too. "My losses amounted to five per cent," he said, and "Mr. Buchanan was highly pleased" with the cattle, which were "in good store condition."[35] Buchanan used the station at Burrandilla to recondition his cattle on roughage and, possibly, some grain, before putting them through the ring.

The Northern Territorians thus were traversing ground that could be at least as daunting as that navigated by the Canadians on their long excursions from the ranges of the West to Great Britain. Remoteness from densely populated markets was just one of the plethora of strikingly similar challenges and circumstances encountered by the graziers in both these regions. In both cases they started out intending to feed the slaughter market and ended up selling a large percentage of their cattle as stores. The Australians seem to have accepted this development – the Canadians perhaps not so much – but the outcome was essentially the same. A harsh climate and difficult ecosystem, uncontrolled breeding on the open range, a shortage of capital during a period of extremely costly operation in the one region (Northern Territories) and of both high costs and high expectations in the other, the uncertainty of grass fattening, and the lack of large quantities of locally produced feed grains also impacted the cattle industry as it struggled to gain a foothold in both places. The next chapter will demonstrate that when they attempted to expand their grazing programs to include horses, the tests pastoralists in these two frontiers faced and the outcomes they achieved were again much the same.

8

THE HORSE TRADE

Many of the first ranchers in both the Canadian West and the Australian north believed that, along with beef cattle, they could produce quality equine stock within just a few years using the open range system. "Cattle and horses thrive well, especially the latter," the Government Resident in the Northern Territory wrote in his quarterly report of May 1886. He was expressing the widely held opinion that, because horses are more mobile than cattle, they are better able to withstand a difficult environment. "In dry seasons they are able to travel further from the water for feed . . . and the same applies to travelling to market." It is only rarely that

> the road to a market is open for travelling stock throughout its entire length. When the first 500 miles is opened by rain, the other half suffers from want thereof. I am of opinion that . . . [the Territory] will eventually be the chief horse-producing district of Australia. Its contiguity to the tropics renders horses more hardy and better able to cope with the heat and other drawbacks attaching to a tropical country than animals bred further south; . . . horses can always be travelled . . . in the most unfavorable season yet experienced. In the course of four or five years, no doubt large numbers will be sent for shipment and use in Northern Territory.[1]

There was merit in the argument that horses were able to adapt to the rigours of life on the open range. In both Australia and in Canada a sizeable wild horse population emerged without human intervention. Some of the first Australian horses were brought from Timor to Port Essington, on the northern tip of the top end, by late eighteenth- or early nineteenth-century British settlers. These were the Timor ponies. Some of their descendants escaped and roamed the Coburg peninsula thereafter like any other feral species. Horses were introduced to southern Australia at about the same time as the Timors, and some of their descendants also escaped or were released from captivity when it was discovered that the camel, which arrived in 1840, was better suited to dealing with desert conditions.[2] Eventually these horses interbred with the Timors to produce what came to be known as the "brumby."[3] Today the majority of the 300,000 feral horses in Australia as a whole are in Queensland and the Northern Territory. They have adapted to the rank vegetation and erratic elements in arid regions. They have little to fear from predators or disease in the outback but can experience high mortality during drought. Still the population has continued to grow. Mares breed in spring to summer and on average produce one foal every two years.[4] In the nineteenth century, pastoralists in the state of New South Wales began domesticating brumbies, breeding them to Old World species and turning them into both harness and saddle horses known as "Walers." Equine historians tell us that the Waler was considered the finest soldier's horse in the world, gaining international acclaim for its stamina and reliability during the Indian Mutiny, the Boer War, and the First World War.[5]

Under at least equally difficult conditions, a similar lot of wild horses survived in the foothills of Alberta. The Canadian herds have not grown as spectacularly as the Australian herds in the century or so since the first of them escaped from the frontier ranches because the animals are at times rounded up and "harvested" by entrepreneurs and conservationists. Wolf predation on newborns and illegal hunting by humans have also taken a toll.[6] Moreover, the human population in this region is considerably more dense than that in the Australian outback. Current estimates peg the number of wild horses currently in the foothills at between five hundred and a thousand.[7] On both continents the stronger, heartier representatives of the species have been able to acclimatize to the surroundings and pass their durable qualities on from generation to generation.

Considering that horse populations were able to adapt on their own to the natural environment on the two continents, it at first seems curious

AUSTRALIAN WALER HORSE ENCAMPMENT ON MOUNT OLIVET AND MOUNT SCOPUS NEAR JERUSALEM, 1918. LIBRARY OF CONGRESS, LC-DIG-PPMSCA-13291-00108.

that the early pastoralists had very limited success in breeding them for commercial purposes. There were two basic types of horses that they tried to produce. One was the purebred (or nearly purebred) – heaviest set animals with a very powerful-looking, well proportioned, and elegant body. These they hoped to sell principally to breeders who desired graceful animals for the show ring or for pulling stylish carriages; or to the British or Indian military for their highest ranking officers or for hauling their most cumbersome long-range artillery. The other type was less elegant but sturdy working horses of mixed ancestry that ranchers needed to control their range herds or that farmers required to plough and cultivate their fields or that ordinary soldiers required in times of war. History would prove that the latter types could be raised on the open range but only if the foundational herds were solid. It was in attempting to produce the former type on the open range that virtually none the ranchers on either frontier succeeded. The reason was simple – in the short term, at least, it is almost impossible to efficiently raise mounts of that sort without close, hands-on management and control.

The Walrond papers in the Glenbow Archives in Calgary provide significant insights into the well-bred horse business in western Canada. Dr. Duncan McEachran raised pedigree Clydesdales on his farm at Ormstown, Quebec, and in the 1880s he began sending out Clydes and Shires to the western ranch with the aim of building up a herd of the

WORKING PONIES, SPENCER BROTHERS' RANCH, MILK RIVER RIDGE, ALBERTA, CA. 1900.
GLENBOW ARCHIVES, NA-2927-1.

highest quality stock, which he hoped would supplement the cattle business. His enthusiasm is evident in the letters he wrote to his head office in London. "The mares and foals are doing well," he reported, "and I am of opinion agreed universally here that this . . . range is the best horse range in Alberta or anywhere else. I hope arrangements will be made for 200 or 300 fillies with stallions for next spring as they are" almost certain to be "immensely profitable."[8] By 1894 McEachran had a core of 546 of these animals on the ranch.[9] For the next few years he ran between 130 and 170 geldings, which he hoped to market in Canada and Great Britain, and 315 to 375 mares and fillies, the most productive of which were for breeding purposes and the rest for selling along with the geldings. The ranch also maintained several stallions, and each year the operation produced well over a hundred foals. The methods gradually developed for nurturing the animals brought modest refinement to the open range system. The older pregnant mares with the younger and frailer foals were cut out of the herd as winter set in and fed oat hay so they would be in better condition and produce more, and more nutritious, milk for their offspring.[10] However, such measures only temporarily protected just a small percentage of the animals from environmental conditions. All the rest felt the full brunt of those conditions. Among them resurgent wolf populations were the most destructive.[11] After all the horses had been rounded up in the fall of 1894, David Warnock reported with obvious incredulity that "we have only gathered forty-nine yearlings out of one hundred and one turned out in May last . . . [We] have thoroughly ridden all the surrounding country within a radius of 20 miles from the ranche and are satisfied that we have found all that are alive . . . The number of wolves in this part of the range at present is I think unprecedented."[12] All the Eastern horses, he noted, are "entirely devoid of the instinct of self-preservation."[13] The ordinary mixed-breed riding horses that were used for working the cattle herds and which had for generations been born and raised in the West were faring much better. The "cayuse[s] are afraid of wolves," and "will fight when cornered." They "seldom get bitten."[14]

The other major challenge confronting the business was the difficulty of producing animals on the open range that showed well to discriminating clients. Buyers of the highest-quality steeds expected them to have a prodigious, powerful-looking body and a smooth, well-groomed, healthy coat. The Walrond animals repeatedly fell well short of the buyers' expectations. From a strictly cosmetic point of view a great impediment was simply the brands on their hides. Branding was necessary under the open range system for reasons not limited to the need to cut down on rustling. Because livestock wandered, and mixed and mingled over a wide area, branding was the means of indicating not only which horses belonged to which ranches but also age and ancestry. The animals were often marked on the flank, the shoulder, the cheek, and under the mane. Eastern buyers viewed this as a form of disfigurement and reacted accordingly. "It is a great pity to number and disfigure the young stock with so many brands," Warnock grumbled. "Some of the best fillies and geldings are branded in no less than four different places – in fact they are covered with brands like a bunch of Texas steers – and their value in the best markets much depreciated in consequence."[15]

Another problem was that, for the animals to exude a very muscular and healthy build, weather conditions needed to be almost perfect. Often, of course, they were not. During the warm summer months, horses, along with the cattle, would overgraze the grass along natural water sources to such a distance that it would become necessary for them to travel almost constantly to satisfy both thirst and hunger. They thus also could end up walking off more energy than they were able to take on. "Although the wolves have not bothered any of them lately the mares and foals are not as fat as they should be," a Walrond employee noted; "Some of the foals are getting footsore with traveling. The days are getting shorter now and the mares do not get as much feed as they should."[16] When the animals went into winter in a poor state the cold weather was bound to cause a higher death rate than would have occurred were they corralled, stabled, and fed. The ones that were most at risk on the plains were those that were imported and then almost immediately left on their own to fend for themselves. In the winter of 1888 one of the recently acquired fillies fell sick due to "exposure to the cold." The men "blanketed" her and gave her "a dose of linseed oil" but to no avail.[17]

The losses to cold weather, though relatively speaking significant, do not seem to have been as great as those from wolf predation. Compared to cattle, horses are reasonably well equipped to survive the harsh elements. They grow a thick coat when temperatures dip for prolonged periods and they are adept at scavenging for food. Unlike cattle, they will "paw" through deep coverings of snow to feed on the grasses below. Consequently most of them managed to get enough to eat on the open range to sustain life. But after going into the winter in less than fit form they certainly were unlikely to improve. Their digestive systems were not capable of ingesting enough energy as they scrounged overgrazed winter pastures to keep them in pristine condition. When they were brought in from the ranges in the spring, their coats were usually dull and their bodies a little on the gaunt side. This problem was compounded by the fact that, before wells and pumps were utilized, the natural water supply was usually not ample in the wintertime, when the creeks and streams froze. "The majority" of the horses "are now on Callum Creek," Warnock told McEachran in January 1894.

> [While] there is good footing . . . the creek is giving a lot of trouble again and today three of us are all . . . chopping a hole [in the ice] for the calves and foals to drink . . . We had to open a new hole and had to cut through ice fully three feet thick to strike water and then cut grades on both sides to

allow the animals to reach water. In spite of all the time and labour spent the stock do not get sufficient water. It requires some one to watch the . . . holes continually as calves and foals are constantly falling in and if not immediately rescued would drown.[18]

Horses, like cattle, can get by without water by eating snow. However, this is not ideal and, in combination with a less than perfect food supply, it negatively affected how they looked. "The 5 years old geldings . . . are rough in their coats, and would not compare favorably with Eastern horses. If they only had three weeks of green grass they would have quite a different appearance," the men would typically warn their manager in the spring.[19] Oscillating temperatures sometimes proved tough for the horses to adjust to as well. "Up till the last night or two, very hard frost has prevailed," Warnock reported in 1895, and "the changeable weather has been extremely trying to stock, of every description . . . I find that our horses are nearly all coughing, and not looking well." A "bad form" of the disease known as "strangles . . . has broken out amongst the yearlings, and I am afraid we will lose several of the weaker ones."[20]

Records are not available to indicate the Walrond's reproduction rate, but considering the quality of the pasturelands it could not have been good, as proper nutrition during the gestation period is so important. One thing is beyond doubt: along with hide disfigurement, poor conditioning consistently kept the overall value of the ranch's equine stock down. Time and again the managers offered the best of the Clydes and Shires for sale, and in nearly every case discussed in their papers either they or their clients were disappointed with the results. In April 1894 McEachran concluded an agreement with Major James Bell to supply the North-West Mounted Police establishment at Indian Head in the Assiniboia region with 16 head of Clydesdale mares.[21] The men selected "the pick of the not-in-foal" mares for the deal. Later Bell complained that they "were too light" and just "not the class he expected." Warnock responded to his complaints by insisting that the Major needed to "take into consideration the fact that these mares had just come through a hard winter. By the middle of June they would have averaged 150 to 200 lbs. heavier and would have had altogether a different appearance."[22]

On a number of occasions McEachran and his onsite manager put some of the finest animals through Eastern sales rings. In November 1893 they tried Glasgow. When Warnock heard the results he expressed his surprise that they had "received such small figures."[23] In the autumn of 1894 they sent geldings overseas and Warnock once again was "very much disappointed" that they had "sold badly."[24] In the fall of 1895 they decided to try the Montreal market in hopes that farmers in Quebec would want the horses as beasts of burden. The men cut out "a very nice lot" that were "well broken" and "fit to go into hard work."[25] McEachran held the horses in Montreal for several months to feed and groom them before the sale.[26] When it was over, he and his manager were "extremely disappointed that the horses . . . met with such a poor demand."[27] Attempts to market the second and third best Walrond animals proved every bit as discouraging. The ranch, like any other frontier breeding operation, always had quite a number in its inventory that could be described generally as "small, unsound or bad doers."[28] This was, in part at least, because of the difficulty of preventing the indiscriminate mixing of herds. Stallions can sense when mares and fillies are in heat and, unless kept in a barn or a corral with a very strong and high fence, they are almost impossible to control. Thus outside stallions often of dubious quality managed to access the Walrond females.[29] Warnock was able to sell most of the resulting offspring locally but at very low prices and in some cases only by offering credit to less-than-credit-worthy brokers.[30] Ultimately McEachran became discouraged with the horse business and decided to abandon it altogether.[31] After some small sales at mediocre prices,[32] he unloaded the bulk of his prized animals – some three hundred head – to local buyers W.H. Fares and Patrick Burns for fifty dollars each.[33] This was just ten dollars per head more than ranchers were paying for "grade" saddle horses of mixed ancestry.[34]

The Walrond experience was typical. When speaking of the attempt by the neighbouring Quorn ranch to supply first-class animals for the British army, local rancher Frederick Ings summed up the problem for all such ventures rather succinctly: "These imported mares were not used to rustling on the range, they were not given the care they needed, and though they produced some pretty fair nags, they were not good enough to make" this kind of breeding program "a success."[35] One partial success that ultimately very clearly illustrates the point was George Lane's purebred Percheron operation on the Bar U ranch. Lane started breeding Percherons in 1908 and he produced some fine animals that won numerous awards in horse shows across North America and in Europe. Two things need to be understood about Lane's program, however. Firstly, on one level it was not an example of the open range or profound neglect approach. All the animals he expected eventually to offer for sale or to show were treated with the greatest possible care and attention. To quote the Bar U's modern chronicler, Simon Evans: "In the spring each youngster was carefully inspected, those showing potential being retained as stallion prospects, while the culls were altered and developed as geldings. Entire horse colts were grain fed even while at pasture during the summer. They ran in large pastures surrounded by fences of woven wire. Feed bunks were installed in each pasture, in which colts received their daily ration of grain." A series of barns and birthing stalls built on the Bar U home place ensured that the marketable animals could be nurtured and fed indoors and generally kept in top condition at all times. Lane must also have used these facilities to practise selective breeding and to carefully time breeding so that the colts were born in the moderate spring weather.

In other words, Lane protected the most valuable of his Percherons from the range summer and winter – in essence he saw to it that they were insulated from the elements that constantly plagued the Walrond Clydes and Shires. That could not be said about the mares that made up his brood herd, however. These were treated with the same loose-handed approach as those on the Walrond. The result, not surprisingly, was about the same. "Weaning fillies were well cared for the first year and then turned out on native pasture, receiving no grain from then on. Brood mares were never pampered. They ranged the hills west of the ranch in the summer and were moved to the Bar U flats for the winter" where they "grazed the prairie wool never receiving hay or grain." Lane paid dearly for this part of his program in lost stock. In any reasonably sophisticated breeding program, one would expect annual reproduction rates of no less than 75 and as high as 90 percent. In the three years for which Dr. Evans was able to find breed books the Bar U produced eleven foals out of fifty mares in 1912, fifteen foals out of forty-six mares in 1913, and thirteen out of forty-two in 1914. By 1913 nine of Lane's original mares had died, 32 percent had not foaled even once, 52 percent had had only one foal, and 16 percent had had two. In 1915 eighty-four foals were born, seventeen died at birth or soon afterwards, one drowned in a slough, and one just disappeared.[36] These are truly dreadful statistics reflecting, one supposes, poor nutrition during the gestation period – particularly in the wintertime. They also, beyond doubt, represent very great financial losses for Lane's horse business as a whole.

The Walrond, Quorn, and Bar U outcomes do not mean that none of the early ranchers in western Canada was able to make money in the horse business during the frontier period. A.E. Cross in Alberta claimed, after the turn of the twentieth century, that it was that side of his operation that had been successful enough in the early days to more than make up for calamity on the beef side. After the disastrous winter of 1886–87, it apparently "paid the total capital invested in three years besides 50 head to the good."[37] Two facts need to be considered about Cross's approach, however. One, he knew his market and had access to the kind of expertise needed to supply the kind of animals it demanded.[38] Two, and probably more importantly, he dealt in the other type of horse mentioned above – the rougher but sturdy type required mainly by neighbouring ranchers and farmers to work their herds or fields. He "did very well" with these by "always watching the *local* demand" and having his "horses ready for any purchaser that might come along, and never lost an opportunity of making a sale if any fair price was offered."[39] In other words, what he was *not* trying to do was supply the very elite animals for the most discriminating, in many cases Old World, buyers.

All the first Canadian cattlemen had access to good working stock from the beginning, which came north with their first cattle from Montana. These horses had descended from Texas origins. They were the ones David Warnock referred to as "cayuses" – a mixed breed that had survived on the open range since the eighteenth century. As the cattle frontier had moved north along the eastern edge of the Rocky Mountains, ranchers had mixed these relatively small (and fast) cowponies with larger varieties, notably Thoroughbreds and Irish Hunters that the big outfits brought in from the East and overseas via the transcontinental railways. The progeny were relatively large and could carry a cowboy loaded with heavy winter clothing and camping gear through deep coverings of snow. They were of sturdy, commercial (rather than pure or nearly pure) stock that had gone through much the same process of natural selection as had the wild horses of Alberta or the brumbies of Australia. Though they

WORKING PONIES, ELBOW PARK RANCH NEAR CALGARY, ALBERTA, CA. 1890S. GLENBOW ARCHIVES, NA-128-4.

would not have shown very well against prized animals in Eastern auction rings, they were exactly what was needed to open the West. Many were also good for draught as well as riding purposes, and when mixed and grain farmers began pouring into the northern extremities of the Great Plains, these animals were crucial to ploughing up the virgin prairie soils.[40] Brokers also apparently bought up quite large numbers of them for British regular soldiers, particularly in the Boer War (1899–1902).[41]

Ultimately one can say that, if managed properly as a relatively low-cost commercial venture aimed at supplying local demand rather than the more prestigious and discriminating national and international markets, the working horse business in western Canada could, at least at times, be a viable supplement to raising cattle that helped to pay the bills. [42]

Even that statement could not be applied to the horse industry in the Northern Territory of Australia. In the beginning at least a number of stations there seem to have agreed with the would-be pundits' optimistic

ROPING HORSES IN ROUNDUP CORRAL, CA. 1890S. GLENBOW ARCHIVES, NA-766-1.

assessments, and some anticipated breeding to the highest standards.[43] Alfred Giles incorporated a breeding program at Springvale soon after setting up operations for W.J. Browne;[44] in April 1881 Abraham Wallace arrived at his Elsey station, some three hundred miles south of Katherine on the edge of the river after which his station was named, with about "1500 well bred cattle and a mob of well bred horses";[45] in the Alice Springs region, Sir Thomas Elder was stocking his Owen Springs run by 1886 with 1,000 horses apparently hoping to produce a "class" of offspring good enough "for the Indian market."[46] And at approximately the same time, owners of Mount Barrell station brought in 1,500 horses that they felt would attract national and international attention.[47]

Few if any of these undertakings were successful. Many of the early investors seem just to have given up the business soon after starting. Elder abandoned the Northern Territory, and the nearly 2,000 horses he left on Owen Springs were offered for sale in 1893 at the incredibly low price of five shillings per head. They must have been in very bad condition, as none of the hundred or so buyers attending the sale was prepared to

HORSES AT DUNBAR RANCH WEST OF FORT MACLEOD, ALBERTA, 1888. GLENBOW
ARCHIVES, NA-2033-1.

take them.[48] Three years later Sidney Kidman bought the run with the
horses still on it. Kidman eventually took most of the stock to the urban
centres of the south to sell, probably at auction. However, he had first
to pasture a large percentage of them for a year at Oodnadatta, presumably in order to bring them up to condition.[49] He sold Owen Springs in
1901. Unquestionably, part of the reason for failure, generally, was due to
the market. Asian demand did not materialize as hoped and in the early
1890s the domestic horse market plummeted as the country sank into
depression. However, the northern environment was also a key factor.
High humidity during the wets was conducive to the development of the
condition known as swamp cancer, and at certain times of the year flies
attacked the horses relentlessly, causing them tremendous stress. The major impediment, however, was that horses suffered like the cattle when the
grasses became overly coarse.

The attempt by the experimental farm at Batchelor, around sixty miles southeast of Darwin, to breed purebred Clydesdales emphatically illustrates the latter problem. "The experience . . . during the past 17 months," the director reported in 1913, "has been that while horses stabled and not allowed to depend on natural pasture for sustenance can be maintained in excellent condition," those placed "on the indigenous rank grasses starve." He went on to document the incredibly high casualty rate among the stock that had been turned loose. "Of the . . . Clydesdale mares which arrived from South [Australia] in August 1912, ten were in foal on arrival . . . Of the pregnant mares one died 25th August 1912 of arsenical poisoning en route to the Farm. One arrived at the farm in very bad condition and died 21st September 1912; a third fell away" until it looked like "a scarecrow." It "got fatally bogged while drinking at a pool on 23rd December 1912; and a fourth died 20th January 1913 from the after effects of foaling." One of the mares that gave birth died in 1913 from "swamp cancer." The director also detailed the low survival rate for the offspring of the mares that lived through gestation: "One foaled 21st October 1912 and the foal lived 10 days; one foaled 21st October 1912 and the foal died within a week; one foaled 27th October and the foal lived only 24 hours; . . . one foaled on 9th Decmeber 1912 and the foal died 10th February 1913; and one foaled 20th October 1912, and foal survives." The director recognized that "fly-time" – when marsh and buffalo flies preyed on the livestock – was a major source of stress for all the animals, and that they "suffered from insufficient water, as the natural holes were too boggy at that time of the year for horses to drink." However, he was also "firmly of the opinion that until the country" had been "improved and stocked heavily enough to change the character of the grasses," it would be "a perilous undertaking to attempt to carry horses on country similar to Batchelor."[50] Interestingly, the answer, he believed, was an intensive agricultural form of production. "Secure paddocks, abundance of wholesome feed, good water and the same personal attention to which farm horses bred for generations on small holdings are accustomed will," he felt confident, "ensure success."

Batchelor is in the top end, where the grasses tend to be the most coarse and unpalatable at maturity. Other parts of the Territory faced long dry spells at least once or a few times virtually every year and then wet, boggy periods at other times. So the environment throughout the Territory was less than ideal for producing breeds which, like McEachran's Clydes and Shires and Lane's Percherons, had over the centuries become highly domesticated and accustomed to pampering. On the Tableland, in the Victoria River region, and around Alice Springs, the grasses usually do not grow quite so tall, rank, and coarse as those in the top end. Therefore the animals were able to survive in those districts without much human intervention, but they tended not to thrive.[51] Sidney Kidman, who dealt a lot in the horse trade (particularly through his celebrated annual auction sale at Kapunda in South Australia), once estimated that quality animals could not be bred successfully in any part of the Northern Territory north of the MacDonnell mountains, which flank Alice Springs in the most southern pastoral region.[52]

Another critical problem, along with the ecological factors, was that breed selection was impossible in the Territory. A "very serious difficulty that has confronted us and, I think, also everyone who has to use horses . . . is that stallions of any and all kinds are allowed to run at large, and it is impossible to obtain at any time of the year a mare that is not in foal," the Bachelor director complained."[53] As late as 1913 a report to the Minister of External Affairs on livestock in the Borroloola and Roper River area stated that "with one or two well marked exceptions, all the horses used as sires on the holdings inspected" are "of inferior quality. . . . Horse-breeding" is "indiscriminate. Mares and stallions" are "turned out into the bush, and the sires" share "chances with the brumby."[54] Some of the stations actually took up a campaign of extermination, principally by gun, in an effort to rid the ranges of roaming animals. This included the brumby males, which, however robust and well adapted, did not live up to the highest Old World standards of body type. They also commonly tempted domesticated mares away from the stations to run off with their feral band.[55] The campaigns could be somewhat successful in some localities but they could hardly rid the Territory of all the horses running at large.

As in Canada then, the production of well-rounded, muscular, and elegant-looking beasts that discriminating foreign buyers would consider suitable for all forms of public display, as well as for the more elite and onerous military duties, was simply unrealistic in an open range system. Unlike in Canada, however, few northern Australians were able even to establish a viable business based on raising the sturdy working horse used by pastoralists and farmers and by rank-and-file soldiers. Demand for that

VERY LIGHT PONY, NORTHERN
TERRITORY, 1912. STATE
LIBRARY OF SOUTH AUSTRALIA,
PRG 280/1/14/501.

type seems almost always to have been brisk, but anyone who hoped to find an abundant supply in the Territory was almost invariably disappointed. The director at Bachelor observed that "the most serious problem that confronts the settler . . . is the scarcity of draught horses." He said that when he first arrived, he "made strenuous efforts to procure . . . a team" for the government experimental farm. "I set out to get horses of any description" but I "found the utmost difficulty in procuring three horses," even at the high price of "twenty-one pounds per head," that would be acceptable for hauling "light spring carts." After a lot of searching, he purchased fifteen horses including mares with foals at foot, and from these, teams were selected to haul supplies and fencing material, and to do a little cultivation. "It took six of the best of the horses to haul a single furrow plough." The director stressed that this situation prevailed throughout the northern frontier. "One has only to observe the teams in any part of the Territory to come to the conclusion that the draught horse as it is known to the southern farmer does not exist" here. "I have seen a wagon with 5 tons of loading . . . with twenty three horses . . . and when one approaches the camp of the ordinary teamster on the road," it has "the appearance of a horse sale."[56] The animals in the photographs below are the sort of creatures to which he was referring. They are very small and rather gaunt for draught or even riding purposes.

From the 1880s onward, the number of horses in the Territory, which included all the regular working and cartage animals on the stations, just barely surpassed 24,000 while cattle numbers rose to more than 500,000.[57] By comparison, southern Alberta and Assiniboia had some 100,000 horses in 1901 along with approximately 350,000 cattle.[58] The dearth of good working horses in the Territory was certainly also due to environmental

BUFFALO HUNTERS AND HORSES, NORTHERN TERRITORY, 1905. NORTHERN TERRITORY LIBRARY, DARWIN, PH0200/0457.

HORSE TEAMS AND DRAY, NORTHERN TERRITORY, 1904. NORTHERN TERRITORY LIBRARY, DARWIN, PH057/0011.

factors. Coarse grasses, low-quality "scrub" stallions, and uncontrolled breeding affected quality at all levels. However, it was to some degree as well a reflection of a relative scarcity of good "grade" stock countrywide. In previous decades Australians had not produced anything like the quantity of regular horses that had originated in Texas and then spread north to the northern Great Plains of North America. Experts repeatedly commented on this shortage from the later nineteenth century on.[59] In 1879, a speaker at the Agricultural Society of New South Wales lectured producers about the need to breed out so many of the defects domestic horses were showing in order to get a type "capable, with suitable mares, of producing a class . . . very useful for general purpose, and with sufficient bone and substance to undergo a large amount of work." These qualities, he said, would be "essential to counteract the weediness which neglect in breeding has permitted so many of the colonial horses to fall into."[60] Five years later, the Director of the Army remount operations in India wrote a letter to Australian stockmen advising them on how "the light weedy horses now being bred in Australia should be improved." He made a number of recommendations that suggest that, at that point, the industry in general was growing at a rapid pace but without much substance. "It cannot be expected that you can change at one moment the mare from which you have been breeding for years past," he wrote, but you really should "look far enough ahead and consider the benefits the next generation might reap."[61] In a 1900 article, a newspaper reporter spoke of the difficulty the military was having finding soldiers' horses in Queensland. That state had recently experienced a great influx of domestic horses, and the writer felt that when they had mixed with the brumbies they had, if anything, actually brought the overall quality down.[62]

> According to the latest returns, there are in Queensland 480,469 horses, yet there has been some little delay in finding a thousand nags . . . [for] our mounted infantry . . . Station owners have made liberal offers of horses, but when experts were sent out to select those suitable for campaigning they found some difficulty in obtaining as many as they want. This was on stations where we had imagined good thoroughbred entries were kept for sires . . . When we consider the kind of sires which roam about the country, and the weedy herds

of brumbies which infest the scrubs, we can well understand that great deterioration is going on. To be kept up to a proper standard, the horse must not only be well and carefully bred, but he must be properly fed. Generally they are allowed to run at pasture in this colony till they are ready for breaking in and it is to be feared there is not that attention given to the character of the grazing ground which seems to be desirable.[63]

It is important to acknowledge that *not all* the regular mounts on the early cattle stations were inferior. The working pony was as necessary to the Texas system in northern Australian as anywhere. Even a relatively small spread like the Elsey, which ran a total of only about 1,500 cattle, had more than 200 head of horses for mustering, droving, pulling supply wagons, and general cartage.[64] "We sat among the camp fires" when out on the range, Jeannie Gunn wrote in her famous memoir, *We of the Never Never*. In the background was the sound of "our horses clanking through the timber . . . forty horses and more, pack teams and relays for the whole company and riding hacks, in addition to both stock and camp horses."[65] The "stock and camp" horses could have matched the general run of working horses on the Canadian spreads. "Frequently, possessing exceptional adaptability for the work," they were kept mainly for their skill and expertise in the cutting corral. Many of them must have been some of the better Walers that had not been taken by the army. These horses usually were not turned loose on the ranges between musters but enclosed in pastures close to the station headquarters and watered and even hand fed wild hay when conditions dictated.[66] They had to have what cattlemen often called "cow sense" as well as the "cat-like" physical agility to "wheel around as on a pivot" over the course of hours when performing their duties in the cutting pen.[67] The observations quoted above and many others illustrate, however, that these better cattle ponies were a relatively small minority on the individual stations and throughout the country. For that reason the average quality of the regular working horses in northern Australia would not rise to the standards in the Canadian West during the frontier period. Ironically, only the pedigree types could do so. That was because, on both continents, standards for those animals were almost universally low.

9

DIVERSIFICATION IN WESTERN CANADA: THE TRIUMPH OF THE FAMILY RANCH/FARM

In their main industry, the cattle business, all the corporation operations in western Canada struggled to the end with high death losses, light carcasses, low quality, and the long trek to market. Had they been able to follow the American practice of selling their cattle on their own continent as feeders they might at least have cut down on some of their expenses and improved their cash flows. The one measure some might have considered was to go into large-scale grain and roughage production themselves, so they could put the last pounds of hard durable fat on their animals themselves and, thereby, raise body weights and prevent some of the shrinkage that occurred en route to the European market. But that not only went diametrically against the Texas system and everything they had claimed to believe in, it was also a very daunting and expensive proposition.

We should not forget that low carcass yield at market destination was not the ranchers' only concern with respect to herd quality. Since inadequate nutrition and harsh weather hindered bovine development at all ages, what they really needed to do was secure enough feed to both fatten their bigger steers after they came off the grass in the fall and also keep the rest of their stock alive and prospering when the grass was inadequate. To be sure, the natural environment in the Canadian West was, and is, conducive to the production of enough grain and both hay and greenfeed to support far more cattle than the ranges were carrying around the turn of the century.[1] The valleys in the high country of southern Alberta and Assiniboia originally produced copious amounts of tall natural grasses that the cattlemen could have cut and stacked. They could also have grown crops of oats and barley on the flatter valley bottoms. The growing season in the hills is short and often the grain is damaged by frost in the early fall, but usually not before it has matured enough for feeding purposes. On the plains to the east and north of the high country the growing season is normally longer and hot enough to ripen both feed grains and wheat (which can be utilized for feeding purposes). A percentage of the land many of the big ranchers leased spilled onto one of those lower, flatter areas. Moreover, before heavy settlement, a lot of that land was still public, vacant, and available.[2]

However, to the big operations the enormous investment required to go into intensive feeding made it seem virtually impossible. While they put up roughage and some oats for their more at-risk stock, none of the corporations ever got even close to being able to feed all their animals through a complete winter. Nor did they feel they could. To simplify the explanation, it is appropriate to illustrate what would have been required if they had utilized hay alone for this purpose. Gestating and/or nursing cows, the bulls that service them, and growing or fattening steers require about a ton and a half of hay apiece to be more or less assured of coming through a long winter on the northern plains in good condition.[3] In the 1880s and early 1890s the Walrond ranch owned on average about 8,500 head in its beef heard, excluding newborn calves. About 5,200 were classified as cows, 300 were bulls, and 3,000 were steers.[4] These cattle would have needed 12,750 tons of hay to keep them all sufficiently satisfied during the hundred or so most inclement days each winter.[5] About 1,000 of the ranch's 1,400 or so calves would also have been mature enough to require feed when pastures were covered with snow. To keep them growing and healthy would have taken about a ton of hay per head, or another 1,000 tons. In total, therefore, the ranch would have required at least 13,600 tons of hay. The cost to procure it, whether by putting up their own or through custom hayers, would have been about $5 a ton, or $68,000 in total.[6] This would have multiplied the ranch's entire annual operational expenditures four times over. For companies that had promised their shareholders that the secrets to ranching success in the

West included low costs and year-round grazing, this was unthinkable. Moreover, since many of the big outfits were running on low and diminishing cash reserves, where were they going to find the thousands of extra dollars required to intensify their systems this way? It scarcely needs to be added that costs were not the only inhibiting factor. To gather 13,600 tons of hay with horse-drawn equipment from natural grasslands scattered over thousands of acres in rough and hilly country would have taken an army of at least three hundred men and then another one perhaps half that size to haul the roughage and fork it to the cattle in the wintertime.[7] That kind of manpower would not have been available before the heavy settlement that occurred in the decade or so after the turn of the century.[8] Regular winter feeding would also have involved hiring extra men to build all the corrals required to enclose the hay and keep the cattle and wild animals from destroying the stacks, and to build the extra fences needed to keep the stock near the feed during bad weather.

The big Canadian ranchers were then left without alternatives other than to continue to send what survived of their under-finished, under-sized stock to distant sales rings at heavily discounted prices. It is usual to blame the ferocious winter of 1906–7 for their demise.[9] That great catastrophe did mark the end for many of them, but it should be seen merely as the last blow in a process of decline that had been underway for at least two decades. The truth of this statement is evinced not just in the fact that when the great ranches left they never returned but also that the system that replaced them, and which has now endured for more than a hundred years in the Canadian West, was and continues to be its nearly exact opposite, agriculturally speaking.

As the great ranchers filed out of the Canadian West, a host of small-scale producers who were to rely on all the diversified operating techniques the Texas system eschewed, filed in. Some of these small operators had actually been on the western plains even before the companies appeared there. And they had continued to arrive in what might be described early on as a trickle and then much more like a stream as the big operations left. Some came as squatters but most as homesteaders taking advantage of the 1872 Homestead Act, which enabled them to claim and, upon "proving-up," to own a 160-acre quarter section of land. Most of the settlers acquired a second quarter section soon after they owned the first, and many also leased a few hundred acres of pastureland.[10] Some started with as few as a dozen cattle and others with as many as several hundred. In the beginning it was mostly young males who came but gender balance slowly improved with the arrival of more and more young women. With that development, the number of families on the homesteads steadily grew.

At first some of the settlers too resisted the process of diversification George Emerson and Tom Lynch brought some of the first herds north, largely to sell to other settlers, and then started up their own ranch west of High River, Alberta. They had had first-hand experience on western American ranges before heading north and they understood (and presumably shared) the high opinion of ranchers and cowboys that pervaded western culture.[11] To them a rancher was someone who worked with "his horse and lasso and branding iron" and stayed away from chickens, hogs, and milk cows and from traditional farming devices such as rakes or pitch forks or "ploughs and binders and threshing machines."[12] All such things were to be spurned because they required the cowboy to get out of the saddle for extended periods during the working day. Many of the ordinary ranchers "say they have not time," a government official observed in 1888; they "will not work on foot" and they show no willingness to "cut hay" or even "to garden" or "attend domestic animals."[13]

However, the cattlemen with smaller operations, like those with big ones, were forced to begin to embrace some farming practices in order to meet major ecological challenges. The changes appeared first as a movement towards the production of feed to secure the herds through winter. In 1884 a lady rancher in the foothills of Alberta wrote the following words to a relative back home in Ontario. A general sense of helplessness during the harshest time of the year is unmistakable.

> There are times when a snow storm has come and spread a cruel depth of snow over the long grass and the cowboys ride late and early driving starving cattle to the nearest hay stack or at any rate driving them from the thickets near a stream where they go for shelter but remain to die . . . This . . . throws a shadow over our days for as long as it lasts – 10 days – even two weeks sometimes but not often – and every ear is listening for the happy sound of the first murmurings of [a warm moist wind known as] a Chinook. One night we were sitting just as I have told you and suddenly someone said,

"the Chinook!" We were all outside in a second, and there was the low roar in the mountains and in twenty minutes the wind had reached the house. We went in and made coffee and were a much more joyful party than an hour before. [14]

Plainly, even at this early date all the cattle people feared massive starvation among the herds. A year or so later the editor of the *Macleod Gazette* implored "every cowman in the country" to "put up enough hay on his range to feed weak stock through any bad storm" in order to "sleep better during the cold and stormy nights of winter."[15]

After the 1886–87 blizzards it was the smaller-scale rancher who not only responded to that advice but also managed to take it to a more logical conclusion. The man who had, say, a hundred cattle would have needed 1.5 x 100 = 150 tons of hay to get all his cattle through an entire winter season. This he could obtain by putting up approximately fifty acres of grassland in an average year. To do so during the summer months would not have been difficult for him, particularly if he had a wife to help out. Many of the cattlemen had less than a hundred head. The small minority who had several times that many might have needed to hire a man or two for a short period. Even so this was doable, and by the 1906–7 winter, when as many as 50 percent of the cattle on the range were lost, almost all of the family ranchers had secured enough roughage to protect their stock properly. The following autumn the commanding North-West Mounted Police officer at Macleod reported: "Last winter was an exceptionally long and cold one. It was said to be the coldest in twenty years. Cattle in consequence suffered a great deal, and large losses" were incurred, "especially by the owners of large herds who could not feed and look after their stock in the way small owners could. These latter suffered very insignificant losses."[16]

This improved the settler rancher's chances of success, but it also initiated the end of the day when he worked only from the saddle. Harvesting hay is labour intensive. In those days it required mowing and raking the grasses with horse-drawn implements and then many hours of work in the hot sun with pitchforks and wagons to stack and store the forage for the winter. Roderick Macleay put up as much hay as he could from the beginning. He both hired men and cooperated with neighbours. Reading through his diary, his grandson, Clay Chattaway (now on one of the two main Macleay ranches west of Nanton), noted:[17]

> The crop was some distance from the buildings so [they] set up a hay camp near a creek . . . With two mowers, a dump rake, a sweep and an overshot stacker, a five-man crew was needed to run a minimal haying operation. . . . The women would have kept them supplied with baked goods such as bread and pies. There may have also been a camp cook and possibly a flunky to catch up fresh horses for the mid day change and sharpen mower sickles. With a minimum of five teams in the field there would be at least twenty horses in camp and more in reserve at the buildings. They started 27 July and after a short rain delay, hayed . . . for the whole month of August . . . They finished 7 September. By measuring the length, breadth and over throw of the haystacks, and applying a standard formula, the tonnage was calculated at 400 T.[18]

Not satisfied with the indigenous grasses, many of the family cattlemen planted fields of mixed domestic varieties such as timothy, brome grass, and clover. To do this they had to break up and cultivate the virgin soils and then work them again every four or five years to replant. Some also began planting, stooking, and stacking oats or oats and barley mixed for greenfeed.[19] This required annual soil cultivation and considerably more fieldwork.

To protect their crops from the cattle and their cattle from cold and hunger, these cattlemen also fenced their holdings. For them this was achievable too. If the average settler owned about 320 acres he had, to be sure, a lot of work to do to fence his property completely. By the Homestead Act the land put aside for settlement was divided into 160-acre parcels with sides a half mile long. Therefore, the average settler had to construct two miles of fences to divide off his home quarter. By working at it consistently when he was not haying or hunting down his livestock, he could expect to do this in one or two years. Then he was able to use the open range for summer pasture and keep all his cattle near home in the wintertime to feed and care for them when necessary. If he continued

POTENTIAL HAY LANDS, SOUTHERN ALBERTA, 1912. GLENBOW ARCHIVES, NA-234-8.

HAY AND GRAIN LANDS, SOUTHERN ALBERTA, 1942. GLENBOW ARCHIVES, NA-4450-17.

HAYING, WALROND RANCH, CA. 1893. GLENBOW ARCHIVES, NA-237-14.

to work at it he might, within the space of another five or six years, enclose the rest of his property including any leased land and do a significant amount of cross fencing. Then he had his entire herd fenced and protected from the open range year round.

By early in the twentieth century the small ranchers who had not yet sufficiently divided up their lands were buying up wire – apparently by the "car load." "Things in the foothills are looking well this year," a small-town paper reported in 1904; "fences are going up in all directions."[20] At Pincher Creek in the southern foothills the following words, written a few months later about fighting the mange, indicate both that the range in that area was now closed and that it was the small-scale cattleman who had completed the job:

> In a range country it is possible for ranchers to take prompt and effectual methods for prevention and cure [of this disease]. Where the range is not intersected with fences it

is easy to handle large herds of cattle, run them through dips, and hold them until every head in that particular district has been dipped. But in [the foothills] . . . the building of public dips . . . would be almost useless. For one thing there . . . [is] not a large enough vacant space of land . . . which could be used for herding any large bunch of cattle; and for another thing, the cattle . . . [are] now held by so many people in small bunches, that it would be almost impossible to see to the treatment of all infected animals.[21]

As they fenced in their pastures, individual cattlemen could treat their own herds and, more importantly, prevent re-infestations by keeping them away from outside stock.

Enclosures also allowed the small ranchers to improve pasture management programs. As they built ever more complex networks of fences they were able to confine their herds to summer pastures, which were usually now in the hills and, in many cases, on relatively distant leased land. In the wintertime they would bring their herds home and confine them to a wind-protected, forested area close to their roughage supplies. This, of course, gave their pastures long seasonal rest periods such as had happened during the buffalo days – though in reverse order. Few if any of the cattlemen practised the sophisticated rest rotational programs being utilized and refined today, but they did keep their cattle numbers in more realistic proportions to the amount of pasture land they controlled; and when necessary they could prevent their stock from accessing overgrazed areas long enough to allow those areas to recoup their pristine health.[22]

Fencing also enabled the cattlemen to drastically improve their breeding patterns. When smaller-scale ranchers began to arrive in large numbers they too brought in their initial cattle from the American West, and this was a setback for overall quality. "It is a great pity that so much inferior stock has been brought in from the United States during the past season by settlers taking their residence here," an employee in the Department of the Interior observed in 1895.[23] A few years later an officer in the mounted police force claimed that "the class of cattle in the country is not generally as good as formerly. The steers offered show less breeding and are smaller . . . Many of the small ranches have too few bulls, and rely on the enterprise of their neighbours to provide new blood, and there are still many wretched looking bulls on the ranges; . . . indeed some of the young bulls imported are not likely to improve matters."[24] Nonetheless, many of the smaller operators were quick to begin upgrading their herds once they were able to stop outside stock from mingling with their animals. They kept undesirable bulls out, and controlled which of their own bulls were able to mix with which cows. As a result of this, and the fact that they both bought up better bulls and culled their cows, they gradually replaced the motley range varieties with heavier-set, more uniform, pure and cross breeds of the Angus, Hereford, and Shorthorn type. "There is no doubt," the above report continued, that the best steers come from areas where "the ranches are small, and stockmen feed hay all winter, and can attend to the breeding of their cows."

Complete networks of fences gave the settler the ability not only to prevent outside bulls from getting to his cows but also to regulate breeding by his own bulls more precisely. He was able first to mix his genders thoroughly in smaller enclosed areas so that, whenever any female cycled into heat, there was a male nearby to ensure that germination could proceed on schedule. The ordinary rancher could also move bulls in and out of his cowherds with more precision so that they would produce calves at the right time of the year. Most of the ranchers wanted to induce calving in March to early April, and so they put bulls with the cows in early July and removed them about six weeks later. This prevented highly risky fall and winter births. It also avoided summer births, which produced calves that were too young at the end of the grazing season to be weaned and put on dry feed.[25]

The man with low livestock numbers and small, well-fenced grazing lands could also see to the proper sorting of his cattle. He could keep some pastures for his older steers, some for his yearlings, and some for his cows. This simplified oversight, enabling him to keep better track of which cows were producing small offspring or none at all, and to do a better job of marketing. This put him in a position to cull his brood stock more scrupulously. He could also weed out poor-quality heifers by spaying them to ensure they did not reproduce. Spaying is somewhat more complicated than castrating; it is normally not done until the young females are at least a year old and, therefore, are bigger and more difficult to handle than the baby bull calves. The heifers had to be thrown to the ground and held there for some time while a veterinarian or well-tutored

SPAYING A HEIFER, MAPLE CREEK AREA, ASSINIBOIA, 1895. GLENBOW ARCHIVES, NA-3811-98.

cattleman cut through their flank with a scalpel to remove the ovaries. The man who had relatively few cattle confined in fenced pastures could sort out any young female stock he did not like and see to the job reasonably efficiently. The neutered heifers were normally fattened like the steers and sold on the slaughter market.

The settler ranchers could maintain a younger, healthier, and higher-quality herd than the great ranchers and, therefore, were almost certainly more productive in almost every sense. In time they brought a degree of specialization to the beef industry. Those in the high country who had some fairly fertile, potentially arable, lower lying lands began to harvest wheat and coarse grains – specifically oats and barley. They found that the calves they were corralling over the winter prospered when given a few pounds of one or more of these grains, suitably processed through a grinder, with their hay and greenfeed. Some ranchers also found that their older steers fattened up quickly when they gave them increasingly greater percentages of grain. Thus many of them got into the feedlot business, finishing their cattle properly before selling them for beef.[26]

The cattle people whose land was exclusively (or nearly so) in the high country tended more to stay away from grain-feeding, sticking mainly to grazing and providing roughage for their stock when necessary. They concentrated on breeding and producing as many calves as they could every year. These they either sold as calves in the early fall or wintered them on hay and marketed them the following spring, summer, or fall as yearlings. It is impossible to give precise dates for all the stages that ranching as a whole went through in the southern prairie livestock regions. However, it can be said with confidence that the modest operations had ended the practice of open range grazing before 1914, had gone into using roughage and grain to finish beef, and were undertaking closely managed selective breeding programs and a measure of rotational grazing.

Many family operations also moved into forms of production that were not associated directly with the beef trade – although that continued to be their primary or staple industry – because they needed to utilize any traditional farming activity that would provide cash to pay the bills between seasonal cattle marketings. They took up sidelines such as raising poultry and producing eggs, dairying, raising hogs, and breeding workhorses. One suspects they had more success breeding workhorses than the great operations did because, after they had closed the open ranges and ended the use of the Texas system, they were able to give this more hands-on attention. On the Rocking P ranch west of Nanton, Alberta, Roderick Macleay normally ran horses along with his cattle herds from the time he started operations in 1901.[27] His idea was to meet local demand for working stock.[28] Macleay was a first-rate businessman and for him this was more than a hobby.[29] By about 1913 the market softened somewhat as the farmlands filled and settlement slowed, and as steam and then gasoline tractors became more common.[30] However, most farmers continued to utilize the horse along with a growing list of machinery until the post–World War II era. Some smaller ranchers were even able to devote enough time, energy, and facilities to the business to breed and nurture a few elite horses such as those pictured below.

The family-controlled ranches were able to get a much better rate of reproduction out of their stock.[31] The men and women who owned a hundred head of cattle and who nurtured them with care and attention

GRACE, ELEGANCE, AND POWER. THESE ARE THE KINDS OF ANIMALS THE BIG RANCHERS
COULD NOT PRODUCE EFFICIENTLY ON THE OPEN RANGE. SOME FAMILY OPERATORS WERE
ABLE TO DO SO BY KEEPING A FEW OF THEM AT A TIME IN A CONTROLLED SETTING,
FEEDING THEM DURING INCLEMENT WEATHER, AND GENERALLY PAMPERING THEM.
CLYDESDALES, RIDDELL RANCH, SHEEP CREEK AREA, ALBERTA, CA. 1902–3. GLENBOW
ARCHIVES, NA-1526-1.

throughout the year – staying up day and night during calving season to
act as midwife whenever a cow had difficulty delivering, and to make
sure that each calf born during inclement weather was dried off and sheltered – could expect to get offspring from around 90 percent of their
cows. Then, after grazing, feeding, and closely attending the animals for
three to five years, they actually *could* keep the death loss down to about 5
percent.[32] Thus they were able eventually to market one animal for some
80 percent of their cows. At an average price of, say, $42 per head for 40
cows this would give them $1,680.[33] Mary Neth has demonstrated that in
the American Midwest in the 1920s the farmer and his wife learned to
exist on very little money.[34] By seldom or never giving themselves proper
recompense in terms of wages for all their work, by growing a large vege-
table garden, keeping a few chickens and pigs for their own consumption,

ELITE WORKHORSE: THOMAS RAWLINSON'S "HAROLD," A SHIRE STALLION, OLDS, ALBERTA, CA. 1907–8. GLENBOW ARCHIVES, NA-3003-1.

and selling milk and eggs for extra "pin money," they could glean enough · to sustain their family. More study needs to be done with respect to the northern Great Plains ranch/farm; however, it would seem reasonable to argue that, with a similar approach, its owner-operators could get by on no more than $400 or $500 out of their yearly beef sales.[35] This left them more than $1,100 to cover their costs of operation. By continually doing their own repair work on sowing, haying, and harvesting equipment and by improving their containment and living facilities with logs cut out of the bush, they could keep their business viable under normal circumstances. Moreover, in years of crop failure and extremely low market prices, one or even both of the farming couple could "work out." He might gain income by working at a larger neighbouring ranch that needed extra labour at haying, calving, or roundup time; or by doing custom farm work with his machinery; or by entering the lumber, mining, or freighting business. "Desperate for cash flow," one group of small southern Alberta ranchers "diversified their business by acquiring a timber berth near St. Leon's south of Revelstoke on Arrow Lake" in the winter of 1907–8. Under contract they cut down the big trees and made ties for railway construction.[36]

Women also worked off the ranch, sometimes as a cook for a neighbouring outfit or as a teacher in a nearby country school or as a clerk in town.[37] Wives and mothers were instrumental in keeping the ranch/farm operative in the Canadian West, and yet their contribution is seldom recognized. There are literally endless examples to make the point that many became true and, in a number of cases, equal partners to their husbands. Home on the ranch, they tackled a whole range of duties simply because there was no one else to do them.[38] Many did not even have the luxury of running water. Laura Macleay's water was "hauled in barrels from a spring three quarters of a mile away. The barrels were loaded on a democrat in the warmer months and on a stone boat in the winter."[39] Vegetables raised on the ranches, eaten fresh in season and canned or stored for the winter months, were an important part of every family diet.[40] The work of establishing and maintaining a garden was arduous, and women usually took responsibility for it. The Macleay's garden, with a variety of green vegetables "and the all important potato crop," was located on the top of a hill about a mile east from the house."[41] One of Evelyn Cameron's immediate tasks, when she arrived from England at their CC ranch on Mosquito Creek near Nanton, was to prepare the gardens for planting. In her diary she recorded the routine of planting, weeding, and harvesting while assisting with outside work and caring for her children.[42] Women also attended to barnyard chores and the care of livestock. In the 1890s, Fred Austin managed to acquire a homestead in the Crowsnest Pass area stocked with a few horses and cattle. His bride, Katherine, joined him in 1901. During that winter he worked for a lumber company in the Pass while she cared for the new baby, looked after their modest home, and fed and nurtured livestock – even donning her husband's clothing so that the milk cow would accept her. It was the farm's output of milk, butter, and eggs, managed by Katherine, that paid the taxes and much of the regular living expenses. In the same area, Johanne Pedersen was frequently left alone to care for the family ranch and her seven children while her husband worked as a freighter. Along with her many domestic chores, she was known to "stack hay, stook grain, clear land, saw wood by hand and brand calves."[43] Jessie Louise Bateman of the Jumping Pound district

BREALY RANCH HOUSE, BIG HILL SPRING, ALBERTA, CA. 1900–1907: NOTE THE BABY IN HER ARMS, THE CHICKENS SCRATCHING IN THE YARD, AND THE HOG AT THE DOORSTEP. GLENBOW ARCHIVES, NA-963-13.

west of Calgary milked cows in an open corral in fair weather and foul. Apparently she "could milk two cows to anyone else's one."[44] Her neighbour, Susan Copithorne, came to Canada from Ireland as a child's maid and then married a rancher. She learned to milk cows, churn butter, and raise chickens.

When domestically raised meat was unavailable, many women turned to hunting and fishing. They were comfortable with guns and accurate marksmen. Evelyn Cameron was a practised shot and rarely rode out without packing a gun. She shot prairie chickens and ducks during the day and stood guard over the poultry house at night to protect her chickens from coyotes and wolves. Mary Alice Halton, who arrived with her large family in the Crowsnest Pass area in 1902, quickly "became a crack shot. She kept the larder stocked with prairie chickens, Hungarian partridge and ducks."[45] Fishing was her specialty; "she often rode down on horseback to

EDITH INGS RECEIVES A SHOOTING LESSON FROM HUSBAND FRED. MIDWAY RANCH, NANTON, CA. 1911–12. GLENBOW ARCHIVES, NA-2368-3.

fill a sack with fish – occasionally even casting from astride her horse."[46] Near Priddis, Monica Hopkins wrote of the "welcome change" the fresh trout she caught while ice fishing made to her and her husband's diet, even though their pantry was well stocked with frozen meat:[47]

> We have hanging in the storehouse a side of beef and one pork, a number of partridge and prairie chickens, and about a dozen roosters. My heart sinks every time I go into the storehouse because whatever I choose has to be thawed out before I can cook it and the meat has to be sawed up into joints. It is all frozen solid and takes at least two days to thaw out and I'm always forgetting to get something in until we are down to the very tag end. It's at times like that that the fish come in handy.[48]

Once children came along they were incorporated into the production process as soon as they were old enough.[49] Elliott West's description of early western American agricultural society could be applied word-for-word to that of western Canada:

> The pioneer household was an economic mechanism of mutually-dependent parts . . . a productive unit, often a remarkably effective and self-sustaining one. Fathers did the heaviest labor – sod busting, construction, and fence-building on a homestead and took off in search of other wage work when necessary. Mothers handled the multitude of domestic duties, cared for barnyard animals, gardened, and earned cash by washing, cooking, and sewing for others. Children filled in wherever they were needed . . . the frontier's popular image is one of individualism and self-reliance . . . but the transformation of the . . . West could be more accurately pictured as a familial conquest, an occupation by tens of thousands of intra-dependent households.[50]

Near Wood Mountain in Assiniboia, the Chamberlain family worked closely together; and after Mr. Chamberlain died his wife and daughter, who "was scarcely out of her teens," were able to take over their operation and keep it going despite heavy debts. They donned men's clothing and proceeded to milk cows; market butter; cut, mow, and rake hay; brand calves; and haul manure. The two were said to have learned to be able to "rope a steer and ride a horse with any rancher in the country."[51] The family approach was instrumental in building and maintaining some of the most productive operations in the Canadian West. Though they paled in size in comparison to the biggest of the great ranches, some of these family operations were much bigger than the average-sized family outfits. The McIntyre ranch on the Milk River Ridge, established in 1894 to the west of what was then the Alberta/Assiniboia border, is an excellent example. It was the co-operative effort by William McIntyre and his sons William Junior and Robert that enabled the ranch to grow and develop during the difficult formative period from the late 1890s to the Depression. Its 55,000 deeded acres stayed in the family until 1947.[52] The McIntyres stuck mainly to the cattle business, but at the same time they saw to the production not just of hay and greenfeed but also of grain to ensure the survival of their stock. Other family operations such as E.A. (Aubrey) Cartwright's D ranch, Tom Lynch's TL, the Rocking P, and the Bar S ran a thousand or more head of cattle over a few tens of thousands of acres in the foothills southwest of Calgary from an early date. The latter two spreads became part of the operation founded by Rod Macleay, who eventually cropped some 4,000 acres and kept hogs and poultry as well as cattle and horses.[53] The degree of family co-operation is illustrated by the contributions of his two daughters, Dorothy and Maxine. Countless entries in the *Rocking P Gazette*, a family newspaper the girls founded when they were respectively only fourteen and twelve years of age, document that they commonly worked alongside the ranch hands and their father, whom they referred to as "Boss":

> Jan 30th was a very hard day for Clem, Max[ine], and her 'pard' [Dorothy]. . . . They worked swift and fast at the Calf Camp separating the fat calves from the beef calves.[54]

> Bert Beacook helped by Max and her 'pard' moved 215 head of steers from Section 33 to the Mountain field Sept. 23. . . . Home field worked by the Boss, Max and her 'pard'

on Feb 19th. Fifty-six head were cut [out] and then taken over to the Bar S feed ground.[55]

Undaunted, the girls, at times, rode out on their own to supplement the work done by the hired cowboys: "Max and her pard rode the west field and found 24 more calves that were missed when the field was rounded up earlier in the month."[56]

The two girls and their mother were equally comfortable in the barn-yard, where they plucked chickens, milked unruly cows, and planted potatoes. However, there is no question that they were more than just hard workers. They were also trusted and true business partners. This was illustrated at times when Rod Macleay needed their support to keep the family holdings out of the hands of creditors. In the 1920s, when he was under constant and heavy pressure from the Bank of Montreal over loans totalling hundreds of thousands of dollars, Macleay branded thousands of cattle with his wife Laura's brand to ensure that the bank could not legally claim them in a foreclosure.[57] When he bought into a small shopping centre in Calgary in 1929 he did so in Laura's name, unquestionably for the same reason.[58] In the 1930s Maxine and Dorothy leased grazing land in their own name and they purchased, branded, and sold their own cattle.[59] Because the two young ladies got involved in all facets of ranch management they were fully prepared to take over when they inherited the Rocking P and Bar S from their father after his death in 1953. They kept alive the tradition of family co-operation, which continues to the present.[60]

The overall movement to more diversified ranching/farming as the twentieth century unfolded is reflected by the variety of livestock record-ed in the Canadian census reports. In all of Alberta and western Assiniboia in 1891 there were 15,511 milk cows, 7,792 hogs, 86,785 chickens, and about 40,000 horses, with more than 200,000 beef cattle. One decade later there were 50,741 milk cows, 48,984 hogs, 265,632 chickens, and nearly 100,000 horses, with just over 355,000 beef cattle. While the number of beef cattle had less than doubled in a decade, all the other livestock had increased by two and a half to six fold. To take a smaller area, virtually all of which was part of the ranching frontier in earlier days, one can con-centrate on the figures for western Assiniboia alone: in 1891 there were just under 10,000 horses, some 5,500 milk cows, 2,627 hogs, and 32,114 chickens, with 67,810 beef cattle. Ten years later there were more than 25,000 horses, just fewer than 9,500 milk cows, 4,820 hogs, and 52,672 chickens, with 72,720 beef cattle. While beef production had expanded only slightly, the other livestock numbers had, on average, increased by close to 100 percent.

The typical rancher/farmer had begun working the 160-acre homestead and possibly a small lease, and then, perhaps after starting a family, doubled or tripled his deeded holdings. He ran thirty to fifty cows from which he raised calves, a dairy herd of about six to ten head, and ten to twenty hogs. He also kept around a hundred chickens and perhaps fifteen to twenty horses, some of which he used to work his own land and others that were bred and raised for the market. He also practised a full spectrum of plant husbandry to attain self-sufficiency in feed. Before the Great War, the era not just of the great ranches but also of what might be termed "pure ranching" in general had thus come and gone. This does not mean that all the skills of the cowboy were obsolete on the high-country spreads of southern Alberta and southern Saskatchewan. Summer pasturing continued to be important on a majority of the operations. Therefore, while the district roundups on the open range had disappeared, it remained necessary for each outfit to have riders who knew how to gather and attend livestock from the saddle. However, cattle grazing was now only one (though, in many cases, the predominant one) of several agricultural techniques being utilized in these regions. By 1909, J.G. Rutherford noted the improvement in herd management techniques that had come with the reduction in size. The "settler farmer," he said, "produces an abundance of feed of all kinds." With his pastures properly fenced "he can keep his cattle under constant observation and control with the result that loss is reduced to a minimum. At the same time the cattle, being at least partly domesticated, and generally to some extent grain fed, handle and ship infinitely better than do the grass-finished range steers which, often, on the long journey from their native prairie to Liverpool or London shrink the profit from their bones."[61] His description would have been more precise if he had prefixed the word "farmer" with "rancher," and he should by rights have acknowledged that one of the secrets to the settler's success was that he did not work alone.[62] When the market seemed to dictate it after World War I, feeders would gather together and try to access buyers in Britain the way they and the big men had done earlier.[63] However, as the

West filled, its cities grew and more packing plants with names like Swifts and Canada Packers entered the picture. The domestic market would take more of their supply and, eventually, restrictions to the American market were to be reduced as well. Furthermore, subsidized freight rates to transport grain east by rail would, at times, make it economically advantageous for farmers in Ontario and Quebec to finish western cattle as the farmers in the corn states of America did.[64]

THE TEXAS SYSTEM AT HOME
IN NORTHERN AUSTRALIA

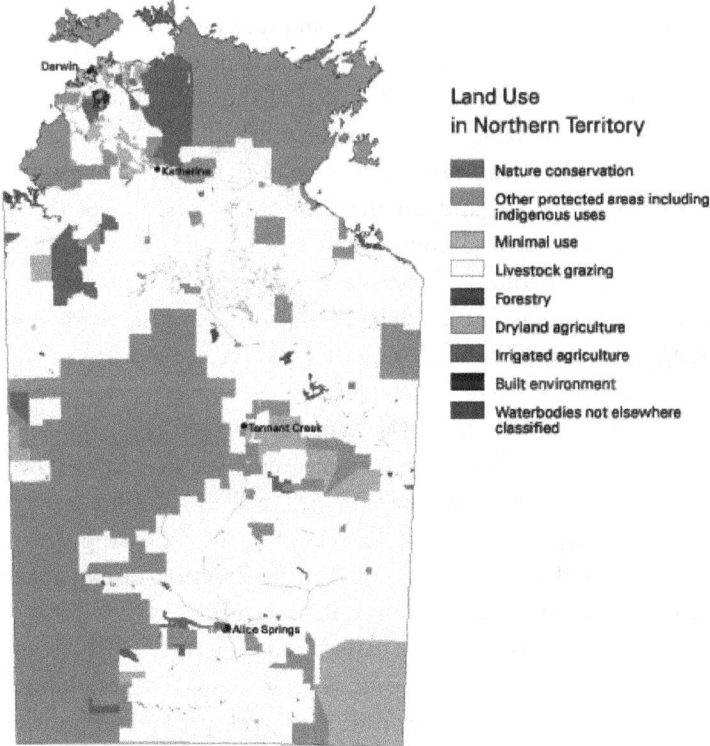

**Land Use
in Northern Territory**

- Nature conservation
- Other protected areas including indigenous uses
- Minimal use
- Livestock grazing
- Forestry
- Dryland agriculture
- Irrigated agriculture
- Built environment
- Waterbodies not elsewhere classified

MAP OF LAND USE IN NORTHERN TERRITORY, 1996–97. AUSTRALIA. "NORTHERN TERRITORY" IN UNDERSTANDING BUSHFIRE TRENDS IN DELIBERATE VEGETATION FIRES IN AUSTRALIA, HTTP://WWW.AIC.GOV.AU/DOCUMENTS/2/E/5/%7B2E5011BF-009F-420B-8435-1A335578CE5A%7DTBP027 _ 09 _ NT.PDF.

As the above map of land use in the Northern Territory 1996–1997 demonstrates, the region was not destined agriculturally to become much of anything but a beef cattle grazing area. Statistics provided with the map indicate that at the most recent turn of the century diversification was almost totally lacking. This is quite obviously due to the climate and terrain more than anything else. Because long dry spells in much of the Territory alternate with heavy rains and floods, domestic crop endeavours are extremely risky. Moreover, the soils generally are not arable. Without mountain and glacial renewal the more than a dozen different soil types have been under continuous weathering for more than a quarter of a billion years.[1] This has robbed them of all the soluble minerals, leaving disproportionate amounts of iron and aluminum oxides, which have reduced the PH and removed or diminished the phosphorus content. The extremely hot northern sun in conjunction with the oxides has also hardened the soil in most areas north of the centre, making it next to impossible to cultivate. In the south, much of the soil is too gravelly or too light (and subject to wind erosion) to be worked.

Deeper soils are found in small areas in the Northern Territory such as parts of the top end and on the Sturt Plateau south of the town of Katherine. Possibly it was knowledge of this and failure to recognize other deficiencies that encouraged some early though futile attempts at arable production. In the 1870s and 1880s an area on the outskirts of Palmerston was designated "the Gardens," with the mission to experiment with "rice, sugar, maize, tobacco, and . . . other tropical products, which would yield handsome returns to the practical farmer."[2] In 1881 the *Northern Territory Times* optimistically reported other ventures: "We may be certain of having a good crushing of sugar cane at Delissaville in August or September, and . . . [another] will probably be ready on the following season at the Daly River. A coffee plantation, under the direction of experienced and competent managers, is being formed at Rum Jungle."[3]

All such undertakings soon failed or just never materialized. Some Chinese took up market gardening, selling their vegetables and fruits in the gold fields and/or in Palmerston. Their ventures were, however, only on a small scale and conducted on lots in areas of reasonably dense settlement rather than in the countryside. On the stations themselves, there was virtually no expansion into traditional farming sub-industries. Sheep raising, as we have seen, failed everywhere. And horses fared only slightly better. One should mention that a handful of graziers do seem to have begun producing a small number of fairly decent working horses by the end of this period by breeding a Waler type of their own. After shooting the wild stallions roaming near their lease, some of the stationers would turn loose better-bred studs to replace them.[4] The result was progeny that aesthetically conformed more closely than the brumby to Old World expectations, was a little easier to handle, and could adapt better than domesticated animals to the tough environment. Near the end of the first decade of the twentieth century, some of these animals started to turn up at southern auction sales. In 1907 newspapers claimed that a few of the "heavy and medium draughts, gunners, remounts, hacks, harness horses, and ponies" that Kidman brought to his annual sale at Kapunda had originated in the Territory. The general run of animals was of varying "dimensions and quality," but some apparently brought cash amounts as high as 34 pounds.[5] It seems doubtful that any of the highest quality were Territorial stock, but a percentage of the decent "grade" animals were. On a number of occasions John Hayes sent horses from Undoolya down to auction that sold quite well. In 1909 one lot brought 15 pounds on average, which was respectable though not competitive with what the elite animals were bringing at the time.[6] A few horses Hayes sold actually came from north of the MacDonnells. "I was cattle buying at Banka Banka Station, 310 miles north of Alice Springs, and . . . [at another] Station 500 miles north of Alice Springs," Hayes wrote in 1911, and I "bought several horses from Messers Bathman and Nugent for 6 to 10 pounds. I used these horses on the road from there to Oodnadatta, 800 miles, and proved them to be the best working horses I had ever ridden. I then gave them two months' spell, sent them to Adelaide, and sold them . . . They realized from 17 to 27 pounds."[7]

The numbers of horses involved in such transactions were very small relative to the grazing industry as a whole, however, and prior to 1911 one cannot speak of an industry of any real significance. Hogs, despite some positive musings by government officials, never really got a start, presumably because their nearly hairless hide was subject to burning under the scorching sun. Some of the early colonists milked cows. However, they did this mainly for personal use and, again in many cases, in the urban setting. When in 1883 the district council in Palmerston passed a "pernicious resolution" enabling charges to be brought against people whose horses and cattle were found "at large in this township," a local resident warned: "It means that there will not be a drop of fresh milk procurable" in the town.[8] Some of the stations had cows that they milked, usually Shorthorns, which are considered dual-purpose animals, as they are marginally good for both beef and milk. But this was to supply a fresh source for the country table and essentially never a commercial enterprise.[9] The population base in the Territory was too sparse to provide an adequate market; and the distances to Palmerston, Borroloola, and Katherine (the only centres that could be called urban) were too great for most stations to ship perishable products during the drys, and the roads were impassable for much of the time during the wets.

Not only did pioneers fail to bring significant diversification to Northern Territory agriculture, they also eschewed even the most fundamental changes within the beef grazing industry. As late as the 1960s two economic surveys of the Northern Territory pastoral industry were undertaken. Three conclusions arising from them are particularly pertinent here: first, most of the cattle stations then functioning had been doing so by 1910;[10] second, though reduced in size somewhat from the earliest frontier period, they were all still very big by anyone's standards; and, third, they were still utilizing the profound neglect approach that had predominated on the coastal plains of southern Texas more than a century earlier.[11]

"The present cattle industry is conducted on a very extensive system," the surveyors concluded, "with large areas (mostly between 1000 and 6000 sq. miles [640,000 – 3,600,000 acres]) in each property . . . and little or no control of cattle movements other than that imposed by distances between watering points." During the wets cattle on some stations grazed the grass down "near the surface waters." Then as those sources dried up, the cattle "moved to the bores" of their own accord. As a result, native grasses in both places were randomly allowed periods of rejuvenation. The only other form of "grassland management" was "the periodic, if somewhat haphazard, burning of some pasture types to destroy coarse material and to encourage the production of small amounts of better-quality fodder."[12] There were only the most modest attempts at quality control in the herds. "Between 23% and 38% of stations culled some cows"; and they seem to have done so in an extremely offhand manner. Graziers tended not to test their cows for fertility but relied on visual inspection alone. They often made mistakes. Indeed, one of the reports acknowledged: "There have been numerous instances of cows consigned to meatworks being found on slaughter to be pregnant."[13] Because bulls and cows were allowed to run together throughout the year, breeding was helter-skelter. No control was exercised over the age at which heifers conceived, nor were efforts made to manage the time of year that breeding took place. Therefore, many of the calves continued to be born during wets and drys, rather than between the seasons when neither drowning during heavy downpours nor over-exposure to direct sunlight would have been so likely.[14] In all districts, some stations practiced pregnancy testing but this was always restricted to a limited number of cows, mainly those used for breeding replacement bulls.[15] Very little if any spaying was done to weed out poorer females, and, therefore, all the surviving heifer calves, whatever their quality, normally became breeders replacing cows as they grew too old or died off.[16] Even weaning was far from universally practised and usually only when the calves were at least a year old; often only the males were weaned – so they could be pulled out of the herd and castrated to combat inbreeding.[17] Few stations produced extra feed to augment natural grasslands and those that did "primarily directed" it "toward drought survival of small numbers of selected cattle." Only a minority of stations even provided phosphate or protein supplements on a regular basis.[18]

Vaccination for pleuropneumonia was common only in the areas where the disease was deemed the most threatening. A vaccination for redwater had been available for decades, but most stations neglected to use it, as few cattle over and above breeding bulls were being imported and major outbreaks of the disease had become quite rare.[19] Some Territorial stations were taking steps to prevent the spread of ticks but a lot more could have been done. "Infestation" was "often serious" in the Victoria River district, which, ostensibly, was the only one of the three where the atmosphere is humid enough for it to prosper. However, even there, only half the stations bothered to dip or spray.[20] Ticks could cause discomfort and stress to the host animal to the point of putting it off its feed. Affected animals decline gradually, however, and thus were not likely to die suddenly. Cattlemen could send the animals to slaughter before they were lost, though few appeared to be very vigilant.[21]

As we have seen, the stations in all three pastoral districts in the Northern Territory upgraded their facilities mainly only by boring

CORRAL ON CATTLE STATION, NORTHERN TERRITORY. NORTHERN TERRITORY LIBRARY, DARWIN, BRUCE CLEEZY COLLECTION, PH0327/0055.

increasing numbers of sub-artesian wells.[22] By the 1920s the better stations, such as Alexandria on the eastern Tableland, had made "good" improvements in the form of bores, massive water storage tanks, and power sources – mainly windmills and pumping engines, the latter of which they had covered to protect from the weather. They also had improved their buildings, and built fairly extensive sets of permanent mustering corrals in their pastures, and containment yards at their headquarters.[23] This type of upgrading continued, and in the 1960s one owner near Alice would be able to boast of "sixty watering points so well placed that there was no area" on his property "without a man made bore."[24] Numerous stations eventually added to their meagre networks of pasture fences, but in most cases only at crucial points on the periphery of their holdings to prevent the cattle from wandering too far. They did little cross fencing.[25]

One of the surveys that was conducted in the 1960s noted that rail service had improved to a limited though significant degree as the decades passed. By 1929 the southern region had service all the way to Alice Springs. At that time those in the other two grazing regions were able to reach rail yards at Dajarra and Mount Isa, both Queensland towns near the eastern Northern Territory border, where stock could be loaded onto cars and shipped to the ports and markets of the east coast and south. By then there was a packinghouse at Wyndham in the northeastern corner of West Australia that had the capacity to take the small fraction of cattle from the closer Victoria River stations that fattened up well enough for killing. However, the majority of the stations from the two northern pastoral districts still had to engage in the arduous process of "walking" their product a good portion of the distance to market and paying for it in carcass weights, though infrastructure on the trails had been substantially improved with watering facilities.[26]

> Stock from the Victoria River and Barkly Tableland districts are sent east to Queensland, whence the original development proceeded. . . . Those from the westernmost properties walk about 1000 miles. They are driven 8 to 10 miles per day along stock routes provided with waterers every 16 to 20 miles and which, by the end of the droving season, are severely overgrazed. Under these conditions only stock old enough and strong enough to walk the distance are marketable and . . . weight losses on the long journey are heavy and the condition of stock normally deteriorates substantially before they reach the killing works.[27]

If the basic grazing system established in southern Texas in the mid- to late nineteenth century thus survived universally in the three grazing districts of the Northern Territory, so too did its most basic assumptions. The first, obviously, was that there would be low input costs. The cattle looked after themselves year round – little was expended on equipment, facilities, medical treatments, or feed supplements. Losses were higher than they might otherwise have been, but, in theory at least, they were acceptable given that expenditures were so light.

This fitted well with the other assumption of the system – that there would be relatively low productivity. Branding percentages – that is, the number of calves branded in a given year relative to the number of cows in the herd – were likely to be "about 40% for all districts."[28] Besides profound neglect, "a major reason" for the low rate "was inadequate nutrition," which was common "throughout" the Territory, particularly near the end of the dry season. Many of the cows aborted or just failed to conceive. The surveyors believed, as well, that a lot of calves were lost between birth and branding. While they could garner little information on the actual numbers, they deduced that, particularly "on the open Mitchell grass plains . . . where shade is scarce and the temperature very high," many calves succumbed to the heat soon after birth.[29]

The general lack of pasture management, poor and fluctuating nutrition, inefficient reproduction, high death rates, and very rudimentary property improvements characterized the industry at the later stage just as in the beginning. The fact that the stations in the Northern Territory that were operating in 1910 lived on indefinitely using the same basic operational practices as did their pioneering predecessors underscores the fact that high startup costs were the main cause of failure in the earliest years. It is clear, moreover, that the industry survived mainly because, by the end of the first decade of the twentieth century, the second- and third-generation pastoralists had been able to surmount most of the more extraordinary challenges associated with beginning anew in a "new" land. First, they had by then discarded most of their poorer holdings and consolidated those that were the more productive. The Victoria River Downs station was typical. When one of the 1895 commissioners asked the representative from that station how much land the run held, he replied, "not so much now as we did . . . because when I was there I found the coast country did not pay – that is, land for 150 miles back from the seaboard . . . therefore we gave up our leases at the [top end] stations of Marrakai and Glencoe."[30] By this time the costs of wages and Native depredations were moderating substantially, in some measure because more and more Aboriginal people were being forced into submission. The "right steps have already been taken," the above witness asserted, as "police protection" is now much better. He did not mention that station employees everywhere had banned together with the forces of law and order to wipe out as many of the hostile Native groups as they could. "A good many" Aborigines "have been put out of the way by bullets," a police chief acknowledged in 1890.[31] The career of the notorious mounted constable W.H. Willshire – who was able to conduct a campaign of terror against the Aboriginal people around Alice in the early 1880s, and to carry it forward to the Victoria River district thereafter – substantiates that statement.[32] Drug and alcohol dependence and sexually transmitted diseases no doubt also helped to temper resistance by the first peoples.[33]

But the most important change was that Aborigines who had endured the onslaught had become one of the mainstays of the pastoral industry. They had gradually shifted from enemy and pillager to needy adherent. "The numbers in constant employment vary . . . from two or three to thirty or forty," a report compiled in 1913 stated: "It is the native living on some of these large pastoral areas who are troublesome in the way of cattle killing, and yet on the other hand it is not too much to say that, under present conditions, the majority of the stations are largely dependent on the work done by black 'boys.'"[34] The report also painted a picture of dependency that went way beyond the small percentage of men and women who actually worked on the stations:

> There is always a native camp in the vicinity of every station where a larger or smaller number of aboriginals is gathered together, attracted by the chance of securing food . . . It is a constant occurrence on practically all stations where cattle are killed to distribute the offal and bones, often with plenty of meat attached to them, amongst the natives, who gather round the killing yard like crows round a dying sheep. Everything is eaten and every bone pounded up to get at the marrow. In addition to this, there are many odd scraps distributed and the few natives who are permanently employed unless special precautions are taken, will share what they receive with the others.[35]

Amanda Nettelbeck and Robert Foster tell us that initially settlers in central Australia "had petitioned the government for officers with Martini-Henry carbines and Colt revolvers" to deal with the Aboriginal population, but by the early 1890s "they wanted flour, tea and sugar to attract" the Native people to work in the cattle industry. That they occasionally killed stock "was of little significance when weighed against the growing importance of their labour."[36] Native manpower was not only essential, it also brought down expenses. Managers and some outside

ABORIGINAL STOCKMEN, NORTHERN TERRITORY. NORTHERN TERRITORY LIBRARY, DARWIN, PETER JAMES COLLECTION, PH0331/0014.

observers remarked particularly on the number of Aborigines the stations fed.[37] When, however, it is considered that the food was mostly what European societies considered waste by-products of the beef industry and that animals killed were almost certainly too old or sick or hurt to be marketed, this appears as considerably less of a burden. True, the stations provided other supplies as well to their workers. "In 1912 the remuneration consisted of two or three suits of clothing yearly, two or three pair of boots, one or two blankets and one or two mosquito nets" over and above edibles such as "flour, tea, sugar, tobacco and pies."[38] But records kept by Goldsborough, Mort and Company indicate that from 1909 to 1911 the company was spending between sixteen and twenty-four pounds per month on its entire "Blacks" workforce when the average full-time white stockman or worker was costing about fourteen and a half pounds per month.[39] The company must have been employing at least a dozen Aborigines at that time, since it had some thirty thousand cattle and the white population in the Territory was so small.[40] This would substantiate estimates that the net cost of keeping a single Aborigine in regular employment ranged from one to two pounds a month.[41]

Any attempt to elucidate the role of Aboriginal labour in establishing and maintaining the northern cattle frontier in Australia will need to give due attention to women. Many stations employed "lubras" not just as domestics or for "chores" around the home place but as stockmen.[42] They are "good, reliable workers, and will stick to a job," a reporter once noted after a visit to Urapunga station near Paddy's Lagoon on the Roper River. "Every house and shed, the wells, and the substantial yards" at the homestead have been built with lubra labour, "and the workmanship is excellent throughout." "Out in the Territory" they "are accounted better stockriders than the boys, they will stick to any horse any boy will, and . . . when in trouble do not resort to any feminine weaknesses by holding on to the horse's neck, . . . but sit upright, and if they are to come off, do so in quite a manly fashion." The reporter singled out for praise one "Princess Polly" on Urapunga "(a strong minded lubra of amazing strength)" who had been appointed head stockwoman.[43] Mary Durack felt sure that the Aboriginal women who worked the cattle herds gained a degree of self-satisfaction and stature. In her first saga about her family's ranching days in the Kimberley area near the Northern Territory border in Western Australian, she claimed that the late nineteenth century was

> probably the heyday of the black women who never before or since enjoyed such status and sense of importance. Small-boned and timid-seeming, they soon proved themselves to have more endurance and intelligence than their men in the cattle game. They loved the life of the stock camps, the thrill of riding the plains . . . and if they served other ends than mustering and holding cattle little evil was prevented by confining them to the boredom of the homestead wurlies on the creek banks.[44]

In the long run, cheap Native labour gave the Australian cattle stations the ability to more than overcome the advantage the great ranches on the northern Great Plains of North America initially had with respect to wage costs. In western Canada the big outfits sometimes employed some Indian cowboys, in part because they were able to pay them less than the white men. On 9 April 1887, William Bell, then ranch clerk on one of the big operations, informed his boss that "we have now two Indians herding, Damien has one at the Bloods" helping to bring in cattle for the beef contract, "and we have one herding the beef cattle at Beaver creek." Bell was very pleased that these men were hired at a bargain basement price. "We give them twenty dollars per month each and board and they furnish their own horses."[45] However, relatively speaking, the number of Indian cowhands on any of the big ranches was small. At this time, this particular outfit had only two on its payroll and more than a dozen whites. In later years it had none.[46]

By the turn of the century the cattle stations in the Northern Territory were also, to a significant if limited extent, reducing in-cartage costs, though in this matter the Canadians would continue to hold the advantage. Some individual stations took their own steps to build and improve transportation facilities. The Victoria River Downs station brought supplies up from southern urban centres by ocean steamer to Port Darwin and then by a smaller steamer along the edge of the Timor Sea and the northwest coast of the Northern Territory to the Victoria River. The ship could go only part of the distance up the river, then goods and people had to be transferred to a "smaller sailing craft" to go another hundred miles to the station's own depot. From there it was necessary to take "drays or horses" some hundred miles to the head station.[47] Overall this obviously was a complex and relatively difficult and expensive trek, but it did help to create some efficiency and bring costs down in comparison to overlanding the nearly six hundred miles from Port Darwin. On the other side of the Territory, the McArthur River station apparently used a somewhat similar setup, transporting goods and people via steamer across the Gulf of Carpentaria to the mouth of the river and then upstream by a smaller vessel.[48] Outside stations were probably allowed to use both of these facilities and, if so, that must have cut costs for all of them. In 1890 the construction of a railway line was completed from Darwin south to Pine Creek, some 150 miles inland. This was particularly helpful in enabling stations such as Newcastle Waters on the western edge of the Barkly Tableland or Wave Hill on the northeast corner of the Victoria River area to bring in supplies.[49] Access to the Alice Springs region improved in the same year, when Oodnadatta in the north central part of South Australia became the terminus of the Great Northern Railway, although, as noted above, the line was not extended the nearly 450 miles further north to Alice until 1929.

The main challenge with respect to out-cartage was, of course, to get the cattle to market, and in this case the Australians had a decided advantage over the Canadians. Drought was the greatest threat when it came to droving stock along one of the four long overland routes. In some years marketing came to a complete halt because the water holes dried up along the way and government bores were neither adequate nor properly maintained.[50] This unquestionably disrupted station incomes. However, as we have seen, men such as William Phillips recognized that their livelihood depended on their ability to get cattle to destination in "good store condition," so when a route was open they took pains to do so. Most years the drovers were able to keep the cattle on the trail by moving them within weeks after the end of the wet season, when the ground had dried out somewhat but the billabongs were still at least partially full.[51]

A regular difficulty even in the earlier period was finding enough good grass along the way to keep the cattle healthy. This was primarily because so much stock travelled these routes that they became overgrazed. Most of the time, though, the stations sent mainly their hardiest animals – the mature bullocks – and the drovers were able to keep them in good enough shape to put on the market as store cattle after their arrival at the place of sale. "From Roxbrough" Downs, just east of the Queensland border, to Marion Downs, some thirty miles further east, "there is not a bite" of grass left, drover H.R. Rose informed his owner in 1909. He knew "two Victoria mobs of cattle" were out there in groups of "800 and 1000" and there were also "5 mobs from Wave Hill about 1200 in each." The trail "is fearful," he said; "I have struck a patch of old stuff today and am making the best of it. From here down there is very little" grass "I am told" and "the old cows are [weakening]." Ultimately, however, he believed he would get by. "I will battle all I know to get a bite to eat for my lot," he continued; "The balance" of the cattle are still "good strong stores." Indeed, he said, "a hundred or more" are "nearly fat" enough to kill.[52] A month later he reported: "I have had a rough time from Birdsville. The feed is all too short and the cattle would not eat the old stuff. I have had to drop a few old cows too weak to travel on. The cattle look pretty rough. But I hope to see them mend a lot from here to Hergott as I have just struck good feed and expect to get it pretty well all the way."[53]

Generally speaking the wear and tear on the stock was acceptable, comparable to that for shipping cattle by land and sea from the northern Great Plains of North America to Great Britain. Many of the drovers were highly experienced by this time, having conducted these treks for years, and they knew to slow down and even stop in areas along the way where the grass was good to allow their cargo to "mend."[54] After the drovers dropped trail-weary cattle at stations along the way, the owners would write to the managers of the stations to retrieve them. Co-operation seems to have been widespread.[55] Moreover, a number of the owners such as W.F. Buchanan and presumably John Lewis, who was the principal shareholder at Newcastle Waters after Dr. Browne lost it, had holding pens near the place where the animals were to be sold so they could rest them, feed them, and get them back in shape before putting them through the ring.

With respect to monetary costs for droving and also transportation, the Australians were in a much better position than their Canadian counterparts. James Cox got figures from a "thoroughly competent authority" on the costs for shipping cattle across the ocean from Chicago. He comprehensively figured in rail charges from the city to the American seaports, ocean freight charges, feed costs, the labour cost for someone caring for the cattle during the voyage overseas, insurance fees, and even the cost of the bucket and rope used to feed and water the animals on the steamer. The total, excluding sales commissions in Britain, was about $20.60 per head.[56] The railroad, feed, and yardage charges to get the animals from Montana to Chicago were about $7.80, so the grand per head total to move cattle all the way from the far West to Britain was something like $28.40.[57] The charges for moving the Canadian cattle via the Canadian Pacific Railway to Montreal and then by ocean steamer to Britain would not have been identical to those for Americans, but they cannot have been much different.[58] The cattlemen from the Northern Territory, on the other hand, paid drovers a mere shilling per head per 100 miles. In 1906 drover Hy Grainger contracted to take 1,360 head over 1,400 kilometres from Newcastle Waters through the Birdsville route to Goyder's Lagoon in northeast South Australia. He got 707 pounds in total, or 10 shillings per head, which would have been equivalent to about $2.50. It would have cost no more than 6 shillings, or $1.50 per head, to drove and rail them the 500 miles from Goyder's Lagoon to Adelaide.[59] That made a total for the entire journey of just over 16 shillings, or about $4.05, per head.[60]

In walking all these cattle to outside markets, the Australians did not have to concern themselves a great deal with the threat of redwater, which had so plagued their predecessors when walking them in. When moving the cattle to market, drovers liked to blame some death loss on that disease as that seemed beyond their control. However, this may often have been a rationalization on their part and, in any case, the numbers involved in single instances were small compared to those that had occurred when the stations were being stocked.[61] There were other types of natural challenges too that, though most damaging to the western Canadian grazing industry, were not of great concern once the Australian pastoralists became established. Cattle losses due to animal predators were tolerable if at times traumatic. Crocodiles swarmed most of the more northern rivers and they did take stock. In the 1870s Arthur Ashwin witnessed a "draught horse" being "dragged" into one of the rivers by a large crocodile, which caught the animal by the head as it was getting a drink. There was a brief struggle, the two animals emerged twice from the water, and then disappeared for good.[62] John Costello called one area – the valley beyond the low hills to the north of Leichhardt's crossing on the Limmen River – "Alligator Plain," in the mistaken belief that the crocodiles that inhabited it were of that species. He related: "Many of the cattle which pastured on this grassy plain" were ambushed "when they came to the river for water." Even though "numbers of these huge reptiles were shot," it was "a common thing . . . to see three or four dead cattle floating about . . . They had been taken by these destructive marauders and were . . . killed – not eaten at the time, but in a day or two." Meanwhile their "inflated carcasses" were left "drifting in the brackish waters." Pioneers believed the beasts preferred their meat in a rotten condition and liked to stockpile food and, like the dingo, enjoyed "the sport of killing" even when "gorged."[63] However, the crocodiles inhabited the more northern rivers and billabongs only. This included the McArthur River on the Tableland and the Victoria River, but even there they were never the threat to stock that the wolves preying on the herds of the Canadian ranchers were. Crocodiles are ambush hunters. They wait in the water or amongst reeds for fish or unsuspecting land animals to come close, and then attack. They move swiftly in the water but they do not hunt in packs and are awkward on land. The cattle were justly afraid of them; during a mustering or drive along a river one of the creatures might appear suddenly, perhaps taking a cow. This would startle the rest of the herd sometimes into a costly stampede. But further kills were unlikely.[64]

The other well-known livestock predators in the Territory were dingoes. Though plentiful, they too did not compare to wolves in terms of kill potential. Generally speaking, dingoes are smaller than wolves and, while they can mercilessly slaughter sheep, they are not capable of inflicting great damage on full-grown cattle.[65] They did at times take a calf, but this required patience and organization to either decoy the mother into running after some of them while others attacked her offspring, or trick the mother into chasing several of them one at a time until she was too exhausted to protect her young. Some cattlemen used poison to control the dingo numbers;[66] but under normal circumstances dingoes were inclined to prey on any number of the 177 species in their Australian diet – including Red Kangaroo; Euro, Swamp, Agile, and Red-necked

Wallabies; wombats; brushtail possums; European Rabbits; and Magpie Goose and other birds and reptiles – rather than cattle.[67]

The most threatening climatic condition with which the cattlemen in the Northern Territory grappled – drought – was also not *quite* as damaging as the severe winters faced on the northern Great Plains of North America. Drought could be very destructive at times, but as the years passed and the stations bolstered their water sources, it did not equal Canada's harsh winter weather during the open range period in terms of total devastation. We have examined the 1886–87 winter in detail, but to comprehend the magnitude of the destruction, it is instructive to look more closely at some of the other years, and to compare, side by side, the damaging effects of climatic extremes on the grazing industry in the Canadian West and in the Australian outback.

What made the winters on the northern Great Plains truly fearsome throughout the open range period was that the storms hit the roaming herds so suddenly and with such force that the cattlemen had very little opportunity to react. This resulted in heavy losses even during winters that have attracted very little notoriety. In March 1892, for instance, "the bitterest blizzard in twenty years, killed many cattle in every district" and then abated for a while and came back again with even more force.[68] On April 24 it began to rain in the evening and poured steadily through the night. The following afternoon the rain turned to snow, which continued to fall all through the next night and the following morning. A strong and bitterly cold north wind magnified the effects of plunging temperatures. Great numbers of cattle that had been thoroughly drenched and chilled by the rain were stressed to the breaking point. As the storm raged, "the poor creatures could do nothing but drift before [it] . . . turning neither to the right hand nor to the left, and if any obstruction, such as a fence, barred their onward progress they simply stood there till they died with the snow drifting over them."[69] One rancher had recently purchased thirty-five head of cows and turned them loose on his pasture west of Macleod. They disappeared in the blizzard, "neither hide nor hoof remaining, the conjecture being that the entire herd was driven over a cut bank and perished."[70] The Circle ranch lost five hundred calves and thirty cows. Later when warm temperatures melted the snow near the ranch, the "water in the springs and small streams was very bad, owing to contamination from the putrefying beef."[71] As so often happened after a tough winter, the losses also vastly exceeded the immediate body count. Many of the surviving cows that suffered and were subjected to stress in the storms later aborted or produced stillborn offspring.

The 1892–93 winter was even worse. In the early weeks of 1893 at least eight thousand cattle succumbed in the foothills districts south of Calgary. And the losses were not confined to the foothills. In writing about their holdings in the Cypress Hills in Assiniboia, manager D.H. Andrews of the Stair ranch told his British directors that this had been "the worst weather I ever experienced: the Tuesday morning . . . the thermometer went down to 64 below zero [Fahrenheit], the next day it was 56 below and a wind blowing there. For 12 days it averaged over 40 below, with snowstorms every third day. Three bulls froze to death in the sheds one night and six calves were lost, at Crane Lake 5 bulls and 12 calves, we had to feed everything all they could eat during the storm, and had to feed inside. . . . We shall have a big loss on the range cattle."[72]

Andrews went on to estimate losses at the ranch properties near Maple Creek and Balgonie, also in Assiniboia, to the foothills of Alberta. A few weeks later, he informed his owners that he might actually have underestimated the damage: "The loss in the Cypress Hills and Mosquito Creek [districts] . . . you will think a very heavy one. What the loss is in the Cypress Hills no one can tell, as we have not been able to ride to where the cattle have drifted since November and cannot tell what the loss is until the snow goes and we can get a wagon and outfit down there; I hope I have overestimated it, but am afraid it will be more than I have taken off. We have had a worse winter than has ever been known before in this country, it has been almost impossible to move about." In the later 1890s the problem of weak cows losing their calves again brought springtime losses that many ranchers previously had not figured on. The "very cold and stormy weather in November 1896, was expected to have disastrous results on stock in some sections of the country," the police commissioner recounted. While "this fear was not directly realized," there was "a considerable decrease in the calf crop." In 1898 an officer at Macleod reported that "the calf brand is smaller than usual . . . a great number of deaths occurred among young stock in the early part of the year. From the depth of snow on the ground during March the cattle became emaciated, and were unable to withstand the cold." The second half of March was especially stormy; "trails were blocked, travel in many localities impossible, and horses as well as cattle showed the effect of the weather."[73] The Stair ranch book count dropped from around 5,700 to 3,553, but the estimate did not adequately reflect numbers in the Cypress Hills where the largest herd was located. On June 5 Andrews estimated the cattle there at 2,300 (down 500 from March 15) but the cowboys could find only 2,100. "This leaves us about 200 short of my estimated tally but I hear a number of our cattle are on the American side of the line, and we are going over to gather them as soon as they commence their beef roundups."[74] Even were they to find the 200 on the American side, the overall drop in the Stair inventory at that point was over 31 percent.

When cows did not produce calves, it meant that all the expenses that had gone into buying, maintaining, and pasturing them and supplying them with breeding bulls went to waste. Moreover, pastures would not be filled in the spring with newborn calves. When that happened the risks derived from winter grazing shot up, as the ranchers were more likely to import highly domesticated doggies from the East that were particularly inept at rustling for feed on their own when the weather was bad.[75] In the late winter to early spring of 1902–3 it was principally both the doggies and the newborn calves that died. Talk among the cattlemen themselves set the losses in the foothills south and west of Calgary at about fifteen thousand.[76] Near Maple Creek,

> Severe weather [in February] compelled ranchers to begin feeding hay to their stock, and March was a severe month: the snow was heavily crusted in some parts, and cattle were reported to be getting low in condition. April opened with snow followed by rain, and heavy frosts were experienced at the end of the month. A very severe storm set in on May 16, and lasted for nearly a week: a great deal of snow fell, particularly in the western part of the district, where it was very deep. There was considerable frost at night and as a consequence of the storm, stockmen sustained considerable loss, chiefly amongst . . . young calves. A great many of the "doggies". . . died from exposure, some in railway cars, some in the stock yards, and larger numbers on the prairie.[77]

DEAD CATTLE, BOW RIVER HORSE RANCH, COCHRANE ALBERTA, 1903 GLENBOW
ARCHIVES, CALGARY, NA-2084-24.

The next spring another late storm at nearby Crane Lake brought considerable destruction to imported yearlings. "No attempt has been made
to hunt up the stock as yet," a reporter wrote, and, therefore, no adequate
picture of the losses could be attained. He estimated, however, that the
average everywhere on the southwestern cattle ranges would be between
10 and 20 percent. "The storm was so heavy and continuous that in many
cases even if the cattle did get shelter under a cut bank they would starve
for the snow was so heavy that they could not travel."[78]

It was on top of this kind of year-after-year destruction that the truly
heartbreaking 1906–7 winter struck. The weather began to turn against
the ranchers on November 15 when rain that had been falling for two
weeks suddenly turned to snow and the temperature plummeted to 15 degrees below zero Fahrenheit. Some three feet of snow fell in a few hours.
Then the temperature climbed above freezing for a few hours and quickly

dropped again, causing a layer of hard crust to form under the fresh snow which made it even more difficult for the cattle to graze. There was no let-up. One blizzard followed another until late spring. By the middle of December all the available hay that had been put up for the cattle was either gone or covered by gigantic snowdrifts.[79] The cattle began to die from starvation and cold. Many pushed south and west in a futile attempt to escape the northern winds and find food. This left them on the open plains without the protection they could have got from the cutbacks and trees in the high country. Near Fort Macleod, Charlie Brewster and his wife spent much of the winter fighting off starving cattle that had come from the vicinity of the Red Deer River. "They almost walked over his buildings, and desperately tried to get at his small feed stack." The couple spent many hours in the bitter cold "urging the moaning animals past their home."[80] Some ranchers attempted to hold the cattle back but in vain as the animals flowed around and past them like a mighty river. Other ranchers tried gathering them in bunches out on the plains to drive them back up into the hills.

> Think of riding all day in a blinding snowstorm, the tem-
> perature fifty and sixty below zero, and no dinner. You'd get
> one bunch of cattle up the hill, and another one would be
> coming down behind you, and it was all so slow, plunging
> after them through the deep snow that way; you'd have to
> fight every step of the road. The horses' feet were cut and
> bleeding from the heavy crust, and the cattle had the hair and
> hide wore off their legs to the knees and hocks. It was surely
> hell to see big four-year-old steers just able to stagger along.[81]

Finally the exhausted riders and horses had to just let the cattle go. As they went they ate everything in their path – small sapling trees sticking through the snow, the hair off the backs of one another. Carcasses piled up everywhere.[82] In the Milk River area "there were so many dead cattle" dotting the landscape when the storms finally broke that one young lady who was still relatively unfamiliar with the countryside "found them very useful" as landmarks for making her "way about the prairies."[83]

Against these sorts of year-after-year losses, what drought took from the Australian range people seems . . . well yes, substantial, but in the

DEAD CATTLE, SHADDOCK RANCH, LANGDON ALBERTA, 1907. GLENBOW ARCHIVES, CALGARY, NA-1636-1.

long run, somewhat less so. When the long dry spells occurred on the Tableland in 1883, 1884, and 1889, the stockmen had to try to move the cattle as their water sources dried up. "All too soon the country was scourged . . . Then the weary ordeal of moving stock from great dams which had dried and travelling them to other portions of the run, where some stale and stagnant water yet remained. In these pools" there were "a number of dead and bogged cattle which had to be continually pulled out." The ones that "died quickly polluted the holes, already putrid with dead fish."[84] In 1893 Walhallow Downs, Corella Downs, Brunette Downs, and Eva Downs trailed some 34,000 animals to the coast of the Bay of Carpentaria where rainfall was more dependable and where the end waters of the Roper and McArthur Rivers continued to flow. They lost many, first on the journey to the coast and then when feeding on the "rank, mineral deficient grasses" that abound in coastal areas.[85] The 5,000 cattle that died on Alexandria in 1897 and the 1,500 on the Alroy run must have been nearly half their inventory, and one supposes that those cases were not atypical.

Over the years, however, the stations continued to sink wells in the areas that lacked permanent surface water, in many cases until they had enough to protect their cattle from desiccation no matter how long the weather refused to co-operate. While first-round owners, such as John Costello on Lake Nash, pushed their financial resources beyond repair in that endeavour, their facilities remained in place for others to build on once they were gone. Of course, depletion of drinking water for stock was not the only adversity that long dry spells created. These spells could also damage the pastures to the point where there was a real threat the cattle would starve. This was particularly true in the Alice Springs region where average annual rainfall is the lowest.

Photographs and news reports of sandy, desert-like conditions in this region have elicited considerable empathy from the public. In 2006 a radio program opened with the headline "central Australian cattle stations struggle to survive."[86] Many stations "are in severe drought," the broadcaster declared, continuing: "Some have received well below their average rainfall over the past three years. The Northern Territory Government this week deemed 11 properties to the south of Alice Springs to be in drought . . . And while they wait for substantial rain, the pastoralists continue to de-stock their properties and prepare for more tough times ahead." To illustrate the difficulties the eleven ranchers were encountering, the program gave the members of the well-known Hayes family, who were living on Deep Well station some fifty miles south of the town, a chance to be heard. They spoke openly of their hardships. Mrs. Tracey Hayes expressed concerns about the impact of drought on future generations: "It can be pretty tough," she said. "We've got 4 boys ranging from one to twelve so they grow up pretty quickly. The two eldest ones go out and give a hand quite a bit and it's quite confronting for them, I guess, to see animals suffering and, you know, the difficulties of running a business in this environmental climate that we face at the moment." The Hayes had been "moving cattle off" their property "for three years now," husband Billy said; "We've trucked a lot of our steers, they went down to Lucindale. Fattened them and sold them down there." He also said that he had "sent 2 or 3 lots to an agistment," and that he was about to rent some Native reserve land that had not been grazed in recent years.

What this indicates, beyond the difficulties associated with drought, is that by keeping a constant watch on their holdings and their herds, cattle owners in the Northern Territory had designed means for handling it. Among those means, what they did *not* do was critical. Along with not overgrazing, they did not follow the Canadian example and replace the drought-resistant grasses Nature selected for the Territory over the course of centuries with less-hardy domestic varieties. Consequently, wandering cattle were normally able to find enough fodder to survive extended periods without rain. Additionally, when drought persisted past a certain point, the owners had practical steps they could take to mitigate the impact. In the above cases, all were adjusting their herd numbers one way or the other. They were finishing some of their cattle on southern feedlots to sell them as fats and leasing land in areas where pasture damage was not so severe, either because it was out of the affected area or because it still had nutritional vegetation that had not been depleted.[87] Moving and marketing cattle added unwanted costs, but, arguably, it also enabled the families to significantly reduce their losses until better conditions prevailed.

Periods of dearth do not last forever. The year after the Hayes interview was conducted, other members of the family who were still on the Undoolya station were basking in the revival of good times. They had been "in drought for six long years, and they're running fewer Polled Hereford cattle, than ever before," a newscaster announced. "But since December 150 millimetres of rain has fallen. Nicole and Benny Hayes and their 5 young children are hopeful recent rains could be the start of a break in the long dry. It's a great relief for the Hayes family to finally see these resilient native flowers blooming once again in central Australia." The world, Nicole Hayes commented, had "changed completely in the last 4 months compared to what it was last year, it was pretty desolate . . . and now it's just a carpet of green."[88]

One final point about drought in Australia: although a constant threat, it has not struck all that often in specific regions – at least not in comparison to the blizzards that overwhelmed the open range cattlemen winter after winter in western Canada. In the Alice Springs district as a whole, long periods without rain have been far from rare, but dry spells extensive enough for the government to designate them as droughts have occurred there just three times from the late nineteenth century through to the 1970s: during 1895–1903, 1918–20, and 1958–68. The Tableland area was struck with such droughts just twice, 1911–16 and 1939–45; and the Victoria River district not at all. While parts of both the Tableland

and Victoria River districts experienced drought-like conditions between 1895 and 1903, they managed to sustain most of their cattle inventories while the Queensland herds next door were largely decimated.[89]

To say all this is not to *minimize* the extent to which periods without rain have hurt the pastoral industry in the Northern Territory. Clearly they have done lots of damage. Generally speaking, however, the native flora combined with human expertise and basic infrastructure have kept the Texas pastoral system alive, if at times not all that well, despite them. In the final analysis, that statement could be applied to all the major challenges pastoralists faced prior to 1911. By that time the second and third rounds of lessees had been able to locate the best grazing lands in their respective areas, and to find ways to deal with the high cost of labour, out-cartage, isolation, and predation as well as deficiencies of water, and they no longer had to pay exorbitantly to build up their cattle inventories. Therefore, they avoided the processes of dissolution and contraction that were occurring on the northern Great Plains of North America. Right through to the present, and despite encouragement from government agents and agricultural authorities, they even evaded subdividing their pastures, taking up controlled and selective breeding programs, and all but the most limited forms of supplementary feeding.[90] In short, they adhered to the precepts of "profound neglect." In the twentieth century, rancher/farmers in the Canadian West had to embrace more refined and diversified agricultural techniques to escape the most devastating manifestations of their northern setting. And they could do so because, unlike their Australian counterparts, they had adequate soils, appropriate weather conditions – at least during spring, summer, and autumn months – and reasonably dependable precipitation year round.[91] The cattlemen of the Northern Territory understood that to take a similar agricultural path was environmentally unnecessary to their survival and, furthermore, would prove a waste of their money because Nature had given them none of the same attributes.[92]

CONCLUSION:
THE FRONTIER LEGACY

While the family was emerging as the main unit of production on the ranch/farms in western Canada, corporations continued to predominate in the Northern Territory. To say this is not to suggest that the family did not have a place in the historical development of the industry in the outback too. First, though there were obviously far fewer family groups generally in the three extremely sparsely populated grazing districts, there were actually more family runs in the Alice Springs area than company runs. A biographer once, quite appropriately, described the families throughout that region with admiration as "battlers" because they eventually made a go of it where the corporations could not.[1] Living as they did in a "new land," lacking extended kinship networks, close neighbours, all luxuries, and most conveniences, they struggled from the beginning to keep their operations going – but the successful ones struggled together. In the Hayes case, every hand counted and the five siblings were expected to contribute in every possible way from an early age. The two girls participated every bit as much as the three boys, and they did not hesitate to cross gender boundaries, as indicated in the following conversation between William and a reporter:

—I understand you acknowledge your daughters to be as good as yourself on the station?

—I do, indeed. There is no phase of bush and station life that they are unable to tackle. There is nothing of the type of girls who want to drive out on Sundays about them. They are thorough horsewomen, with or without saddles, and can muster cattle with the best men I ever had.

—Can they shoe a horse?

—Of course they can shoe a horse. That's easy.

—Can they brand cattle?

—Yes; and shoot and dress a beast when the beef has run out. They also break in colts and go out for a week or two at anytime with a couple of lubras mustering cattle. They think nothing of camping under the stars and, in fact, can do anything with stock that men can do.

William knew his daughters were mentally tough as well. "'I can tell you that if they were bosses of a station things would have to be carried out their way.'"[2] When his children were old enough William built up his holdings by establishing them all on separate runs. In 1913 John was at Undoolya, William Junior at Owen Springs, Edward at Mount Burrell, and Miaa and Mary (Adams nee Hayes) were at Maryvale station with the elder couple.[3]

The following story recounted by a stockman in 1905 illustrates that, on the family operations that did exist in northern Australia, collaboration between man and wife during hard times could bring to the fore the same desperate strategy for fending off creditors as in the Canadian West.

I was present during the 1900 drought in the taking over by the mortgagees of a station away out. The owner of the property was a married man, and his wife possessed stock in her own name, and these were running on the station with her husband's cattle. When the representative of the mortgagees arrived I was at the station taking delivery of a mob of horses bred by the wife of the station-owner, and I went out with the muster when the first camp was put on. As soon as the cattle were steadied down and the chap who was taking delivery rode in amongst them to have a look through the lot, the station head stockman began "cutting out" for all he was worth. This naturally excited the curiosity of the mortgagee's representative, who asked him what he was at. The reply came quick and prompt, "Oh, only cutting out a few of Mrs.'s cattle." Then many more questions were asked, and brands and ear-marks were referred to and discussed but the result was that when Mrs.'s cattle were cut out of the mob, very few remained for the mortgagees. The reason was easily explained. After the mortgage was given over the property, the wife's brand was the only one used on the station.[4]

While the big corporations in the Victory River and Tableland districts were more dependent than those around Alice on outside hired labour, in some cases a man and wife co-managed. At Urapunga, John and Kate Warrington Rogers were equally reliant on each other in an operational sense.[5] A reporter once visited the station when John was away droving cattle to a distant market. "This droving takes from ten to eleven months every year," he wrote, "and during this time Mrs. Warrington Rogers, with her staff of lubras is in sole charge of the station. This means that for months at a time the lady is out mustering and branding her beasts, building cattle yards, rounding up 'fats' for the markets and attending to the hundred and one other jobs of a big station."[6] What Kate "does not know about cattle station management is not worth bothering about," one well-known neighbouring grazier commented. "If energy, daring, fine horsemanship, nerve, and shrewd common sense are qualities to make a capable cattle station manager, then this remarkable lady" is "well up to the mark and to her reputation." When asked if "she did not at times feel nervous in such lonely and dangerous surroundings and living solely with 'lubras,'" she replied, "nervous! It would not do for me to be silly and nervous; and besides, I have no time to be nervous, there is always so much to do and it must be done."[7]

One attribute the rancher/farmers in western Canada and the graziers in northern Australia seem almost all to have shared throughout their history is a similar level of economic attainment. That is to say, neither has been able to consistently show healthy annual profits. In the mid-1960s the average farm income in the Alice Springs region was $–4,109, in the Barkly Tableland region, $38,344, and in the Victoria River district, $34,193.[8] The Alice Springs area was in the midst of a three-year rainfall shortage, so for it the figures may be abnormally low. However, climatic conditions in the other two districts were about average. Considering that 50 percent of the stations were running 15,000-plus cattle and all were leasing huge areas of land and maintaining a sizeable labour force, the percentage return on investment was very low indeed.[9] Dependable figures for the Canadian West are hard to find until more recent times. However, those supplied by statistics Canada indicate that from 2005 to 2009 average net operating income from agricultural production for the 30,000 or so family farms (and ranch/farms) in Alberta varied from $16,292 to $22,935 while off-farm income ran from $79,307 to $94,509.[10] In Saskatchewan average net operating income for the 25,000 or so farms varied from $13,352 to $31,145 while off-farm income ran from $58,474 to $75,301.[11] To put what this means in blunt terms – the average farm family would have been living in abject poverty were it not for the fact that its members were able to take paid outside work.

The truth is that for most of the producers in the two areas of concern in this study, survival rather than wealth has always been the primary objective. In a sense these rancher/farmers have endured despite, rather than because of, their natural setting. It is evident that the frontier period was when survival proved most elusive and when the means by which it was most likely to be achieved had to be worked out. One of the outstanding features of frontiers pretty much anywhere is that the incoming peoples have a relatively poor understanding of the new area's qualities and, therefore, they will make mistakes and are liable to fail at an inordinate rate, historically speaking. In that respect the frontier works with nature to put limits on success. The first big Canadian ranchers were not familiar enough with their surroundings to understand that a grazing system that had shown great potential in the Deep South would not work on the northern extremities of the Great Plains. They had to learn that the winters were too severe, predation too widespread, the mange too persistent, and the grass not nearly productive enough to sustain grazing on the levels they anticipated. The first pastoralists in the Northern Territory had a better grasp of the weather-related factors in their country's hinterlands, but they also underestimated the magnitude of problems such as unforeseeably coarse grasses, scarcity of accessible natural water sources, disease, duffers, and racial conflict.

The extent to which, from the beginning, the frontier worked with Nature not just to exacerbate economic failure but also to shape the overall development of the cattle industry on both continents must be acknowledged. The Canadians chose the Texas system for the northern Great Plains to some degree because of the rich rough fescue grasslands that naturally abounded there. However, they were persuaded to embrace the idea of open range grazing in part because that was the easiest and cheapest way to get started in an undeveloped region that had no infrastructure. Moreover, while the elements did much to force the big ranchers out of business, it was to a considerable degree because the unrefined, open range system subjected their herds unreasonably to extremes of weather, predation, and disease and also because it made selective and controlled breeding impractical. It was for the same reasons that the movement to family ranching/farming was necessary. The Australian pastoralists were also attracted to the Northern Territory by the grasslands but they too unquestionably saw the open range system as the course of least resistance. It subjected their cattle to Nature's destructive power as well, mainly in the form of long periods of tremendous heat and little rain. In reaction they had to upgrade their facilities somewhat, mainly by incorporating increasing numbers of man-made water sources and, particularly in the Alice Springs district, by managing their stock more closely. On both continents the cattlemen also had to respond to low population density and their remote situation – the Canadians by supplying store cattle over land and sea to European farmers and the Australians by largely walking their stock to grain growers via Charleville, Hergott Springs, and Oodnadatta.

Despite its impact throughout the American West as well as in Australia and Canada, the frontier as a concept, as noted above, is largely absent from modern historiography. North American historians have basically given up talking about it: Americans in part because they feel that Fredrick Jackson Turner's work is passé if not discredited, Canadians because the concept is too American;[12] and Australian historians have treated their frontiers almost solely as a place where invading and indigenous races met, mingled, and clashed. In these societies, however, its attributes not only affected virtually all aspects of life in its day but they cast a shadow over time that continues to be felt through to the present. Arguably that shadow could be seen for years in political/constitutional, gender, and religious developments.[13] Such subjects are outside the scope of this study, but a few more words can appropriately be said about cultural manifestations. In that general area the frontier's influence is still palpable. The rough and unruly crew culture has been tempered on both ends of the globe as the institutions of law and order and the family have become stronger. However, in some noticeable respects, pioneering customs and traditions endure.

To grasp how these customs and traditions first became entrenched, we need to be cognizant of the process of selection the frontier imposed on the society of its day. Some types of people it rejected and others it not only accepted but actually raised to heroic stature. The ones it tended to reject were those who people considered to be the most firmly restrained by Old World values. In western Canada, people felt that their society was virtually the antithesis of that in the East or overseas. Whereas the latter were refined and sophisticated, and catered to the polite and courteous, the West was rough-hewn, rugged, and both mentally and physically demanding. It thus militated against the sort of new arrivals who were unable, for whatever reason, to thoroughly alter their ways. "Though the spirit of sheer adventure has sent many young men to Canada, and there made good and contented Canadians of them," many are not "of the quality that wears well," warned a writer from London after a visit to Calgary in 1904. "Among the derelicts . . . in the west," there were "young fellows whose sole equipment was manifestly their spirit of adventure. They hung about the town looking picturesque and with . . . leggings and cowboy hats on, inept . . . and waiting for some pleasant leisure for shooting prairie chicken or catching trout."[14] Some westerners learned to look with deep suspicion on almost anyone from the East but particularly Great Britain. "After residing here and reading your newspapers for a few months past, it would seem to me many take a deep delight in fanning the flames of hatred towards the British nation," Alfred Cross wrote in 1895. It was, he felt, "a pity one has to carry back such an opinion to one's native land to harm the respect and friendship due so great a nation."[15] From time to time employers advertised job openings with the stipulation "no English need apply."[16] In most cases, such prejudices were directed towards a very specific kind of Englishman. He was the spoiled, well-heeled "remittance man" who had been sent west by his family because he was an embarrassment at home. The West was supposed to encourage him to mend his childish and indolent lifestyle. Stories about remittance men were commonly repeated in the newspapers and in the correspondence of people who became part of the ranching fraternity.

Time and again they reiterated the opinion that "such chaps should be kept at home."[17] They were convinced that too many young men who were relatively well-to-do, physically weak, and naive about the workings of the world had come out from the mother country. Most were not just awkward and out of place but predestined to fail in a land where only the strongest could compete. "The slow-moving brains of some, the lack of initiative, of originality, marked the general run of them as hopeless for Western life, where necessity is ever forcing and developing the inventive genius, the adaptability, and the power to make one thing do work for a dozen other articles."[18] Unquestionably, there was a bias here but there seemed to be lots of evidence to support it. Numerous disparaging eyewitness comments came from British ranchers themselves. Monica Hopkins, who along with her husband had a 640-acre ranch near Millarville, was one. Her descriptions of her rather pathetic neighbours, named Bolts, painted a grim picture. "I never would have believed that anyone could live in such discomfort in such an appalling place if I hadn't seen it for myself," she told one of her fellow countrymen.

> The house built by Mr. Bolts is of course built of logs, the ends of which have never been cut off and stick out at various angles at each corner. The roof has a dip in the middle and the stovepipe sticks out like a crooked handle. Instead of plaster or moss between the logs, odd bits of newspapers have been shoved in [and from the inside] the daylight could be seen between most of the logs. . . . Mr. Bolts is hopeless out here, so stupid and ignorant of anything connected with country life. In Manchester where he comes from he would probably be quite an ordinary young man, dressed in blue serge and a bowler hat and travelling by train or bus to an office.[19]

David Warnock wrote of a ranch hand named Brown who wanted badly to go back to England. "Out of wages paid him since coming here I don't think he has saved a dollar!" Warnock said. "He lost one cheque by giving it to" a fellow worker and countryman, "to take to town and get it cashed for him." The man "went to town, cashed the cheque, got drunk, stayed in town and spent the money."[20] They never saw him again.

Story after story recounted British business failures too. D.H. Andrews told of a man who "could not make a success grazing cattle and sold out at a loss." He had allowed himself to become so broke that when he "took the opportunity to go home" he was forced to ride with the cattle "in order to save the expense of paying for railroad tickets and passage on a steamer."[21] In 1903 the *Calgary Herald* published an article on a well-known British experiment – the Barr Colony – proclaiming that its colonists are "Rich in Everything Except Knowledge of Their New Condition in Life." The author's main conclusion was that "Education leads to Disillusion."[22] Such examples were so numerous that at least one school was started to provide young Britons with a realistic idea of what to expect and how to cope. Someone told Cross in 1906 of a scheme to bring together "the members of the British public schools in Canada" to help and advise them. He liked the idea. "We have a large proportion of public school men coming from the British Isles," he told the people behind the scheme. "Many of them do not seem to get along very well owing to their lack of knowledge of what is required to make a success in the new country."[23]

Comparing attitudes towards the British with those towards Americans provides a sharp and interesting contrast. Anyone who searches the correspondence of this era or reads the newspapers cannot help but be impressed by the high esteem in which Americans were held because of their affinity for, and ability to deal with, conditions peculiar to the cattle industry. Few cases of American failure were cited by contemporaries, while a disproportionate number of success stories centred on families such as the McIntyres or men like E.H. Maunsell, John Franklin, John Ware, George Emerson, or D.H. Andrews who were born or had spent a considerable portion of their lives south of the border. All of them had worked cattle either as hired hands or as owners and were thus equipped to deal with all the challenges associated with establishing the beef industry.

One British rancher who came to the Canadian West in the 1880s after living for a considerable period of time in California, Arizona, Mexico, and Texas estimated that by 1886 "and prior to that date some of the ranch managers were Americans, all the foremen, nearly all the cowboys, nearly all the cattle and horses, all the saddles, rifles, revolvers and cowboy outfit in general were American."[24] Specific examples of British and Eastern owners hiring Americans to manage their herds are numerous. The Walrond brought in James Patterson from Montana as foreman.[25] The Bar U contacted the Montana Cattle Association to acquire George Lane.[26] Responsibility for the Cochrane cattle at Waterton was eventually turned over to James Dunlap.[27] E.C. Johnson, who took "charge of the Bar U herds for some years," worked for D.H. Andrews "both in Wyoming and this country." He was a "first rate cow man, in fact about the best all round cow man" around.[28] Andrews himself had many years' experience on the American ranching frontier before he came north to manage the Stair outfit for British owners. Frank Strong, who came to Alberta from Montana in 1880, ran the I.G. Baker stock business while operating a horse ranch of his own.[29] John Ware is one of many American cowboys who helped make up the most highly skilled segment of the day-to-day labour force. Because he was black, Ware had always felt threatened by vigilante groups in the United States that commonly hanged men suspected of cattle rustling. However, his decision to stay on at the Bar U was also undoubtedly because his expertise was in demand there, just as it had been in the south.[30] One of the same ranch's most famous hands was the notorious outlaw Harry Longabaugh, better known as the Sundance Kid. He was employed to break horses in 1890 and was considered very good at the job.[31]

Americans became role models and, in time, as the frontier selection process did its work, the more capable among the non-Americans adopted their skills and know-how.[32] Then admiration was transformed into an appreciation for anyone who was able to master the craft of the cowboy. In 1896 the *Montreal Witness* published an article based on an interview with Fred Stimson, then manager of the Bar U ranch. It started with a description of the superb effects of Western life on his physical condition, noting that when he had lived in Quebec he had been "a thin, delicate young man who feared consumption." Now, after more than a decade on the ranch, he was "colossal, hearty, and humorous." He had learned not only to "disdain . . . the 'biled shirt' of civilization" but also to enjoy sleeping "on the bare ground." The article described Stimson's deep knowledge of and faith in cattle grazing in the foothills of Alberta.[33] This sort of reasoning was endemic throughout the North American West.

After ranching himself in Montana and North Dakota, future president of the United States Theodore Roosevelt wrote that there are "very few businesses so absolutely legitimate as stock-raising and so beneficial to the nation at large." The rancher must not only be "shrewd, thrifty, pliant, and enterprising but he must also possess qualities of personal bravery, hardihood, and self-reliance to a degree not demanded in the least by any mercantile occupation in a community long settled." The cattlemen are "the pioneers of civilization, and their drive and adventurousness make the after settlement of the nation possible." They are "much better fellows and pleasanter company than small farmers or agricultural labourers." The "mechanics and workmen" of the cities should not even "be mentioned in the same breath."[34]

But adoration for the capable cattle frontiersman was demonstrated most forcefully in an endless number of dime and romantic novels originally published in North America and/or Great Britain, all of which in one way or another developed the theme that in the demanding and challenging setting of the West certain individuals had been transformed both physically and mentally into almost super-human beings. This was the central message in a host of works such as *The Boys of the Rincon Ranch*,[35] *Son of Rosario Ranch*,[36] *The Giant Cowboys*,[37] *The Chief of the Cowboys*,[38] *Sunset Ranch*,[39] and *The Virginian*, the latter by noted author Owen Wister.[40] American authors wrote most of the stories. However, their impact was equally profound on both sides of the international border. A few of the publications were Canadian. In *Sky Pilot* the acclaimed author Ralph Connor described the "Noble Seven," a group of Britons and certain "approved colonials" who had made their way to the foothills of the Rockies where, "freed from the restraints of custom and surrounding," they had "soon shed all that was superficial in their make-up . . . stood forth in the naked simplicity of their manhood," and learned the ways and culture of the cowboy. "Never have I fallen in with men braver, truer or of warmer heart . . . Throughout that summer and the winter . . . I lived among them, camping on the range . . . and sleeping in their shacks, bunching cattle in the summer and hunting wolves in the winter." Yes they went on sprees of drinking and debauchery but "through all not a man . . . ever failed to be true to his standard of honor in the duties of comradeship and brother hood."[41] So taken were the public with ranchers and cowboys that every aspect of their existence became subject to public depiction. Aesthetic qualities were everything. In all the novels intricate descriptions painted these frontier heroes in living colour and helped to grant them legendary status.

> Long dark-brown hair hung, in wavy masses, low over his well-rounded shoulders, while a goatee and mustache, silky in fineness and gloss, added to the manly beauty of his face, which was tanned by sun and wind . . . Buckskin breeches, fringed, and ornamented with silver buttons down the outer seams, were sustained about his waist by both belt and silken red sash. The breeches were thrust into the top of high-legged boots of calfskin, upon the heels of which were buckled a pair of silver spurs, with but medium-sized rowels. A blue woolen shirt, with wide collar loosely confined at the neck by a black kerchief and a black wide-brimmed sombrero, made up his . . . costume.[42]

It is indicative of the selection process associated with the frontier environment that in Australia the public underwent exactly the same basic pattern of disdain for Old World types who could not adapt and, eventually, outright veneration for all those of any origin who could. The centre of negative comment for ineptitude were young Britons who, very much like the remittance men in Canada, were sent out to the frontier by their family in hopes that they would find themselves. The family often paid stations to take them and subject them to outback challenges. "Some of the old time pastoralists" apparently "charged as much as 200 pounds and 300 pounds per annum for allowing" them "the privilege of breaking down their shaky fences, galloping the legs off their horses after kangaroos and emus, and violently making love to their sisters, servants, daughters, cousins, and maiden aunts."[43] It was widely believed that in most cases these young men in training, the so-called "jackaroos," did not learn the trade of the stockman and stationer but ultimately, like numerous of their countrymen in North America, returned to England with little or nothing to show for their colonial experience. They were considered overindulged children from wealthy families who showed virtually no interest in living up to their parents' hopes. "Who comes from home, devoid of sense, to gain regardless of expense, Colonial Experience? The Jackaroo."[44]

Here too, some of these men eventually adjusted their habits to fit their New World setting. "After a few years sojourn in this sunny land of tremendous distances most of them returned to merry England to settle down in their respective spheres of respectability." But "some . . . came out with a purpose to study pastoralism and invest capital" in the grazing business. "Many of the latter" invested wisely and were able to reap the rewards "of their studies on station properties throughout Australasia."[45] Eventually the good and capable jackaroo shared the public stature of the career stockman, just as the best of the remittance men in Canada enjoyed the immense esteem of the American cowboy. This brought him an equal level of well-published acclamation. Though "his relatives were located in the mother land," he was known to be "courageous as a bulldog, taciturn of speech, and a deep thinker." He had become a true man of the outback, "born with the love of a horse, a dog, and cattle . . . of which he was an astute judge." A "bold, fearless rider he . . . would tear through the bush at a full gallop either by day or" by night. "Every full moon he was out with two or three blackfellows, mounted his offside, as he termed" his horse, "and with a small mob of tailers" he "skirted the scrubs," and rounded up "the semi-wild cattle" that others had been unable to capture.[46]

It speaks to the universality of the frontier selection process that in Australia too writers provided an eager audience with vivid and intricate depictions of their heroes' style and dress. Except for a few of the terms used, the following description could easily have appeared in a northern Great Plains novel.

> Who has not seen either in the body, or depicted in various illustrated papers, the traditional stockman? To look at him as he stands, lightly resting his hand on the arched neck of his docile steed, is to wish to be that stockman. See him in all the glorious panoply of buckskin breeches, faultless, without a wrinkle, cabbage-tree hat, with long black sash with long scarlet pendants, kneeboots carefully greased (your traditional stockman eschews blacking), and an immaculate scarlet or pink-striped shirt! [This is the epitome of] wild freedom . . . devoted to careering on fiery steeds across boundless

plains, chasing wild cattle whose speed and ferocity are only
equalled by the lion.[47]

One cannot tell the whole story, however, without mentioning that the
tendency for people to be captivated by the cowboy generally was an Old
as well as a New World manifestation. The truth is that this noble knight
of the ranges came along at precisely the right moment in history. The
nineteenth century as a whole was a time when creeping industrialism
and/or urbanization seemed to be blotting out the sun and creating ghast-
ly slums in crowded centres of eastern North America, southern Australia,
and a host of European cities.[48] It was no accident that as these trends gathered strength, a multitude of romantic poets with names likes Byron,[49]
Shelley,[50] and Wordsworth[51] stated their regret at the loss of a bygone existence when people had been able to feel closer to nature. In that context,
any individuals who were able to go out into the vast wilderness in distant
parts of the world and handle its hardships and dangers seemed larger than
life. Adventurers, explorers, big game hunters, trappers, and bushmen held
a special place in the public view. Works such as G.O Shields' *Rustlings
in the Rockies: Hunting and Fishing by Mountain and Stream*,[52] W.F. Butler's
*The Great Lone Land: A Narrative of Travel and Adventure in the North-West
of America*,[53] A.D. Richardson's *Beyond the Mississippi: from the Great River
to the Great Ocean. Life and Adventure on the Prairies, Mountains and Pacific
Coast*,[54] Giles Seagram's *Jack Halliday, Stockman: A Story of Australian Bush
Life*,[55] A.B. Patterson's *The Man from Snowy River and other Verses* and *Old
Bush Songs*,[56] along with many others sold in the thousands.[57]

   The able cowboy or stockman was thus just one, though quite clearly
the most widely recognized, of a number of adventurous types who captured the hearts and minds of the reading public beyond as well as within
the frontier environment that had made his name. So firmly was admiration for him entrenched that time would not erode his stature. Today men
and women in ranching communities in Canada and Australia (and, of
course, the United States) commonly aspire to his image. They regularly
don wide-brimmed hats, bandanas, high-heeled riding boots, and special
belts and buckles in their everyday lives. They also maintain a lexicon of
their own, much of which is a carryover from the pioneer days. Terms
like "axle grease" (butter), "belly wash" (weak coffee), "doggie" (calf),
"buck out" (to die), "wrangler" (the guy who looks after the horses), and

"fixin' to," (do something) persist in western Canada, as do "jackaroo" (stockman in training), "cocky" (small grazier), "duffer" (cattle rustler), "buckjumper" (bucking horse), "roughrider" (stockman riding bucking animal), and "ringer" (very capable stockman) in Australia. This, and a particular parochial accent, set the rancher/farmers on the high plains of western Canada and the graziers in the outback of Australia apart from urbanites and regular farmers alike. Moreover, country music and cowboy poetry,[58] which developed out of young men's attempts to entertain their fellow cowhands around the campfire when droving or rounding up in the earliest frontier days, still command a substantial following.[59] Among the performers, Lee Kernaghan and Gina Jeffreys are as popular down under as Ian Tyson, Terri Clarke, and Stompin' Tom Connors up top. For samples of country poetry in modern times, see Appendix A below.

Perhaps nothing symbolizes the frontier today more than the resilience and vigour of the rodeo or stampede. It too originated and emanated from the time when the Texas system was first established. On the western plains of North America, spontaneous competitions of roping, racing, bucking, and/or cutting often took place during the general roundups when several ranches came together. The *Yellowstone Journal* in Montana commented on one such event in 1885. "Will G. Comstock in town from the nine-six-nine ranch reports a grand time on Saturday and Sunday at the Capital X Ranch on Mezpah Creek. Over seventy-five cowboys were present and the roping and cutting 'matches' both offered prize money for the winners." People from far and wide were sometimes invited to attend. "There were race meetings . . . and, at intervals between races, roping the wild steer, riding the bronco and other events peculiar to a great stock country were indulged in." In this manner the rodeo, first established in the American South, proliferated across the northern states and into the Canadian territories. By the early 1890s, professional cowboy athletes were appearing at these events along with local working ranch hands. A Canadian North-West Mounted Police officer recalled: "The competitors . . . had often come from a long distance and were past-masters at the games, sometimes champions of the great stock regions south of the line and in our country from the ranches in the vicinity."[60]

In Australia rodeo had its start with "campdrafting" and "rough-riding" during mustering when the stockmen were also inclined to display their riding skills and the quality of their horses.[61] Stock was taken from the cattle camps at night to compete in drafting, or cutting out. "Roughriding" evolved from these competitions. It featured bull and bronc riding and steer wrestling and eventually roping. These events started on stations in New South Wales and then spread through Queensland to the Northern Territory. We close with five photographs – the first two Australian and the other three Canadian. Only the keenest expert eye could tell which is which.

National Library of Australia, Canberra, NLA.GOV.AU/NLA.PIC-VN3108382.

GLENBOW ARCHIVES, PA-3465-32.

GLENBOW ARCHIVES, PA-4015-4.

GLENBOW ARCHIVES, NA-3279-11.

COWBOY POETRY

More evidence of the universality and durability of frontier cowboy culture is found in the continuing popularity of a great array of Western or country music and art that emanated from the early days, as young men tried to entertain themselves on roundup or muster or on the droving trail. What follows is some relatively recent poetry from both continents that, like the enduring culture of the rodeos, speak volumes. The first two compositions reflect the close relationship that often formed between man and his indispensable friend, the horse. The second two mirror the working lives of men who trailed the herds to pasture or market. Only minor peculiarities of language make it possible to discern from which continent any of these poems originated.

Horses and People – A Cowboy's Poem

We were all gathered at the sale barn
waitin' for the horse sale to get underway
When this old hand sat amongst us,
it was easy seein' "Cowboy" was on his resume
He watched the horses come and go
With an easy, patient horseman's eye.
He studied each horse as they came through,
but he never nodded or attempted to buy.

I found myself watchin' the old man
When to my surprise he turned and spoke.
"Horses are a lot like folks I've known,
some's honest and true, others can't be broke."

Then he pointed out a nice sorrel filly
as she swatted her tail and gave a squeal.
"She's like Miss Milly down at the diner,
plenty of good looks and sex appeal.

And that skinny lookin' ole horse,
actin' all touchy, nervous and rank,
he reminds me of old Mr. T. Wad
the loan officer at the bank.

Now that old mare, she's a kid's horse
She'd teach 'em and they'd never come to harm
She's sure a lot like old Mrs. Beachem
a grand lady, and my first school marm.

See that little two-year-old
boy, he'd like to break and run.
All he wants is away from here,
He reminds me of my son."

It seemed like we sat for hours,
Talkin', laughin' and comparin' notes,
About honest horses and people we knew,
Those we like and those not worth the oats.

About that time, an old bay entered the ring,
the old hands voice began to soften.
"If he was a man, I'd call him friend
and that's just somethin' I don't do often.

"A little thin and gray around the muzzle,
Like me, he's gotten on in years
But there's a heap of know-how restin'
between that old horse's ears.

"That old horse is some ole cowboy's pal,
Sellin' him, would be like committin' a sin.
So if you'll excuse me boys,
think I'll just buy him back again!"[1]

"Cowboy Blues"
GRAEME KING

I dropped a quarter in the slot and pressed A-42,
the bass line started hummin' from afar,
the guy behind the counter mixed me up another brew,
I saw my teardrops splashin' on the bar.

The pain was like a bullwhip – just one year ago today
my little Dolly lost her gallant fight,
the angels came 'a callin' and they took my little girl away
and still I cry most every single night.

Her favourite song, I still recall her eyes aglow at me
each time I hummed that sentimental tune,
I'd put my arms around her neck and hold her tenderly,
but then she went and left me way too soon.

The images flashed through my mind of just a year before,
it broke my heart to lay her in the ground,
we had three happy years but there would never be no more,
I hung my head and howled like a hound.

The song upon the jukebox ended, everything was still,
that barroom was as quiet as a mouse,
the bar man looked at me and said: "Ole buddy drink your fill,
and everything tonight is on the house."

A cowboy brought a bottle over, stood there by my side.
He said: "Here's to your grief I see it's bad."
I blinked through tears. "One year ago today my Dolly died –
the best danged horse a cowboy ever had.[2]

"The Ballad of the Drover"
HENRY LAWSON

Across the stony ridges,
Across the rolling plain,
Young Harry Dale, the drover,
Comes riding home again.
And well his stock-horse bears him,
And light of heart is he,
And stoutly his old packhorse
Is trotting by his knee.

Up Queensland way with cattle
He's traveled regions vast,
And many months have vanished
Since home-folks saw him last.
He hums a song of someone
He hopes to marry soon;
And hobble-chains and camp-ware
Keep jingling to the tune.

Beyond the hazy dado
Against the lower skies
And yon blue line of ranges
The station homestead lies.
And thitherward the drover
Jogs through the lazy noon,
While hobble-chains and camp-ware
Are jingling to a tune.

An hour has filled the heavens
With storm-clouds inky black;
At times the lightning trickles
Around the drover's track;
But Harry pushes onward,
His horses' strength he tries,
In hope to reach the river
Before the flood shall rise.

The thunder, pealing o'er him,
Goes rumbling down the plain;
And sweet on thirsty pastures
Beats fast the splashing rain;
Then every creek and gully
Sends forth its tribute flood
The river runs a banker,
All stained with yellow mud.

Now Harry speaks to Rover,
The best dog on the plains,
And to his hardy horses,
And strokes their shaggy manes:
"We've breasted bigger rivers
When Hoods were at their height,
Nor shall this gutter stop us
From getting home tonight!"

The thunder growls a warning,
The blue, forked lightning's gleam;
The drover turns his horses
To swim the fatal stream.
But, oh! the flood runs stronger
Than e'er it ran before;
The saddle-horse is failing,
And only half-way o'er! . . .[3]

"Tales of the Trail"
PAUL KERN

As time rushes over a concrete bridge.
It slows to a walk on rocky ride.
Since just a boy barely five feet tall.
I have followed this backcountry call.

Imprinted young at eight years old.
To follow the tales of the trail I was told,
Those old-time trails that still ride.
Burned deep their brand into my hide.

Up ahead in the next drainage over,
The past meets up with a mounted drover.
Ghost riders of pintos untracked and unshod,
Rise up through the dust of unplowed sod.

Faint rings in the bottoms along a stream,
Come into view in the morning gleam.
Teepee rings face the rising sun –
Circles of home before the ride is done.

Vices of those, whose legends were made,
In rendezvous camps of the beaver trade,
Echo through canyons and fade in the trees,
Where a rusty old trap still holds the keys.

Of a cook fire ring that's still neatly made –
A circle of homes lies there in the shade,
Of a trapper blowing coals on his knees,
Over rocks in a clearing back in the trees.

And of time-worn tracks and dusty trails,
Where an old-time path is there – then pales.
Dust has settled followed by grass,
It comes into view and then seems to pass.

Those worn-out trails of olden date,
Spread over grassland in paths of eight.
Riders and wagons rolled side by side,
To check the dust where the trail gets wide.

Dust that rises, takes wing, then falls,
Signals the past and quietly calls,
To tell the tale of those yesterdays,
And the circle of home over bygone ways.

Trails rocky and steep then easy and wide,
Circle me back each time I ride.
They circle me back each time I roam.
The tales of the trail are of going home. [4]

NOTES

1 "Horses and People – A Cowboy's Poem," http://www.equisearch.com/article/eqpoem647.
2 "Graeme King, Cowboy Blues," http://kingpoetry.com/cowboy_blues.htm.
3 "Featured at the Bar D Ranch, Classic Cowboy Poetry," http://www.cowboypoetry.com/henrylawson.htm#Drover.
4 "Cowboy Poetry and Western Verse," http://www.paulkern.com/2008/03/tales-of-trail.html.

OFFICIALLY DECLARED DROUGHTS ON THE AUSTRALIAN CONTINENT

"Drought in Australia," National Climate Centre, Australian Bureau of Meteorology, http://www.abs.gov.au/AUSSTATS/abs@.nsf/Lookup/1301.0Feature+Article151988.

1864–66 (and 1868)	The little data available indicate that this drought period was rather severe in Victoria, South Australia, New South Wales, Queensland, and Western Australia.
1880–86	Victoria (northern areas and Gippsland); New South Wales (mainly northern wheat belt, northern Tablelands, and south coast); Queensland (1881–86, in south-east with breaks; otherwise mainly in coastal areas, the central highlands, and central interior in 1883–86); and South Australia (1884–86, mainly in agricultural areas).

1888	Victoria (northern areas and Gippsland); Tasmania (1887–89 in the south); New South Wales; Queensland (1888–89); South Australia and Western Australia (central agricultural areas).
1895–1903	Practically the whole of Australia was affected, but most persistently the coast of Queensland, inland areas of New South Wales, South Australia, and central Australia. This was probably Australia's worst drought to date in terms of severity and area. Sheep numbers, which had reached more than 100 million, were reduced by approximately half and cattle numbers by more than 40 percent. Average wheat yields exceeded 8 bushels per acre in only one year of the nine, and dropped to 2.4 bushels per acre in 1902.
1911–16	Victoria (1913–15 in north and west); Tasmania (1913–15); New South Wales, particularly inland areas; Queensland; Northern Territory (mainly in the Tennant Creek–Alexandria Downs area); South Australia (some breaks in agricultural areas); and Western Australia (1910–14).
1918–20	Queensland, New South Wales, South Australia, Northern Territory (Darwin–Daly Waters area and central Australia), Western Australia (Fortescue area), Victoria, and Tasmania.

1939–45   New South Wales (severe on the coast), South Australia (persistent in pastoral areas), Queensland and Tasmania; also (more particularly in 1940 and 1944–45) in Western Australia, Victoria, and central Australia; Tennant Creek–Alexandria Downs area in 1943–45.

1958–68   This drought was the most widespread and probably second to the 1895–1903 drought in severity. For more than a decade from 1957, drought was consistently prominent and frequently made news headlines from 1964 onwards. This was treated as one major drought period, but could be subdivided into two which overlapped, both in time and area. Central Australia and vast areas of adjacent Queensland, South Australia, Western Australia, New South Wales, and northern Australia were affected, with varying intensity, 1957–66; and southeastern Australia experienced a severe drought, 1964–68.

1982–83   This extensive drought affected nearly all of eastern Australia, and was particularly severe in southeastern Australia. The lowest-ever 11-month rainfall occurred over most of Victoria, much of inland New South Wales, and central and southern Queensland; and the lowest-ever 10-month rainfall occurred in much of South Australia and northern Queensland. Total losses were estimated in excess of $3,000 million.

SELECT BIBLIOGRAPHY

I. Manuscript Collections

AMERICAN HERITAGE CENTER ARCHIVES, LARAMIE.
Frewen papers.

BAR S RANCH, NANTON, ALBERTA.
Macleay family papers.

GLENBOW ARCHIVES, CALGARY.
A.E. Cross papers.
Billy and Evelyn Cochrane papers.
Canadian Agricultural, Coal and Colonization Company papers,
Stair Ranch Letterbook.
Herbert M. Hatfield papers.
Mrs. Charles Inderwick, Diary and Personal Letters from the
North Fork Ranch.
New Walrond Ranche papers.
Sergeant S.J. Clarke diary.
Western Stockgrowers Association papers.

GOVERNMENT OF SOUTH AUSTRALIA STATE RECORD OFFICE, ADELAIDE.

GRS–1: In-letters (1870–1910) of the Minister Controlling the Northern Territory: P. Foelsche to E.W. Price, 3 August 1882.

GRS–1: In-letters (1870–1910) of the Minister Controlling the Northern Territory (Minister of Education), Quarterly Report of G.R. McMinn, Acting Government Resident, 7 July 1883.

MONTANA HISTORICAL SOCIETY LIBRARY AND ARCHIVES, HELENA.

Memoirs of Lady Kathleen Lindsay.

T.C. Power papers.

NATIONAL ARCHIVES, CANBERRA, AUSTRALIA.

Commonwealth Government Records about the Northern Territory Archives Service, Darwin, "Report of the Northern Territory Commission; together with the Minutes of Proceedings, Evidence and Appendices," *South Australia Parliamentary Papers* (1895), vol. 2, paper 19.

"Department of External Affairs, File of Papers, Subject: Batchelor Demonstration Farm Report on results of operations conducted at Darwin, 19 July 1913.

Goldsbrough, Mort & Company papers.

Prospects of Agriculture in the Northern Territory; Report of the Forster Committee. Canberra: Department of Territories, 1960.

"Report of the Department of Agriculture for year ending December 31," (1912).

NORTHERN TERRITORY ARCHIVES SERVICE, DARWIN.

Borroloola Police Station Letter Book, 1886–1924.

Graeme Bucknall, "A Documented Short History of Undoolya: The First Legal Cattle Station in the Northern Territory" (National Trust of Australia, Northern Territory, 1983).

South Australian Government and Administrators Reports.

"Government Resident's Quarterly Report on Northern Territory," 7 July 1883; 12 August 1884.

Government Resident's Report on Northern Territory for the
Year . . ." (1879–1910).
"Half Yearly Report on Northern Territory to December 31st
1886."

PROVINCIAL ARCHIVES OF ALBERTA, EDMONTON.
72,27/SE: Violet LaGranduer, "Memoirs of a Cowboy's Wife."

STATE LIBRARY OF SOUTH AUSTRALIA, ADELAIDE.
Alfred Giles' Diary.
Alfred Giles papers.
Alfred Giles, "The First Pastoral Settlement in the Northern
Territory compiled principally for his own experiences
as an overlander and pioneer pastoralist with special
references to the founding of the Springvale, Delamere,
Elsey and Newcastle Waters runs, 1870–1895 with
extracts from his diary 1879–1895."
"Arthur C. Aswhin's Recollections of Ralph Milner's
Expedition from Kopperamanna to the Northern
Territory with sheep and Horses in 1870/71 with an
account of his subsequent experiences in the Northern
Territory" (1927).
Lewis family papers.

II. Newspapers

Advertiser

Argus

Australian Town and Country Journal

Brisbane Courier

Brisbane Daily Mail

Cairns Post

Calgary Herald

Central Queensland Herald

Clarence and Richmond Examiner

Daily Courier

Daily News

Edinburgh Courant

Great Falls Tribune

Kilmore Free Press

Lethbridge Herald

Macleod Gazette

Maitland Mercury & Hunter River General Advertiser

Medicine Hat News

Morning Bulletin

Morning Chronicle

Napean Times

North Australian

Northern Argus

Northern Miner

Northern Standard

Northern Star

Northern Territory Times

Pincher Creek Echo

Queenslander

Regina Leader

Rockhampton Bulletin

Rocky Mountain Husbandman

South Australian Register (later *The Register*)

Sydney Morning Herald

Townsville Daily Bulletin

Wallaroo Times and Mining Journal

Warwick Examiner and Times

Western Mail

Western Star and Roma Advertiser

III. Books and Articles

Abbott, Edward C., and H. Huntington Smith. *We Pointed Them North: Recollections of a Cowpuncher.* 2nd ed. Norman: University of Oklahoma Press, 1955.

Adams, B.W., Richard Ehlert, Darlene Moisey, and Ron L. McNeil. *Range Plant Communities and Range Health Assessment Guidelines for the Foothills Fescue Natural Subregion of Alberta, Foothills Fescue Range Plant Community Guide, Alberta.* Lethbridge: Alberta Sustainable Resource Development, 2005.

Angus, Beverly M. *Tick Fever and the Cattle Tick in Australia, 1829–1996.* Brisbane: Queensland Department of Primary Industries, 1998.

Attwood, Bain, and S.G. Foster, eds. *Frontier Conflict.* Canberra: National Museum of Australia, 2003.

Barker, H.M. *Droving Days.* Melbourne: Pitman, 1966.

Belich, James. *Replenishing the Earth: The Settler Revolution and the Rise of the Anglo-World, 1783–1939.* Oxford and New York: Oxford University Press, 2009.

Binney, Keith R. *Horsemen of the First Frontier (1788–1900) and the Serpent's Legacy.* Neutral Bay: Volcanic Publications, 2005.

Bolton, G.C. *A Thousand Miles Away.* Canberra: Australian National University Press, 1970.

Bowen, Jill. *Kidman: The Forgotten King.* Sydney: Harper Collins, 2007.

Breen, David H. *The Canadian Prairie West and the Ranching Frontier, 1874–1924.* Toronto: University of Toronto Press, 1983.

Brisbin, James S. *The Beef Bonanza or How to get Rich on the Plains; being a description of cattle-growing, sheep-farming, horse-raising, and dairying in the West.* Philadelphia: J.B. Lippincott & Co., 1881.

Buchanan, Gordon. *Packhorse and Waterhole.* 2nd ed. Sydney: Angus and Robertson, 1934.

Butler, W.F. *The Great Lone Land: A Narrative of Travel and Adventure in the North-West of America.* London: Sampson, Low, Marston, Low and Searle, 1874.

Carruthers, Fiona. *The Horse in Australia.* Sydney: Random House, 2008.

Cartwright, Max. *The Never Never Country: A History of the Roper River and Urapunga.* Alice Springs: M. Cartwright, 1999.

Connor, J. *The Australian Frontier Wars.* Sydney: UNSW Press, 2002.

Connor, Ralph. *Sky Pilot: A Tale of the Foothills.* Chicago: R.H. Revell, 1899.

Costello, Michael J. *Life of John Costello, Being the Adventures of a Pioneer, Pastoralist and Explorer in Queensland and the Northern Territory.* Sydney: Dymock's Book Arcade, 1930.

Coupe, Sheena, ed. *Frontier Country: Australia's Outback Heritage.* Vol. 1. Willoughby, NSW: Weldon Russell, 1989.

Cox, James. *Historical and Biographical Record of the Cattle Industry and the Cattlemen of Texas and Adjacent Territory.* St. Louis, MO: Woodward and Tiernan, 1895.

Cranfield, H.S. *The Boys of the Rincon Ranch.* New York: Century, 1902.

Cross, Alfred Ernest. "The Roundup of 1887." *Alberta Historical Review* 13, no. 2 (Spring 1965): 23.

Cunfer, Geoff. *On the Great Plains: Agriculture and the Environment.* College Station: Texas A&M University Press, 2005.

Dawson, John. *Washout: On the Academic Response to the Fabrication of Aboriginal History.* Sydney: Macleay Press, 2004.

Dale, Edward Everett. *The Range Cattle Industry: Ranching on the Great Plains, 1865–1925.* Norman: University of Oklahoma Press, 1960.

Dempsey, Hugh A. "Cypress Hills Massacre." *Montana Magazine* 3, no. 4 (Autumn 1953): 1–9.

———. *The Golden Age of the Canadian Cowboy.* Saskatoon and Calgary: Fifth House, 1995.

Duncan, Ross. *The Northern Territory Pastoral Industry, 1863–1910.* Melbourne: Melbourne University Press, 1967.

Durack, Mary. *Kings in Grass Castles.* London: Constable, 1959.

Elofson, Warren M. *Cowboys, Gentlemen and Cattle Thieves: Ranching on the Western Frontier.* Montreal and Kingston: McGill-Queen's University Press, 2000.

———. *Frontier Cattle Ranching in the Land and Times of Charlie Russell.* Montreal and Kingston: McGill-Queen's University Press, 2004.

———. "Not Just a Cowboy: The Practice of Ranching in Southern Alberta, 1881–1914." *Canadian Papers in Rural History* 10 (1996): 205–16.

———. *Somebody Else's Money: The Walrond Ranch Story, 1883–1907.* Calgary: University of Calgary Press, 2009.

Evans, Simon M. "American Cattlemen in the Canadian West, 1874–1914." *Prairie Forum* 4, no. 1 (1979): 121–35.

———. *The Bar U and Canadian Ranching History.* Calgary: University of Calgary Press, 2004.

———. "Canadian Beef for Victorian Britain." *Agricultural History* 53, no. 4 (October 1979): 748 –62.

———. "The End of the Open Range in Western Canada." *Prairie Forum* 8, no. 1 (1983): 71–87.

———. "Grazing the Grasslands: Exploring Conflicts, Relationships and Futures." *Prairie Forum* 26, no. 1 (Spring 2001): 67–84.

———. "The Origins of Ranching in Western Canada: American Diffusion or Victorian Transplant?" *Great Plains Quarterly* 3, no. 2 (Spring 1983): 79–91.

———. "Stocking the Canadian Range." *Alberta History* 26, no. 3 (Summer 1978): 1-8.

————. "Tenderfoot to Rider, Leaning 'Cowboying' on the Canadian Ranching Frontier during the 1880s." In *Cowboys, Ranchers and the Cattle Business: Cross-Border Perspectives on Ranching History*, eds. Simon Evans, Bill Yeo, and Sarah Carter. Calgary: University of Calgary Press, 2000, 61–80.

Fitch, L., B. Adams, P. Ag, and K. O'Shaughnessy. *Caring for the Green Zone: Riparian Areas and Grazing Management*. New 3rd ed. http://www.cowsandfih.org/riparian/caring.html.

Foothills Historical Society. *Chaps and Chinooks: A History West of Calgary*. Calgary: Foothills Historical Society, 1976.

Foran, Max. *Trails and Trials: Markets and Land Use in the Alberta Beef Cattle Industry, 1881–1918*. Calgary: University of Calgary Press, 2003.

Forrest, Peter. "A History of Elsey and Locality." Unpublished manuscript, State Library of the Northern Territory.

————. *A Rush for Grass*. Ilfracombe: Murranji Press, 1988.

————. *Springvale's Story and Early Years at Katherine*. Darwin: Murranji Press, 1985.

Fort Macleod History Book Committee. *Fort Macleod – Our Colourful Past: A History of the Town of Fort Macleod from 1874 to 1924*. Fort Macleod History Book Committee, 1977.

Foster, Robert, and Amanda Nettelbeck. *Out of the Silence: The History and Memory of South Australia's Frontier Wars*. Kent Town: Wadefield Press, 2007.

Gaber, Stan. *The Last Roundup: Memoirs of a Canadian Cowboy*. Saskatoon: Fifth House, 1995.

Groom, A. *One Mountain after Another*. Sydney: Environbook, 1992.

Groves, Mary. *An Outback Life*. Sydney Arena Books, 2011.

Gunn, Jeannie. *We of the Never-Never*. 10th ed. 2003. http://www.gutenberg.org/ebooks/4699.

Hall, S.S. *Stampede Steve; or, the Doom of the Double Face*. New York: Beadle and Adam, 1884.

Henniker Heaton, John. *Australian Dictionary of Dates and Men of the Time: containing the history of Australasia from 1542 to May, 1879.* http://archive.org/details/australiandicti00heatgoog.

Hine, Robert V., and John Mack Faragher. *The American West: A New Interpretive History.* New Haven and London: Yale University Press, 2000.

Hopkins, Monica. *Letters from a Lady Rancher.* Halifax: Formac Publishing, 1983.

Idriess, Ion L. *The Cattle King: The Classic Story of Sir Sidney Kidman.* Sydney: Angus and Robertson, 1936.

Ings, Frederick. *Before the Fences (tales from the Midway Ranch): Autobiography.* Ed. J. Davis. Calgary: McAra Printing, 1980.

James, Barbara. *No Man's Land: Women of the Northern Territory.* Sydney: Collins Australia, 1989.

Jameson, Sheilagh. *Ranchers, Cowboys and Characters: The Birth of Alberta's Western Culture.* Calgary: Glenbow Museum, 1987.

Jordan-Bychkov, Terry G. "Does the Border Matter? Cattle Ranching and the 49th Parallel." In *Cowboys, Ranchers and the Cattle Business: Cross-Border Perspectives on Ranching History*, eds. Sarah Carter, Simon Evans, and Bill Yeo. Calgary: University of Calgary Press, 2000.

———. *North American Cattle-Ranching Frontiers: Origins, Diffusion, and Differentiation.* Albuquerque: University of New Mexico Press, 1993.

Kelly, J.H. *Beef in Northern Australia.* Canberra: Australian National University Press, 1971.

Kelly, Leroy V. *The Range Men.* 75th anniversary ed. Calgary: Glenbow-Alberta Institute, 1988.

Klassen, Henry C. "A Century of Ranching at the Rocking P and Bar S." In *Cowboys, Ranchers and the Cattle Business: Cross-Border Perspectives on Ranching History*, eds. Sarah Carter, Simon Evans, and Bill Yeo. Calgary: University of Calgary Press, 2000.

———. "Entrepreneurship in the Canadian West: The Enterprises of A.E. Cross, 1886–1920." *Western Historical Quarterly* 22, no. 3 (August 1991): 313–33.

Klein, Kerwin Lee. "Reclaiming the 'F' Word, or Being and Becoming Postwestern." *The Pacific Historical Review* 65, no. 2 (May 1996): 179–215.

Kowald, Margaret, and William Johnston. *You Can't Make it Rain: The Story of the North Australian Pastoral Company 1877–1991.* Brisbane: Boolarong Publications with North Australian Pastoral Company, 1992.

Latham, Hiram. *Trans-Missouri Stock Raising: The Pasture Lands of North America, Winter Grazing.* Omaha: Daily Herald Steam Printing House, 1871.

Lavington, Harold "Dude." *Nine Lives of a Cowboy.* Victoria: Sono Nis Press, 1982.

Lawrence, H.F. "Early Days in the Chinook Belt." *Alberta Historical Review* 13, no. 1 (Winter 1965): 3–17.

Limerick, Patricia Nelson. "Going West and Ending Up Global." *Western Historical Quarterly* 32, no. 1 (Spring 2001): 4–23.

———. "Turnerians All: The Dream of a Helpful History in an Intelligible World." *American Historical Review* 100, no. 3 (June 1995): 697–716.

Linklater, W. *Gather No Moss.* Melbourne: Macmillan, 1968.

Macdonald, James. *Food from the Far West.* New York: Orange Judd, 1878.

MacEwan, Grant. *John Ware's Cow Country.* Nanoose Bay, BC: Greystone Books, 1995.

Makin, Jock. *The Big Run: Victoria River Downs.* London: Hale, 1970.

Manne, Robert, ed. *Whitewash: On Keith Windschuttle's Fabrication of Aboriginal History.* Melbourne: Black Inc., 2003.

Maurovic, Richard. *The Meat Game: A History of the Gepps Cross Abattoir.* Kent Town: Wakefield Press, 2007.

McCoy, Joseph. *Historic Sketches of the Cattle Trade of the West and Southwest.* Kansas City: Ramsay, Millett and Hudson, 1874.

McEachran, Duncan. *A Journey Over the Plains: From Fort Benton to Bow River and Back.* Montreal, n.p.: 1881.

McGrath, Ann. *"Born in the Cattle": Aborigines in Cattle Country.* Sydney: Allen and Unwin, 1987.

McIntyre, Stuart. *A Concise History of Australia.* Cambridge: Cambridge University Press, 1999.

McIntyre, William H. *A Brief History of the McIntyre Ranch.* Lethbridge: *Lethbridge Herald*, 1948.

McLaren, Glen, and William Cooper. *Distance, Drought and Dispossession: A History of the Northern Territory Pastoral Industry.* Darwin: Northern Territory University Press, 2001.

Merrill, A., and J. Jacobson. *Montana Almanac.* Helena, MT: Falcon Books, 1997.

Nelson, J.G. "Some Reflections on Man's Impact on the Landscape of the Canadian Prairies and Nearby Areas." In *The Prairie Provinces*, ed. P.J. Smith. Toronto: University of Toronto Press, 1972.

Nettelbeck, Amanda, and Robert Foster. *In the Name of the Law: William Willshire and the Policing of the Australian Frontier.* Kent Town: Wakefield Press, 2007.

Nielson, Kris, and John Prociuk. *From Start to Finish: A History of Cattle Feeding in Alberta.* Calgary: Alberta Cattle Feeders Association, 1999.

Patterson, A.B. *The Man from Snowy River and Other Verses.* Sydney: Angus and Patterson, 1895.

———. *Old Bush Songs.* Sydney: Angus and Patters, 1906.

Patterson, Paul E., and Joy Poole. *Great Plains Cattle Empire: Thatcher Brothers and Associates, 1875–1945.* Lubbock: Texas Tech University Press, 2000.

Perry, H.C. *Pioneering: The Life of the Hon. R. M. Collins, M.L.C.* Brisbane: Watson-Ferguson, 1923.

Perry, T.M. *Australia's First Frontier: The Spread of Settlement in New South Wales, 1788–1829.* Melbourne: Melbourne University Press, 1963.

Pincher Creek Historical Society. *Prairie Grass to Mountain Pass.* Pincher Creek, AB: Pincher Creek Historical Society, 1974.

Powell, A. *Far Country.* 2nd ed. Melbourne: Melbourne University Press, 1988.

Price, A. Grenfell. *The History and Problems of the Northern Territory, Australia.* John Murtagh Macrossan Lecture. Brisbane: University of Queensland Press, 1930.

Rathborne, St. George. *Sunset Ranch.* London: Shurmer Sibthorp, 1902.

Reynolds, Henry. *The Other Side of the Frontier: Aboriginal Resistance to the European Invasion of Australia.* Sydney: University of New South Wales Press, 2006.

Richardson, A.D. *Beyond the Mississippi: From the Great River to the Great Ocean. Life and Adventure on the Prairies, Mountains and Pacific Coast.* Hartford, CT: American Publishing Co., 1869.

Riley, Herbert William. "Herbert William (Herb) Millar." *Canadian Cattlemen* 4, no. 4 (March 1942).

Roberts, S.H. *The Squatting Age in Australia, 1835–1847.* Melbourne: Melbourne University Press, 1964.

Roberts, Tony. *Frontier Justice: A History of the Gulf Country to 1900.* Adelaide: University of Queensland Press, 2005.

Roosevelt, Theodore R. *Ranch Life and the Hunting Trail.* London: T. Fisher Unwin, 1888.

Sergison, Albert William. *The Northern Territory and Its Pastoral Capabilities.* Melbourne: Sands and McDougall, 1878.

Sharp, Paul. "Three Frontiers: Some Comparative Studies of Canadian, American, and Australian Settlement." *Pacific Historical Review* 24, no. 4 (November 1955): 369–77.

Shields, G.O. *Rustlings in the Rockies: Hunting and Fishing by Mountain and Stream.* Chicago: Clarke and Co., 1883.

Slatta, Richard. "Taking Our Myths Seriously." *Journal of the West* 40, no. 3 (2001): 3–5.

Stanley, George F.G. "Western Canada and the Frontier Thesis." *Canadian Historical Association* 19, no. 1 (1940): 105–17.

Steele, Samuel. *Forty Years in Canada: Reminiscences of the Great North-West, with some account of his service in South Africa.* Ed. M.G. Niblett. 2nd ed. Toronto: Prospero Books, 2000.

Stegner, Wallace. *Wolf Willow: A History, a Story, and a Memory of the Last Plains Frontier.* New York: Penguin Books, 1955.

Stuart, Granville. *Forty Years on the Frontier, as seen in the journals and reminiscences of Granville Stuart.* Vol. 2. Ed. P.C. Philips. Cleveland: A.H. Clark, 1925.

Summers, Anne. *Damned Whores and God's Police.* 2nd ed. Melbourne: Penguin Books, 1991.

Thompson, John Herd. *Forging the Prairie West: The Illustrated History of Canada.* Oxford: Oxford University Press, 1998.

Turner, Frederick Jackson. *The Frontier in American History.* Austin, TX: Holt, Rinehart and Winston, 1962.

Voisey, Paul L. *Vulcan: The Making of a Prairie Community.* Toronto: University of Toronto Press, 1988.

von Richthofen, Baron. *Cattle Raising on the Plains of North America.* New York: D. Appleton & Co., 1885.

Vrooman, C.W., G.D. Chattaway, and Andrew Stuart. *Cattle Ranching in Western Canada,* publication 776, Technical Bulletin 778. Ottawa: Department of Agriculture, Marketing Services, Economic Division, in co-operation with the Experimental Farm Service, 1946.

Ward, Russell. *The Australian Legend.* Melbourne: Oxford University Press, 1958.

West, Elliott. "Families in the West." *Organization of American Historians Magazine of History* 9 (Fall 1994): 18–21.

Wheeler, David L. "The Texas Panhandle Drift Fences." *Panhandle-Plains Historical Review* 55 (1982): 25–35.

White, C. *Revolution on the Range: The Rise of a New Ranch in the American West.* Washington: Island Press, 2008.

Williams, H.L. *The Chief of the Cowboys.* New York: R. Midewitt, 1870.

———. *The Giant Cowboys.* London: General Publishing, 1890.

Windschuttle, Keith. *The Fabrication of Aboriginal History: Volume One, Van Diemen's Land 1803–1847.* Sydney: Macleay Press, 2003.

Wister, Owen. *The Virginian: A Horseman of the Plains.* New York: Macmillan, 1902.

Zalums, Elmer. *A Bibliography of South Australian Royal Commissions, Select Committees of Parliament, and Boards of Inquiry, 1857–1970.* Bedford Park: The Flinders University of South Australia, 1975.

IV. Theses and Dissertations

Evans, Simon M. "The Passing of a Frontier: Ranching in the Canadian West, 1882–1912." PhD diss., University of Calgary, 1976.

Herbert, Rachel. "Ranching Women in Southern Alberta, 1880–1930." MA thesis, University of Calgary, 2011.

Rudd, F. Albert. "Production and Marketing of Beef Cattle from the Short Grass Plains Area of Canada." MA thesis, University of Alberta, 1935.

Turner, Leland. "Grassland Frontiers: Beef Cattle Agriculture in Queensland and Texas." PhD diss., Texas Tech University, 2008.

Wilson, William R. "A Force Apart: A History of theNorthern Territory Police, 1870–1920." PhD diss., Northern Territory University, 2000.

V. Government Reports

Alberta. Department of Agriculture, *Annual Reports*, 1905–13.

Australia. *The Northern Territory Beef Cattle Industry: An Economic Survey, 1962–63 to 1964–65*. Melbourne: Commonwealth Scientific and Industrial Research Organization, 1968.

———."Preliminary Report on the Aboriginals of the Northern Territory." *Bulletin of the Northern Territory* 7. Melbourne: Department of External Affairs, July 1913.

———. "Report of Preliminary Scientific Expedition to the Northern Territory." *Bulletin of the Northern Territory* 1. Melbourne: Department of External Affairs, March 1912.

Bauer, F.H. *Historical Geography of White Settlement in Part of Northern Australia* 2, "The Katherine Darwin Region." Canberra: Commonwealth Scientific and Industrial Research Organization, 1964.

Bishop, F.A.C. *Report on an Inspection of the Pastoral Holdings, Stock Routes, Bores and Dips on the Barkly Tableland, Northern Territory*. Melbourne: Government Printer, 1923.

Canada. *Sessional Papers*, North-West Mounted Police Annual Reports, 1905–1913.

Muir, G. *The Winter Feeding of Beef Cattle in Ontario*. Ottawa: Department of Agriculture, Animal Husbandry Division, 1922.

Newton, L.G., and R. Norris. *Clearing a Continent: The Eradication of Bovine Pleuropneumonia from Australia*. Melbourne: Commonwealth Scientific and Industrial Research Organization, Primary Industries Report Series, 2000.

Perry, R.A. *Pasture Lands of the Northern Territory, Australia*. Melbourne: Commonwealth Scientific and Industrial Research Organization, 1960.

United Kingdom. "Agricultural Interests Commission, Reports of the Assistant Commissioners presented to both Houses of Parliament by Command of Her Majesty." *British Parliamentary Papers, Area Studies: United States of America*, 1. Agriculture, 1878–99.

United States. *Range and Ranch Cattle Traffic of the United States.* New York: Office of Poor, White and Greenough, 1885.

NOTES

··

1 INTRODUCTION

1 Frederick Jackson Turner, *The Frontier in American History* (Austin, TX: Holt, Rinehart and Winston, 1962), one of many editions of the paper "The Significance of the Frontier in American History," which Turner originally presented to the American Historical Association in 1893; Russell Ward, *The Australian Legend* (Melbourne: Oxford University Press, 1958).

2 Though one may dispute some of the specific ways in which they applied it.

3 See, for instance, G.F.G. Stanley, "Western Canada and the Frontier Thesis," *Canadian Historical Association Report*, 1940, 111; David H. Breen, *The Canadian Prairie West and the Ranching Frontier, 1874–1924* (Toronto: University of Toronto Press, 1983), 21–23; John Herd Thompson, *Forging the Prairie West: The Illustrated History of Canada* (Oxford: Oxford University Press, 1998), 43–103. A more recent work, Simon Evans' *The Bar U and Canadian Ranching History* (Calgary: University of Calgary Press, 2004), lauds the federal government's lease legislation, which in fact changed so often that the ranchers seldom had any faith in it. Evans also plays down the role of the natural environment in controlling the destiny of the great ranches.

4 Henry Reynolds, *The Other Side of the Frontier: Aboriginal Resistance to the European Invasion of Australia* (Sydney: University of New South Wales Press, 2006).

5 Reynolds' main antagonist is Keith Windschuttle; see, for instance, *The Fabrication of Aboriginal History, Vol. 1: Van Diemen's Land 1803–1847*

(Sydney: Macleay Press, 2003).
For the rest of the debate see J.
Connor, *The Australian Frontier
Wars* (Sydney: University
of New South Wales Press,
2002); Bain Attwood and S.G.
Foster, eds., *Frontier Conflict*
(Canberra: National Museum
of Australia, 2003); Robert
Manne, ed., *Whitewash:
On Keith Windschuttle's
Fabrication of Aboriginal History*
(Melbourne: Black Inc., 2003);
John Dawson, *Washout: On
the Academic Response to the
Fabrication of Aboriginal History*
(Sydney: Macleay Press, 2004);
Robert Foster and Amanda
Nettelbeck, *Out of the Silence:
The History and Memory of South
Australia's Frontier Wars* (Kent
Town: Wadefield Press, 2007).

6   Terry G. Jordan-Bychkov,
*North American Cattle-Ranching
Frontiers: Origins, Diffusion and
Differentiation* (Albuquerque:
University of New Mexico
Press, 1993), 217.

7   Jordan-Bychkov, *North
American Cattle-Ranching
Frontiers*, 208; Robert V. Hine
and John Mack Faragher,
*The American West: A New
Interpretive History* (New Haven
and London: Yale University
Press, 2000), 302–4.

8   "Stock Raising," *Texas Almanac
for 1861* (Galveston, 1860),
148–52.

9   "Stock Raising," 150–52.

10 Jordan-Bychkov, *North
American Cattle-Ranching
Frontiers*, 210.

11 "Stock Raising," 150.

12 Warren M. Elofson, *Frontier
Cattle Ranching in the Land
and Times of Charlie Russell*
(Montreal and Kingston:
McGill-Queen's University
Press, 2004), 25–41; "Stock
Raising," 150.

13 Jordan-Bychkov, *North
American Cattle-Ranching
Frontiers*, 217–36.

14 Jordan-Bychkov uses the term
"profound neglect" (210).

15 *The Pastoral Review* was
originally titled *The Australasian
Pastoralists' Review* then
successively *The Pastoralists'
Review*, *The Pastoral Review*,
and finally *The Pastoral Review
and Grazier's Record*. Still in
production, it is commonly
known simply as *The Pastoral
Review*.

16 "The United States," *The
Argus*, 25 October 1873.

17 See chapter 10.

18 Ross Duncan, *The Northern
Territory Pastoral Industry, 1863–
1910* (Melbourne: Melbourne
University Press, 1967),
139–56.

19 Max Foran, *Trails and Trials:
Markets and Land Use in the
Alberta Beef Cattle Industry,
1881–1948* (Calgary:
University of Calgary Press,
2003), 1–56.

20 Foran, *Trails and Trials*, 9.

2 THE SHORT HISTORY OF THE TEXAS SYSTEM IN WESTERN CANADA

1 Prior to this the industry was very small in Montana. The state saw its first cattle in the early 1860s as small traders tried to meet the demand for food from miners searching for gold and silver around the fledgling urban centres of Bannack, Virginia City, and Helena. In the beginning these cattle were mostly exhausted and lame animals that migrating settlers sold off or abandoned on their trek to regions farther west. Then traders started to trail cattle called "westerns" in from the Pacific seaboard via the Oregon Trail.

2 See Warren M. Elofson, *Frontier Cattle Ranching in the Land and Times of Charlie Russell* (Montreal and Kingston: McGill-Queen's University Press, 2004), 3–24. For the earlier movement of Californian cattle to Oregon see Terry G. Jordan-Bychkov, *North American Cattle-Ranching Frontiers: Origins, Diffusion and Differentiation* (Albuquerque: University of New Mexico Press, 1993), 249–55.

3 Leroy V. Kelly, *The Range Men*, 75th anniversary ed. (Calgary: Glenbow-Alberta Institute, 1988), 47–49.

4 For an overview of this period see also Warren M. Elofson,

Cowboys, Gentlemen and Cattle Thieves: Ranching on the Western Frontier (Montreal and Kingston: McGill-Queen's University Press, 2000), 3–22.

5 E.C. Abbott and H. Huntington Smith, *We Pointed Them North: Recollections of a Cowpuncher*, 2nd ed. (Norman: University of Oklahoma Press, 1955), 64–65.

6 All types of cattle in all of Montana: A. Merrill and J. Jacobson, *Montana Almanac* (Helena: Falcon Books, 1997), 309.

7 All types of cattle in all of Alberta and Assiniboia: Simon M. Evans, "Stocking the Canadian Range," *Alberta History* 26, no. 3 (Summer 1978): 1; Canada, *Fourth Census*, 1901, vol. 2, 52–53.

8 Cresswell, Henry Whiteside (1830–1904). Hank Cresswell, range cattleman in the Texas Panhandle, the son of John Cresswell, was born at Fairfield House, Lancashire, England, in 1830 (http://www.tshaonline.org/handbook/search/results/Cresswell).

9 Elofson, *Frontier Cattle Ranching*, 13–24.

10 Elofson, *Cowboys, Gentlemen and Cattle Thieves*, 38, 49; Simon M. Evans, "Tenderfoot to Rider, Learning 'Cowboying' on the Canadian Ranching Frontier during the 1880s," in *Cowboys, Ranchers and the Cattle Business:*

Cross-Border Perspectives on Ranching History, ed. Simon Evans, Bill Yeo, and Sarah Carter (Calgary: University of Calgary Press, 2000), 61–80.

11   The best-known Canadian novel is Ralph Connor, *Sky Pilot: A Tale of the Foothills* (Chicago: R.H. Revell, 1899). For a summary of the literature generally, see Elofson, *Frontier Cattle Ranching*, 25–40.

12   G. Stuart, *Forty Years on the Frontier, as seen in the journals and reminiscences of Granville Stuart*, vol. 2, ed. P.C. Philips (Cleveland: A.H. Clark, 1925), 188.

13   The Bar U survived under George Lane's stewardship until his death in 1925 and thus longer than any of the above (Simon Evans, *The Bar U and Canadian Ranching History* [Calgary: University of Calgary Press, 2004]). At that time, however, the banks took possession of all its livestock and lands and sold them to pay Lane's massive debts. Simon Evans insists that the operation did well financially until a plethora of unlucky events struck in the last several years. A postwar depression, the bankruptcy of Gordon, Ironsides and Fares, which cut into Lane's personal wealth and then forced him to come up with some $650,000 to buy them out, and bad weather, Evans believes, produced a near perfect storm that robbed Lane of the net worth he had built up over the course of a lifetime. Two things need to be recognized, however. First, though Evans uses the word "flourishing" and "prosperous" over and over again he produces no hard evidence – no account books, no assessments of inventory to debt ratios, no bank records. Secondly, even if he is right, we should not forget that Lane operated with special advantages that the others lacked. Throughout most of his career as a cattle baron he had the support of one of the wealthiest families in Canada. For the Walrond collapse and the others see see Warren M. Elofson, *Somebody Else's Money: The Walrond Ranch Story, 1883–1907* (Calgary: University of Calgary Press, 2009), 228–30.

14   Evans, *The Bar U and Canadian Ranching History*, xiii, 2, 18.

15   Figures provided by Statistics Canada (www.statcan.gc.ca/pub/11-516-x/sectionm/M228_238-eng.csv).

16   James Cox, *Historical and Biographical Record of the Cattle Industry and the Cattlemen of Texas and Adjacent Territory* (St. Louis, MO: Woodward and Tiernan, 1895), 136.

17   David L. Wheeler, "The Texas Panhandle Drift Fences," *Panhandle-Plains Historical Review* 55 (1982): 25–35.

18 Glenbow Archives, A.E. Cross papers, M8780, 108: A.E. Cross to A.R. Springett, 10 November 1902.

19 Kelly, *The Range Men*, 100–101.

20 A.E. Cross, "The Roundup of 1887," *Alberta Historical Review* 13, no. 2 (Spring 1965): 23.

21 Kelly, *The Range Men*, 100.

22 Elofson, *Cowboys, Gentlemen and Cattle Thieves*, 79–84. As this study demonstrates, even the relatively mild winters could be difficult for cattle. Calves born in the colder months, for instance, often died from pneumonia, or they succumbed to malnutrition, mainly because their mothers had struggled during the gestation period to find enough good feed under even a light snow cover.

23 See J.G. Nelson, "Some Reflections on Man's Impact on the Landscape of the Canadian Prairies and Nearby Areas," in *The Prairie Provinces*, ed. P.J. Smith (Toronto: University of Toronto Press, 1972), 43.

24 The severe losses the Walrond took from them in both cattle and horses inclines one to empathize with modern-day livestock owners who have vociferously resisted government efforts to reintroduce and revive the species in Idaho, Montana, and Wyoming. The ranchers' stand against wolf recovery programs has been well covered by the media in ranching areas; see, for instance, "Ranchers Want Feds to Start Killing Wolves," *Bozeman Daily Chronicle*, 16 April 2004; "Livestock Losses Leave Ranchers Worn Down by Wolves," *Billings Gazette*, 16 May 2004; and "Impact of Wolves Grows," *Casper Star Tribune*, 18 January 2005. The advocates of recovery are many; see B.H. Lopez, *Of Wolves and Men* (London: J.M. Dent, 1978); T. McNamee, *The Return of the Wolf to Yellowstone* (New York: Henry Holt, 1997); R. Bass, *The Ninemile Wolves: An Essay* (Livingstone: Clark City Press, 1992); K. Jones, *Wolf Mountains: A History of Wolves along the Great Divide* (Calgary: University of Calgary Press, 2002); M.A. Nie, *Beyond Wolves: The Politics of Wolf Recovery and Management* (Minneapolis: University of Minnesota Press, 2003).

25 Cross, for instance, commonly lost 10 percent of his colts to wolves (Kelly, *The Range Men*, 189). The wolves would sneak up on one of the defenceless animals and kill it with ease.

26 Glenbow Archives, New Walrond Ranche papers, M8688-3: Warnock to McEachran, 31 July 1894.

27 M8688-4: Warnock to J.G. Ross, 13 December 1897.

28 Elofson, *Somebody Else's Money*, 141–51.

29 Kelly, *The Range Men*, 160.

30 "What Causes Mange in Cattle," http://www.ehow.com/list_6143115_causes-mange-cattle_.html.

31 Sometimes an ointment made of sulphur, tar, and linseed oil was applied ("'Mange,' at Gleichen," *Calgary Herald*, 16 February 1904).

32 "Mange," *Rocky Mountain Husbandman*, 24 April 1902. The paper went on to suggest that government officials should make sure that all infected animals on the range are "close-herded" by their owners to keep them separated from healthy herds and "compel all cattle to be dipped twice" every year.

33 "Dipping of Cattle Recommended for Mange," *Calgary Herald*, 12 April 1904.

34 "Dominion of Canada, Order of the Minister of Agriculture," *Calgary Herald*, 19 August 1904.

35 Harold "Dude" Lavington, *Nine Lives of a Cowboy* (Victoria: Sono Nis Press, 1982), 18–19.

36 "Canada's Cattle: An Interview with her Chief Inspector of Livestock," *Morning Bulletin*, 31 March 1887.

37 Elofson, *Somebody Else's Money*, 85–89.

38 Elofson, *Somebody Else's Money*, 216–19.

39 "Mange in cattle: causes and treatments," http://www.helium.com/items/1495957-mange-in-cattle.

40 Cox, *Historical and Biographical Record*, 136. See also Paul E. Patterson and Joy Poole, *Great Plains Cattle Empire: Thatcher Brothers and Associates, 1875–1945* (Lubbock: Texas Tech University Press, 2000), 91–93.

41 Cox, *Historical and Biographical Record*, 137.

42 Ibid.

43 Cox's estimate of $30 to $35 per head for the start-up cattle seems right on. In Canada, for instance, the Walrond ranch paid broker T.C. Power in Montana $32 a head across the board for cows with calves at foot, young heifers, and yearling to three-year-old steers (Elofson, *Somebody Else's Money*, 40–43). Years later the Walrond would sell slaughter steers, heifers, and cows for an average price of just over $35 per head (Elofson, *Somebody Else's Money*, 156).

44 Elofson, *Cowboys, Gentlemen and Cattle Thieves*, 8.

45 Elofson, *Somebody Else's Money*, 35–37, 159.

46 Elofson, *Cowboys, Gentlemen and Cattle Thieves*, 11.

47 Cox, *Historical and Biographical Record*, 137. "Beef," he said, they confidently predicted would sell "at as high as thirty cents and thirty–five cents a pound in London," providing a margin of thirty to thirty-five dollars.

48   Cox, *Historical and Biographical Record*, 137.

49   The *Daily Courier* in Liverpool, for instance, claimed that the live cattle trade between Britain and America was so valuable that "anything calculated to curtail its limits could not be regarded as other than a national calamity" ("Treatment of Cattle," 15 July 1880); and the Scottish agricultural writer James Macdonald told his readers to expect profits in the Trans-Mississippi West to run around 25 percent annually (*Food from the Far West* [New York: Orange Judd, 1878], vii, xiv, 47).

50   James S. Brisbin, *The Beef Bonanza or How to get Rich on the Plains; being a description of cattle-growing, sheep-farming, horse-raising, and dairying in the West* (Philadelphia: J.B. Lippincott & Co., 1881).

51   Walter, Baron von Richthofen, *Cattle Raising on the Plains of North America* (New York: D. Appleton & Co., 1885).

52   Hiram Latham, *Trans-Missouri Stock Raising: The Pasture Lands of North America, Winter Grazing* (Omaha: Daily Herald Steam Printing House, 1871).

53   Joseph McCoy, *Historic Sketches of the Cattle Trade of the West and Southwest* (Kansas City: Ramsay, Millett and Hudson, 1874).

54   Brisbin, *The Beef Bonanza*, 79.

55   In 1880 a Royal Commission laid a report before the British Parliament on the conditions of both Canadian and American agriculture. Unlike many other reports, it made an attempt to sound realistic by speaking of some of the major flaws of farming in America. Severe winters, dangerous droughts, harmful insects, and an inadequate supply of good drinking water for livestock can and do cause problems, it said. However, in assessing the potential of the plains for grazing, it simply repeated the supposed wisdom of earlier writers. "These vast plains appear to the stranger in the autumn fearfully scorched and sterile. . . the short stunted herbage is quite brown and looks burnt to a cinder." However, "this apparently worthless grass is in reality *self-made hay*. It grows rapidly in the spring, and is *cured* by the sun before it ripens." The report also parroted the theories about year-round grazing. "Lovely open weather may prevail until Christmas," it stated. "Great falls of snow are rare. When they happen cattle suffer severely, but more generally the snow quickly drifts into the hollows and the stock can get at the grass without much trouble": "Agricultural Interests Commission, Reports of the Assistant Commissioners

presented to both Houses of Parliament by Command of Her Majesty," *British Parliamentary Papers, Area Studies: United States of America,* 1 (Agriculture, 1878–99), 67.

56 McCoy, *Historic Sketches of the Cattle Trade,* 238–39.

57 Elofson, *Somebody Else's Money,* 113–17.

58 von Richthofen, *Cattle Raising on the Plains of North America,* 80.

59 Cox, *Historical and Biographical Record,* 140.

60 Ibid., 145. The witness was "Mr. Dudley H. Snyder, the well-known cattle drover, residing at Georgetown, Texas." Another witness stated: "a few years ago large fortunes were realized in the herding of cattle in all sections west of the Missouri River, and capital from New England, the Middle States, England, Scotland, and the Continent was recklessly invested in this new enterprise. Men without experience bought whole herds by brands and book account, supposing they were receiving what they actually paid for, and it is generally conceded that in few instances would the actual count of the animals exceed seventy-five per cent of the number shown by the book account. Because of the great demand for ranches, and consequently inflation of cattle values, investors often paid for such cattle greatly above their actual value."

61 Cox, *Historical and Biographical Record,* 140. "All these features were not without effect on our supply of native cattle . . . And what was the result of this? Simply that the business was overdone, and the end was what invariably follows over production."

62 Montana Historical Society Library and Archives, Helena, Power papers, MC55–448–2: McEachran to Power, 4 September 1884.

63 Elofson, *Frontier Cattle Ranching,* 81–85.

64 M8688-4: Bell to McEachran, 9 October 1887. In the same letter he also implied that there were a lot more substandard cattle still left. "We have cut out every old cow with a barren udder or frozen teats, and have put them on good pasture . . . and will wean their calves as soon as they can live. And let them fatten for . . . contracts before winter sets in and will feed the calves during part of winter if need be."

65 Herbert William Riley, "Herbert William (Herb) Millar," *Canadian Cattlemen* 4, no. 4 (March 1942): 168.

66 Elofson, *Frontier Cattle Ranching,* 47.

3 THE SHORTER HISTORY OF THE TEXAS SYSTEM IN NORTHERN AUSTRALIA

1   State Library of South Australia, Adelaide, Alfred Giles papers, PRG 1389/2: Giles, "The First Pastoral Settlement in the Northern Territory compiled principally for his own experiences as an overlander and pioneer pastoralist with special references to the founding of the Springvale, Delamere, Elsey and Newcastle Waters runs, 1870–1895 with extracts from his diary 1879–1895," 54–55.

2   The commission was the Royal Pastoral Lands Commission (1897–1898) appointed by the Australian government: Elmar Zalums, *A Bibliography of South Australian Royal Commissions, Select Committees of Parliament, and Boards of Inquiry, 1857–1970* (Bedford Park: The Flinders University of South Australia, 1975).

3   Bagot and Gilbert were out by 1876 after starting up in 1872; Nat Buchanan at Wave Hill sold out to his brother William F. Buchanan in 1884 after setting up with Gordon Brothers in 1883; Browne by 1887; Fisher and Lyons at Glencoe, Victoria River Downs, and other stations by 1887; Tennant and Love at Undoolya by 1891. Thomas Elder at Mount Burrell and Owen Springs was out by 1894. John Costello lost or gave up Valley of Springs, Lake Nash, Wickham Park, and Wangalara between the late 1880s and late 1890s (see below, pp. 55-57).

4   "Cattle Distributions 1912," in Griffith Taylor, *Railways and stock routes, with later additions, also shown* (Commonwealth Bulletin II), quoted in A. Grenfell Price, *The History and Problems of the Northern Territory, Australia* (Adelaide: A.M. Acott, 1931), 36.

5   See below, p. 41-42.

6   John Henniker Heaton, *Australian Dictionary of Dates and Men of the Time: containing the history of Australasia from 1542 to May 1879*, 31, http://archive.org/details/australiandicti00heatgoog.

7   F.H. Bauer, *Historical Geography of White Settlement in Part of Northern Australia* 2, *The Katherine Darwin Region* (Melbourne: Commonwealth Scientific and Industrial Research Organization, Division of Land Research and Regional Survey Division, 1964).

8   See R.A. Perry, *Pasture Lands of the Northern Territory, Australia* (Melbourne: Commonwealth Scientific and Industrial Research Organization, 1960); Australia, *The Northern Territory Beef Cattle Industry: An Economic Survey, 1962–63 to 1964–65* (Melbourne: Commonwealth

Scientific and Industrial Research Organization, 1968).

9 National Archives, Canberra, Goldsbrough, Mort and Company papers, GMRBV/4, 1: "This Transcript is probably part of the evidence given to the 1895 Royal Commission into N.T. affairs conducted by SA govt."

10 Referring principally to dam construction, someone asked the VDR representative, "would it not be an encouragement to you if at the end of your lease the Government or incoming lessee had to pay you for the improvements?" He replied, "decidedly, it would be to any lease" (GMRBV/4, 9). In modern times virtually all stations have secured their water supply with bores; see, for instance, "AA co. A world-leading provider of cattle, beef and agricultural products since 1824," https://www.aaco.com.au/operations/properties/nt/delamere-station/.

11 For all the major costs see Chapter 4.

12 Perry, *Pasture Lands of the Northern Territory,* 30.

13 Ibid.

14 H.C. Perry, *Pioneering: The Life of the Hon. R. M. Collins, M.L.C.* (Brisbane: Watson-Ferguson, 1923); A. Groom, *One Mountain After Another* (Sydney: Environbook, 1992); "The North Australian Pastoral Company," http://www.napco.com.au.

15 Over 12,000 square miles; the infamous outlaw Harry Redford drove the first 3,000 cattle to Brunette Downs in 1883. Redford stayed on as manager. John Macansh, Captain Charles Smith, and John McDonald took up the leases of Brunette Downs ("A Man Who Blazed the Trail," *Northern Standard,* 1 June 1904). James White took over the leases from McDonald, Smith and Company and brought in his brothers, Frank and George, as partners. The Whites went into partnership with Alfred J. Cotton, who became the managing director ("Brunette Downs; Subdivision Scheme," *The Register,* 11 December 1926).

16 Perry, *Pasture Lands of the Northern Territory,* 18, "the south is largely desert wasteland with spiny-leaved tussock forming grasses loosely referred to as inland spinifex."

17 "Drys": an Australian term referring to the entire dry season.

18 Ross Duncan, *The Northern Territory Pastoral Industry, 1863–1910* (Melbourne: University of Melbourne Press, 1967), 49. During the 1891–92 drought, "possibly every herd on the tableland was shifted to various coastal streams, some of them remaining away from their

home stations for up to sixteen or eighteen months." (p. 51). Mustering and droving took their toll, and heavy losses on the rank, mineral-deficient coastal grasses must also have been a problem.

19 Margaret Kowald and William Johnston, *You Can't Make it Rain: The Story of the North Australian Pastoral Company 1877–1991* (Brisbane: Boolarong, 1992), 34. In 1877, Englishmen John Warner and Sir William Ingram joined Queenslanders William Collins, William Forrest, and Sir Thomas McIlwraith to form a partnership, the North Australian Pastoral Company (NAPCO). Descendants of the original partners are among the current shareholders. In 1877, the NAPCO partners were the original lessees of Alexandria Downs station in the Northern Territory (Kowald and Johnston, *You Can't Make it Rain*, 32–47).

20 This also occurs in parts of the Victoria River area where tree vegetation is sparse, though ostensibly less frequently.

21 Alice Springs is completely reliant on groundwater, and such water is costly to supply because the bores source water from around 150 metres underground. Unfortunately, much more water is taken from these aquifers than they receive from rainfall or river recharges. As a result, water

levels in the Mereenie Aquifer at the Roe Creek borefield are dropping about a metre every year. There's still a lot of water in the basin, but as the level drops, bores have to be deepened and new bores drilled, which is very expensive and uses considerable energy ("Power Water, Mereenie Aquifer Alice Springs," https://www.powerwater.com.au/community_and_education/mereenie_aquifer).

22 "In this non-eucalypt region, vast areas are characterized by various perennial drought resisting species of Triodia or Plectrachne, which are sclerophyllous grasses forming large tussocks and collectively often called Spinifex" (Perry, *Pasture Lands of the Northern Territory*, 17–18).

23 Australia, *The Northern Territory Beef Cattle Industry*, 8. "Cattle stations in the Alice Springs district are generally owner-operated and smaller than those in the other districts. The average area of the station is 1,359 square miles, compared with 2,064 square miles for the Barkly Tableland and 2,239 for Victoria River District. At the time of the survey most stations in the Alice Springs district were carrying under 2,500 cattle. In contrast, about one-half of stations in the Barkly and Victoria carried more than 15,000. Alice Springs district is the only one where there were

stations with fewer than 1,000 cattle – mostly 500 to 2500 with a concentration at around 1200."

24 See below, p. 187-88.

25 The MacDonnell Ranges are the headwaters of the Todd, Finke, and Sandover Rivers.

26 A 1935 report by the Northern Territory Pastoral Leases Investigation Committee gave the area of the Undoolya leases owned by Hayes and Sons as 1,299 square miles (Northern Territory Archives Service, Darwin, NTRS 636 BUC: Graeme Bucknall, "A Documented Short History of Undoolya: The First Legal Cattle Station in the Northern Territory," National Trust of Australia, Northern Territory, 1983, 11). "With the exception of the dwelling, the buildings though of sound construction are very old. The main buildings are being very well maintained and the whole place looks what it is, a very long established homestead. Estimated value 1020 pds."

27 "Flinders Ranges Research, Victoria River Downs (VRD) The Big Run," http://www. southaustralianhistory.com. The station was eventually taken over by the multinational Bovril liquid meat company; Nathaniel (Nat) Buchanan and the Gordon brothers took up Wave Hill on the Victoria River in 1883, one of the first stations established west of the Telegraph Line. Nat later partnered on the run with his brother William F. Buchanan, who then bought him out (Gordon Buchanan, *Packhorse and Waterhole*, 2nd ed., Sydney: Angus and Robertson, 1934). Delamere station was founded by one of the pastoral industry's earliest participants (and best known failures), Dr. William J. Browne of Melbourne (below, p. 42).

28 After the railway reached Kapunda in 1860 Bagot became a station agent there; thousands of horses and cattle, many driven from Queensland, and sheep passed through his sale yards. In 1888 the firm of E. M. Bagot & Co. merged with that of James Shakes (1807–1900) and John Lewis (1844–1923) (*Australian Dictionary of Biography*, http://adb.anu.edu. au/biography/lewis-john-599).

29 Giles, "The First Pastoral Settlement in the Northern Territory," 58. Browne lived in South Australia from 1836 to 1866. Then he moved back to England. When he took the leases in the Northern Territory he was actually living at his family estate at Buckland Filleigh, Devon.

30 See Advertisement, *Northern Territory Times*, 28 April 1893.

31 "Mr. Alexander Forrest's Expedition," *South Australian Register*, 23 September 1879.

32 Albert William Sergison, *The Northern Territory and Its Pastoral Capabilities* (Melbourne: Sands and McDougall, 1878).

33 Northern Territory Archives Service, Darwin, South Australian Government and Administrators Reports, "Government Resident's Report on Northern Territory for the Year 1893."

34 "Notice," *Northern Territory Times*, 10 July 1886.

35 National Archives, Canberra, Goldsbrough, Mort and Company papers, GMC 2/876: "Sundry Papers Re. C.B. Fisher and Northern Territory Properties, 1886–1892."

36 GMC 2/176/12/62: 14 November 1889.

37 "The McArthur River Tableland," 30 January 1886.

38 "From our Correspondent," *Brisbane Courier*, 13 August 1879.

39 "Through Texas," *Northern Star*, 27 March 1880. The Australian press also acknowledged the devastating effects of both overgrazing and bad weather in the northwestern states. In an article on 14 October 1887 the *Morning Bulletin* stated that the life of the American cowboy had been great "while employment was assured and wages were good." However, "now, alas, it is different. Cattlemen have lost heavily and the cowboy is as pronounced a sufferer as his employer . . . The cattle industry in consequence of overstocked ranges, three dry summers, and a winter of unexampled severity has practically collapsed" ("Cattle and Cowboys, Horses and Horsemen in Western America").

40 David H. Breen, *The Canadian Prairie West and the Ranching Frontier, 1874–1924* (Toronto: University of Toronto Press, 1983), 58.

41 Warren M. Elofson, *Cowboys, Gentlemen and Cattle Thieves: Ranching on the Western Frontier* (Montreal and Kingston: McGill-Queen's University Press, 2000), 19.

42 Northern Territory Archives Service, South Australian Government and Administrators Reports, "Half Yearly Report on Northern Territory to December 31ˢᵗ 1886." Browne, originally from England and living in Melbourne, was a speculator, farmer, and pastoralist who owned a chain of stations in South Australia by 1884.

43 South Australian Government and Administrators Reports, "Half Yearly Report on Northern Territory to December 31ˢᵗ 1886."

44 Under the names T. McIlwraith, W. Collins, and W. Forrest (South Australian Government and

Administrators Reports, "Half Yearly Report on Northern Territory to December 31st 1886").

45 Giles, "The First Pastoral Settlement in the Northern Territory," 60.

46 In 1904, J.C. White (who had also held separate Brunette Downs leases since 1878) and F.C. White became the owners of Brunette Downs. The Whites went into partnership with A.J. Cotton in 1912 ("Sale of Station Properties. No Offer for Brunette Downs. Walhallow and Eva Downs Realise 15,000 pounds," *Townsville Daily Bulletin*, 11 May 1918).

47 The average farm size in Alberta was around 360 acres (Elofson, *Cowboys, Gentlemen and Cattle Thieves*, 157).

48 Bucknall, "A Documented Short History of Undoolya," 11.

49 Under the names of F.A. Grant and F.W. Stokes (Northern Territory Archives Service, South Australian Government and Administrators Reports, "Half Yearly Report on Northern Territory to December 31st 1886").

50 F.A.C. Bishop, *Report on an Inspection of the Pastoral Holdings, Stock Routes, Bores and Dips on the Barkly Tableland, Northern Territory* (Melbourne: Government Printer, 1923), 3.

51 Ibid., 5

52 Ibid., 8.

53 Ibid., 7.

54 30,000 cattle and 500 horses on 8,264 square miles (GMC 2/876/4/6, 4).

55 "The Northern Territory Quarterly Report," *South Australian Register*, 15 August 1883. It had 4,000 cattle and 200 horses. Land held equalled 1,100 square miles ("Northern Territory Pastoral Blocks," *Northern Territory Times*, 28 September 1889). In 1935 the Northern Territory Pastoral Leases Investigation Committee reported that the operation near Alice Springs was running less than two animals per square mile (Bucknall, "A Documented Short History of Undoolya," 11).

56 For South Australia see Strangways Springs Station, http://www.poltalloch.com.au/history.htm; Wilpena Station, http://www.southaustralianhistory.com.au/wilpena.htm; Kanyaka Station, http://www.youtube.com/watch?v=dNLCKWWEmYQ; Poltalloch Station, http://www.poltalloch.com.au/history.htm; Anna Creek Station, http://en.wikipedia.org/wiki/Anna_Creek_station. For Southeast Queensland see Tinnenburra Station, http://www.qhatlas.com.au/category/keywords/pastoral-industry; Darling Downs, http://www.

heritageaustralia.com.au/
magazine.php?article=381.
For southern Queensland,
see Noela Corfield, "The
Development of the Cattle
Industry in Queensland, 1840–
1890," unpublished honours
thesis, Class Library, University
of Queensland, Brisbane, 5.

57 Historical records are
incomplete, but we do know
that during the period 1864–66
and again in 1868, major
districts of Victoria, South
Australia, New South Wales,
Queensland, and Western
Australia were severely
affected; and as occupation
of the Territory was taking
place between 1880 and 1886,
various parts of Victoria, New
South Wales, Queensland, and
South Australia were struck
(Appendix B).

58 Jeannie Gunn, *We of the Never-
Never*, 10th ed. (2003), 89,
http://www.gutenberg.org/
ebooks/4699.

59 Northern Territory Archives
Service, Darwin, South
Australian Government and
Administrators Reports,
"Government Resident's
Report on Northern Territory
for the Year 1890."

60 "Country Mining and General
News," *North Australian*, 19
October 1883.

61 "Northern Territory Pastoral
Areas," *The Advertiser*, 18
November 1903.

4 THE OUTBACK FRONTIER

1 State Library of South
Australia, Adelaide, Alfred
Giles papers, PRG 1389/2:
Giles, "The First Pastoral
Settlement in the Northern
Territory compiled principally
for his own experiences as
an overlander and pioneer
pastoralist with special
references to the founding
of the Springvale, Delamere,
Elsey and Newcastle Waters
runs, 1870–1895 with extracts
from his diary 1879–1895," 55.

2 "Report of the Northern
Territory Commission;
together with the Minutes of
Proceedings, Evidence and
Appendices," *South Australia
Parliamentary Papers* (1895),
2, no. 19. "On 15 January
1895 the South Australian
Government appointed a
Royal Commission to inquire
into all matters relating to
the Northern Territory with
a view to further developing
its resources and establishing
better government. The
Commission held 35 meetings
and heard from 69 witnesses
before reporting later that
year" (National Archives,
Canberra, Commonwealth
Government Records about
the Northern Territory,
http://guides.naa.gov.au/
records-about-northern-
territory/part1/
chapter1/1.6.aspx#chap1
note14).

3 National Archives, Canberra, Goldsbrough Mort and Company papers, GMRBV/ 4, 4–5. The disease was redwater or Texas tick disease.

4 Such grasses might be referred to as "rank," a term used a lot at the time, meaning foul or nutritionally worthless.

5 "The Northern Territory," *South Australian Register*, 28 August 1877.

6 "Palmerston, June 20," *Northern Territory Times*, 23 June 1877; No title, *Northern Territory Times*, 11 August 1877; "Money and Wool Markets," *Rockhampton Bulletin*, 22 November 1877; "The Northern Territory," *South Australian Register*, 6 September 1877; "Palmerston," *Northern Territory Times and Gazette*, 10 February 1877. "The Northern Territory," *South Australian Register*, 6 November 1877, reported that the two men had taken a lease of 10,000 square miles.

7 See, for instance, "Money and Wool Markets," *Rockhampton Bulletin*, 22 November 1877. "The party have returned to the Katherine, and report some magnificent country between the Victoria and the Junction of the Daly and Katherine." The next year Sergison published *The Northern Territory and Its Pastoral Capabilities* (Melbourne: Sands and McDougall, 1878).

8 Giles, "The First Pastoral Settlement in the Northern Territory," 148.

9 "News and Notes," *Northern Territory Times*, 10 December 1881.

10 Gordon Buchanan, *Packhorse and Waterhole*, 2nd ed. (Sydney: Angus and Robertson, 1934), 69.

11 In 1890 Glencoe was acquired by two cattlemen named Lawrie and Armstrong. In about 1910 the Byrne family acquired the station. Vestey brothers of the world-renowned Bovril canned meat company bought the station in 1920 and used it as a depot for cattle being railed to Darwin via nearby Fountainhead Trucking Yards. Later, the station was absorbed into Ban Ban Springs, a nearby grazing property.

12 Goldsbrough, Mort and Company papers, GM 2/876/7: B. Blair to Goldsbrough, Mort and Company, 24 October 1889.

13 Alfred Giles papers, PRG 1389/3: W. Brown to Giles, 24 March 1886; Browne to Giles, 15 May 1887.

14 Peter Forrest, *Springvale's Story and Early Years at Katherine* (Darwin: Murranji Press, 1985), 55–56. Delamere was absorbed into the nearby Willeroo station and later regained its status as a single operation, and John Lewis

purchased Newcastle Waters (State Library of South Australia, Lewis family papers, PRG 247/2). The Browne years can also be documented in correspondence between Browne and Giles (Alfred Giles papers, PRG 1389/3).

15 Pastoral leases in the Kakadu area to the east of Glencoe were given up successively from 1889. The site of Oenpelli was originally established in 1906 when Paddy Cahill set up a station on which to raise cattle and hunt buffalo. The government took over the lease in 1916 and handed the land over to the Church Missionary Society in 1925 ("Kakadu National Park," New World Encyclopedia, http://www. newworldencyclopedia.org/ entry/Kakadu_National_Park).

16 R.A. Perry, *Pasture Lands of the Northern Territory, Australia* (Melbourne: Commonwealth Scientific and Industrial Research Organization, 1960), 17–30.

17 Australia, *The Northern Territory Beef Cattle Industry: An Economic Survey, 1962–63 to 1964–65* (Melbourne: Commonwealth Scientific and Industrial Research Organization, 1968).

18 Goldsbrough, Mort and Company papers, GMRBV/4, 6–7.

19 Northern Territory Archives Service, South Australian Government and Administrators Reports, "Government Resident's Report on Northern Territory for the Year 1893."

20 By 1894 the reduction in amount of land leased in fact bottomed out as pastoralists began to pick their new leases more wisely. "At the close of the year 1892 the area held under lease was 141,999 square miles, while at the close of last year it was 145,000 square miles. The area declared stocked at the end of 1892 was 80,048 square miles, while last year shows 74,305 square miles as stocked. The area applied for in 1892 was 13,040 square miles as against 16,340 square miles applied for in 1893. Leases comprising 20,656 square miles were forfeited during 1892, while the area forfeited last year was 15,300 square miles. The sum of 11,622 pounds 11 shillings, 2 pence was received from rents of pastoral lands for the year 1892, and during the year 1893 the rents received . . . amounted to about 9,000 pounds" ("Government Resident's Report on Northern Territory for the Year 1893").

21 See Duncan MacEachran, *A Journey Over the Plains: From Fort Benton to Bow River and Back* (Montreal: n.p., 1881).

22 The manager of the Walrond ranch, Duncan McNab McEachran, wrote about the route he, Matthew Cochrane,

and other easterners took in order to choose their locations before the arrival of the railway. He also described the natural advantages in foothills country (*A Journey Over the Plains: From Fort Benton to Bow River and Back* [Montreal: n.p., 1881]).

23 Goldsbrough, Mort and Company papers, GMRBV/4, 6–7.

24 "Cattle and Sheep in the Territory," *Northern Territory Times*, 2 April 1881.

25 "The Territory's Pastoral Wealth?" *Northern Territory Times*, 11 October 1901.

26 Northern Territory Archives Service, South Australian Government and Administrators Reports, "Government Resident's Quarterly Report on Northern Territory," 12 August 1884.

27 "Government Resident's Report on Northern Territory for the Year 1885."

28 "Government Resident's Report on Northern Territory for the Year 1893."

29 Perry, *Pasture Lands of the Northern Territory*, 21.

30 Goldsbrough, Mort and Company papers, GMRBV/4, 31.

31 Northern Territory Archives Service, South Australian Government and Administrators Reports, "Government Resident's

Report on Northern Territory for the Year 1890."

32 Peter C. Thomson, "The behavioural ecology of dingoes in north-western Australia," III, "Hunting and Feeding behaviour, and diet," *Wildlife Research* 19, no. 5 (1992): 531–34 (http://www.publish.csiro.au/paper/WR9920531.htm). See also Peter C. Thomson, IV, "Social and spatial organization, and movements," *Wildlife Research* 19, no. 5 (1992): 543–63.

33 Michael J. Costello, *Life of John Costello, Being the Adventures of a Pioneer, Pastoralist and Explorer in Queensland and the Northern Territory* (Sydney: Dymock's Book Arcade, 1930), 188. The stock in this case were cattle. When sheep were caught the destruction was even worse as the smaller animals were even more easily caught.

34 "At present, however, the Tableland has the drawback of a scarcity of permanent waters, and until this is overcome by artesian boring, sinking, or construction of dams, pastoralists in this district must always labour under a disadvantage" ("The Territory's Pastoral Wealth," *Northern Territory Times*, 11 October 1901).

35 Giles, "The First Pastoral Settlement in the Northern Territory," 151-53.

36 Ross Duncan, *The Northern Territory Pastoral Industry, 1863–1910* (Melbourne: University of Melbourne Press, 1967), 158–60.

37 Leroy V. Kelly, *The Range Men*, 75th anniversary ed. (Calgary: Glenbow-Alberta Institute, 1988), 82; Warren M. Elofson, *Frontier Cattle Ranching in the Land and Times of Charlie Russell* (Montreal and Kingston: McGill-Queen's University Press, 2004), 189.

38 Giles, "The First Pastoral Settlement in the Northern Territory," 1.

39 The station was about 125 miles north of Adelaide.

40 Giles, "The First Pastoral Settlement in the Northern Territory," 70–71.

41 Ibid., 138.

42 Ibid., 65–66. Giles estimated that the total cost of all the "stations formed" by these two men, including "yards, paddocks, homesteads and station expeditions," was about 245,000 pounds sterling.

43 Buchanan, *Packhorse and Waterhole*, 61.

44 Ibid., 68.

45 In 1887 W.J. Brown's son Leonard wrote to Giles to inform him that wages were going to have to be reduced to cut costs. "You must see," he wrote, "that supposing you were willing to remain at reduced salary, it would be out of the question to bring your wife and child to live in such miserable quarters" (Alfred Giles papers, PRG 1389/3/9: L.G. Browne to Giles, 15 May 1887).

46 Northern Territory Archives Service, South Australian Government and Administrators Reports, "Government Resident's Report on Northern Territory for the Year 1891," statement by J.S. Little at Austral Downs. On 19 October 1912 a government representative forwarded to the administration in Adelaide an evaluation of the "improvements" at a home place near Alice Springs: "Lease. No. 1 Managers house of 2 rooms each about 16 X 15 stone walls, veranda on front and one side, iron roof. Est. value 140 pounds. Kitchen and dining room stone walls thatched roof fair condition est. value 70 pounds. Harness room and Blacksmiths shop rough stone walls thatched roof, well 30 ft., 20 pounds. . . yard 30 pounds and well with whip, bucket and troughing 15 pounds. Lease No 2. Simpson's Gap, tailing yard 20 pounds. Lease No. 17. Nil" (Northern Territory Archives Service, NTRS 636 BUC: Graeme Bucknall, "A Documented Short History of Undoolya: The First Legal

Cattle Station in the Northern Territory," National Trust of Australia, Northern Territory, 1983, 6).

47 Alfred Giles papers, PRG 1389/3: 24 March 1886.

48 Warren M. Elofson, *Somebody Else's Money: The Walrond Ranch Story, 1883–1907* (Calgary: University of Calgary Press, 2009), 43. For the most notable exception see the Cochrane cattle drives in the early 1880s: Warren M. Elofson, *Cowboys, Gentlemen and Cattle Thieves: Ranching on the Western Frontier* (Montreal and Kingston: McGill-Queen's University Press, 2000), 9–15.

49 Indeed, eventually, the Canadian government subsidized the rates. The Crow's Nest Pass Agreement, dated 6 September 1897, was an agreement between the CPR and the Canadian government. The CPR was given a cash subsidy of $3.3 million and title to pass into the province of British Columbia in exchange for reducing, in perpetuity, eastbound rates on grain and flour and westbound rates on a specified list of "settlers' effects" ("Crows Nest Pass Agreement," http://www.thecanadianencyclopedia.ca).

50 See chapter 9.

51 National Archives, Canberra, Goldsbrough, Mort and Company, GMC 87/2/1: account books. Labour at Victoria River Downs for February 1909 – top stockman 41 pounds, 2 others 15 pounds, 1 at 13 pounds, 4 at 10 pounds, 12 at 6–8 pounds. If the bottom 12 averaged 7 pounds or $35 that would be about average in western Canada too (Elofson, *Somebody Else's Money*, 39, 309–10). However, the rest on VRD ran from over $200 for the top man and $75 for others – well above the Walrond average. The entire "Blacks acct." on VRD tended to run from 16–20 pounds in the average month.

52 Northern Territory Archives Service, South Australian Government and Administrators Reports, "Government Resident's Report on Northern Territory for the Year 1910," 15; Elofson, *Cowboys, Gentlemen and Cattle Thieves*, xviii, 149.

53 See chapter 5.

54 See chapter 5 .

55 William Beahen and Stan Horrall, *Red Coats on the Prairies: The North-West Mounted Police, 1886–1900* (Regina: Centax Books, 1998), 14.

56 Australia, *The Northern Territory Beef Cattle Industry*, 27.

57 Margaret Kowald and William Johnston, *You Can't Make it Rain: The Story of the North Australian Pastoral Company 1877–1991* (Brisbane: Boolarong, 1992), 41. More

sophisticated methods
followed. For the definitive
history see L.G. Newton
and R. Norris, *Clearing the
Continent: The Eradication
of Bovine Pleuropneumonia
from Australia* (Melbourne:
Commonwealth Scientific
and Industrial Research
Organization, Primary
Industries Report Series,
2000).

58   Beverly M. Angus, *Tick
Fever and the Cattle Tick in
Australia, 1829–1996* (Brisbane:
Queensland Department of
Primary Industries, 1998), 5–7.

59   Australia, "Report of
Preliminary Scientific
Expedition to the Northern
Territory," *Bulletin of the
Northern Territory* 1 (March
1912), 15–22.

60   "Report of Preliminary
Scientific Expedition to the
Northern Territory," 19.

61   Buchanan, *Packhorse to
Waterhole*, 113.

62   "Report of Preliminary
Scientific Expedition to the
Northern Territory," 19.

63   Goldsbrough, Mort and
Company papers, GMRBV/4,
31.

64   Government Resident's
Report quoted in "Report
of Preliminary Scientific
Expedition to the Northern
Territory," 20. "During the
past few years," the disease "has
attacked overlanding mobs of

cattle, and in some cases has
swept off a very large number."

65   "Report of Preliminary
Scientific Expedition to the
Northern Territory," 23.

66   Glen McLaren and William
Cooper, *Distance, Drought
and Dispossession: A History of
the Northern Territory Pastoral
Industry* (Darwin: Northern
Territory University Press,
2001), 33.

67   Below, p. 179.

68   "Diseases," *Yellowstone
Journal*, 14 September 1887.
Among the cattle the most
frightening plagues were
pleuropneumonia – for which
both Canadian and American
cattle were eventually
embargoed in Britain –
blackleg, and foot and mouth
disease.

69   "The Grange," *Rocky Mountain
Husbandman*, 12 February 1880;
"Black Leg," *Rocky Mountain
Husbandman*, 15 April 1880;
"Local Notes," *Yellowstone
Journal*, 6 August 1885; Kelly,
The Range Men, 160; "Disease,"
Yellowstone Journal, 4 April
1886; "Vaccination of Calves,"
Rocky Mountain Husbandman, 12
September 1901.

70   See Elofson, *Frontier Cattle
Ranching*, 144–47. In 1892
the British placed import
restrictions on Canadian cattle
with the rationalization that
they were protecting home-
grown stock (Max Foran, *Trails
and Trials: Markets and Land*

Use in the Alberta Beef Cattle Industry, 1881–1948 [Calgary: University of Calgary Press, 2003], 21–22, 24–25).

71   Costello, *Life of John Costello*, 95.

72   Ibid., 96.

73   Ibid., 97.

74   Ibid., 97.

75   Ibid., 121–22.

76   Ibid., 118.

77   Ibid., 119.

78   Ibid., 123–89.

79   Ibid., 190–95.

80   Ibid., 191.

81   Ibid., 217–18.

82   Ibid., 219.

83   Ibid., 220.

84   Butlin, *Investment in Australian Economic Development* (Cambridge: University of Cambridge Press, 1964); W.A. Sinclair, *The Process of Economic Development in Australia* (Melbourne: Cheshire Publishing, 1976); Richard H. Timberlake Jr., "Panic of 1893," in *Business Cycles and Depressions: An Encyclopedia*, ed. David Glasner and Thomas Cooley (New York: Garland Publishing, 1997), 516–18.

85   Buchanan, *Packhorse and Waterhole*, 133.

86   Ibid., 176.

87   Northern Territory Archives Service, South Australian Government and Administrators Reports, "Government Resident's Report on Northern Territory for the Year 1890."

88   See David H. Breen, *The Canadian Prairie West and the Ranching Frontier, 1874–1924* (Toronto: University of Toronto Press, 1983), 11–19.

89   Elofson, *Cowboys, Gentlemen and Cattle Thieves*, 9–10; "Town Topics," *Calgary Herald*, 19 September 1888; "The Week's Local News," *Calgary Herald*, 26 September 1888; H.F. Lawrence, "Early Days in the Chinook Belt," *Alberta Historical Review* 13, no. 1 (Winter 1965): 12.

90   J.J. Young, "A Visit to the Cochrane Ranch," *Alberta Historical Review* 22, no. 3 (Summer 1974): 28.

91   That is, the Creswell outfit managed by A.G. "Tony" Day. See Kelly, *The Range Men*, 172, 192; Elofson, *Frontier Cattle Ranching*, 157; Elofson, *Cowboys, Gentlemen and Cattle Thieves*, 86.

5 THE SOCIAL ENVIRONMENT

1   Jeannie Gunn, *We of the Never-Never*, 10th ed. (2003), 59, http://www.gutenberg.org/ebooks/4699.

2   Ibid., 88.

3   Ibid., 92–93.

4   Michael J. Costello, *Life of John Costello, Being the Adventures of a Pioneer, Pastoralist and Explorer in Queensland and the Northern Territory* (Sydney: Dymock's Book Arcade, 1930), 196–97.

5 Theodore Roosevelt, "The Round-Up," in *The Complete Cowboy Reader: Remembering the Open Range*, ed. Ted Stone (Red Deer: Red Deer College Press, 2002), 206.

6 One Australian stockman was intrigued when he viewed the roping on a North American roundup. He later described it with considerable admiration to an Australian Newspaper:

Soon we got amongst the cattle – tidy looking shorthorns, mostly young, and looking like between 600 lbs. to 1000 lbs. each. They were genuine bush cattle that got but a little alfalfa and barley straw during the very coldest of winter. The stockmen used the riata as Australians do the stockwhip, letting it fly out towards the cattle that lagged behind . . . By mid-day the round-up, or muster, was complete, and after a hearty dinner we saw the manner in which the cattle are lassoed, either for quieting, branding, or killing. In cutting out beasts from the mob, the process was similar to that usual in Australia. Soon as the beast to be cut out was seen, a stockman dashed in between it and the crowd, and seldom failed to drive the animal where he desired it to go. When an extra cute or refractory customer was met, the riata came into play. This riata is of green-hide plaited precisely as a stockman's whip. It is from 40 to 60 feet in length, and about the thickness of the little finger of a man, or say five-eighths of an inch. From its suppleness and great strength, it is evident that the Mexicans use the very best hides that they can get in order to make riata. One end is fastened to the fore part or horn of the saddle. The other end is a noose, made to slip upon a polished metal ring. When about to use the riata, a noose fully six feet in diameter is opened out, and with this in his right hand the horseman darts after the [animal] . . . Gradually he brings himself nearer and nearer the beast . . . Then the rider makes a spurt – his horse is splendidly trained and knows all about his duty – and when about the length of a horse behind his prey, away shoots the riata, the noose circling in the air. I never saw it fail to fall clean upon the horns of the beast. The rider then tightens his line, and the movement is understood by the horse, who "props" instantly, and turns himself slightly, so that he stands with his two off legs as struts to brace back his body. The rider also braces back. But in one-tenth of the time it takes to read this, the climax has come. The whole maneuver is quick as a flash. The rope runs out, and as the shock comes with a snap upon the saddle, the bullock or cow upon the other end, running head down, is brought up with a jerk on the head that throws the hindquarters round with centrifugal force, and the beast rolls over. He seldom rises just then . . . He lies still. He may be thinking that something more sudden is to happen. Should he rise, a second horseman drops a second riata over a hind foot – then they have him. Animals to be branded are served in this way, and they certainly make good work of their branding. By the way, the brands – mostly initial letters of the owners – are registered in the County Clerk's office ("Mining and Stock Farming in America," *The Queenslander*, 3 November 1877).

7 When a corral was unavailable on the Costello roundup, presumably because of a scarcity of trees for building one, the boss himself "roped the calves, in Texas style and then, with the assistance of his men and boys, successfully completed the branding of all his unmarked young stock" (Costello, *Life of John Costello*, 200).

8 After starting up Elsey station, the men began building "draughting lane[s] and branding pens," out in the open pastures (Gunn, *We of the Never-Never*, 89).

9 Sometimes called "cabbage palm hat" – a straw hat made from the leaves of the Australian cabbage tree first produced around 1800 ("Cabbage Tree Hat," *The Queenslander*, 5 January 1938).

10 For a discussion of the importance of environment and tradition in moulding ranching practices on the northern Great Plains see Terry Jordan-Bychkov, "Does the Border Matter? Cattle Ranching and the 49th Parallel," in *Cowboys, Ranchers and the Cattle Business: Cross-Border Perspectives on Ranching History*, ed. Simon Evans, Sarah Carter, and Bill Yeo (Calgary: University of Calgary Press, 2000), 1–10; Terry Jordan-Bychkov, *North American Cattle-Ranching Frontiers: Origins, Diffusion, and Differentiation* (Albuquerque: University of New Mexico Press, 1993), 267–307.

11 Present-day historians have stressed the impact of climate, landscape, and region in encouraging cultural developments and a sense of self in the borderlands of the northwestern United States and western Canada. This chapter is meant to supplement their work by emphasizing that social forces also played a crucial role in moulding the way people thought and behaved; see Benjamin Johnson and Andrew Graybill, eds., *Bridging National Borders in*

North America: Transnational and Comparative Histories (Durham: Duke University Press, 2010); Sterling Evans, ed., The Borderlands of the American and Canadian Wests: Essays on Regional History of the Forty-ninth Parallel (Lincoln: University of Nebraska Press, 2006); Carol Higham and Robert Thacker, eds., One Myth, Two Wests, 2 vols. (Calgary: University of Calgary Press, 2004, 2006); John Finlay and Ken S. Coates, eds., Parallel Destinies: Canadian-American Relations West of the Rockies (Seattle: University of Washington Press, 2002); Beth Ladow, The Medicine Line: Life and Death on a North American Borderland (New York: Routledge, 2001); Paul Hirt, ed., Terra Pacifica: People and Place in the Northwest States and Western Canada (Pullman: Washington State University Press, 1998).

12 Henry Reynolds, The Other Side of the Frontier: Aboriginal Resistance to the European Invasion of Australia (Sydney: University of New South Wales Press, 2006).

13 See James Belich, Replenishing the Earth: The Settler Revolution and the Rise of the Anglo-World, 1783–1939 (Oxford and New York: Oxford University Press, 2009).

14 The figures for each year are posted in the Southern Australia Government Gazette.

15 Ross Duncan, The Northern Territory Pastoral Industry, 1863–1910 (Melbourne: University of Melbourne Press, 1967), 158–60.

16 "Indigenous Australians were excluded from the Constitution in 1901 and in federal censuses were counted with flora and fauna. This was not reversed until the referendum of 1968 when the constitution was changed to include Indigenous Australians. Put simply their numbers in the Northern Territory were not known with accuracy until 1968" (Dr. Glenn Mitchell, Faculty of Law, Humanities and the Arts, Wollongong University, 2014).

17 Besides the following note, Northern Territory Archives Service, Darwin, Borroloola Police Station Letter Book, 1886–1924, NTRS 2210/P1: C. Power to P. Foelsche, 24 February 1889 and 28 February 1889; and M. Donegan to Foelsche, 22 May 1888.

18 NTRS 2210/P1: C. Power to P. Foelsche, 21 November 1888.

19 For which see Northern Territory Archives Service, NTC 363.2099429 WLS: William R. Wilson, "A Force Apart: A History of the Northern Territory Police, 1870–1920" (PhD thesis, Northern Territory University, 2000), 175–83.

20 Rabbits were a major pest in Australia. The 1890 Rabbit Act required all farmers to surround all lands declared by government proclamation to be rabbit infested with rabbit-proof netting ("The Rabbit Act," *Evening News*, 30 May 1891; "Regulations Under the Rabbit Act," The Riverine Grazier, 13 February 1891).

21 Wilson, "A Force Apart," 175–83.

22 "Letter to the Editor," *Northern Territory Times*, 12 February 1881. See also "Letter to the Editor," *Northern Territory Times*, 5 March 1881; "Letter to the Editor," *Northern Territory Times*, 12 March 1881.

23 For Montana, Alberta, and Assiniboia see Warren M. Elofson, *Frontier Cattle Ranching in the Land and Times of Charlie Russell* (Montreal and Kingston: McGill-Queen's University Press, 2004), 67–68.

24 Belich, *Replenishing the Earth*, 324.

25 Montana Historical Society Library and Archives, Helena, SC 1692: Memoirs of Lady Kathleen Lindsay.

26 Belich, *Replenishing the Earth*, 324.

27 Samuel Steele, *Forty Years in Canada: Reminiscences of the Great North-West, with some account of his service in South Africa*, ed. M.G. Niblett, 2nd ed. (Toronto: Prospero Books, 2000), 177.

28 Glenbow Archives, M229: Simon John Clarke papers.

29 Government of South Australia State Record Office, Adelaide, GRS-1: In-letters (1870–1910) of the Minister Controlling the Northern Territory (Minister of Education), Quarterly Report of G.R. McMinn, Acting Government Resident, 7 July 1883.

30 Northern Territory Archives Service, South Australian Government and Administrators Reports, "Government Resident's Report on Northern Territory for the Year 1910," 15.

31 "Conclusion of Murder Trial," *Northern Territory Times*, 30 April 1909.

32 State Library of South Australia, Adelaide, D7478: "George Byng Scott's Reminiscences of life in the Northern Territory during his term of office as Government Resident, 1873–1876," 2.

33 Frederick Ings, *Before the Fences (Tales from the Midway Ranch): Autobiography*, ed. J. Davis (Calgary: McAra Printing, 1980), 48.

34 Borroloola Police Station Letter Book: J. J. Roberts to W.G. Stretton, 25 July 1889.

35 See Andrew Gillett, "Opium and Race Relations in Queensland," 5, www.siq.qld.gov.au; *Harvest of Endurance:*

A History of the Chinese in Australia, 1788–1988 (Sydney: Australia-China Friendship Society, 1988), 5–6, http://www.multiculturalaustralia.edu.au/doc/yimei_1.pdf.

36 "To the Editor," Northern Territory Times, 1 May 1880; "Opium Trade in the Northern Territory," Burra (South Aus.) Record, 5 August 1887; "Opium Traffic in the Northern Territory," Kalgoorlie (Western Aus.) Miner, 5 October 1895. See also Baldwin Spencer, "Preliminary Report on the Aboriginals of the Northern Territory," Bulletin of the Northern Territory 7 (Melbourne: Department of External Affairs, July 1913), 16.

37 The Queenslander, 28 August 1886, quoted in Dawn May, Aboriginal Labour and the Cattle Industry: Queensland from White Settlement to the Present (Cambridge: University of Cambridge Press, 1994), 47.

38 Wilson, "A Force Apart," 254.

39 Charles M. Russell, Trails Plowed Under: Stories of the Old West, introduction by William Rogers and Brian W. Dippie (Lincoln: University of Nebraska Press, 1996), 159.

40 For Alberta, see Steele, Forty Years in Canada, 167–68; "Is Gambling Prevalent Throughout the City," Calgary Herald, 17 October 1906.

41 "Looking Round in the NT," Northern Territory Times, 28 May 1887.

42 "Chinese Gambling," Northern Territory Times, 26 July 1884. See also "Keeping a Gambling Home" and "To the Editor," 1 May 1880; "To the Editor," 11 March 1882; "Law Courts," 19 June 1882.

43 "Chinese Gambling."

44 James Gray, Red Lights on the Prairies (Scarborough: The New American Library of Canada, 1973); E.C. Abbott and H. Huntington Smith, We Pointed Them North: Recollections of a Cowpuncher, 2nd ed.(Norman: University of Oklahoma Press, 1955), 103, 105, 106.

45 Char Smith, "Crossing the Line, American Prostitutes in Western Canada," in One Step Over the Line: Toward a History of Women in the North American Wests, eds. Elizabeth Jameson and Sheila McManus (Edmonton: University of Alberta Press, 2008), 241–60.

46 The same was true on the mining frontier. For Butte, Montana, see Mary Murphy, "Private Lives of Public Women," in The Women's West, eds. Susan Armitage and Elizabeth Jameson (Norman: University of Oklahoma Press, 1987), 191–205.

47 Frank W. Anderson, Sheriffs and Outlaws of Western Canada

(Calgary: Frontier Publishing, n.d.), 48.

48 Hugh A. Dempsey, *Golden Age of the Canadian Cowboy* (Saskatoon and Calgary: Fifth House, 1995), 56.

49 The seminal work for Australia is Anne Summers, *Damned Whores and God's Police*, 2nd ed. (Melbourne: Penguin Books, 1991).

50 Barbara James, *No Man's Land: Women of the Northern Territories* (Sydney: Collins Publishers, 1989), chap. 4; Wilson, "A Force Apart," 255.

51 Gray, *Red Lights on the Prairies*, 183; Abbott and Huntington Smith, *We Pointed Them North*, 108.

52 Government of South Australia State Record Office, Adelaide, GRS-1: In-letters (1870–1910) of the Minister Controlling the Northern Territory: P. Foelsche to E.W. Price, 3 August 1882.

53 Abbott and Huntington Smith, *We Pointed them North*, 145–46.

54 "Our Annual Visitation," *Northern Territory Times*, 25 June 1881.

55 Borroloola Police Station Letter Book: P. Foelsche to G.R. McMinn, 7 July 1883.

56 Ann McGrath, *"Born in the Cattle": Aborigines in Cattle Country* (Sydney: Allen and Unwin, 1987), 91.

57 Tony Roberts, *Frontier Justice: A History of the Gulf Country to 1900* (Adelaide: University of Queensland Press, 2005), 137.

58 Elofson, *Frontier Cattle Ranching*, 124–26.

59 Northern Territory Archives Service, Government Resident Inward Correspondence, NTRS 1467: W.L. Hutton letter, 15 August 1889.

60 "To the Editor," *Northern Territory Times*, 16 July 1881.

61 Quarterly Report of G.R. McMinn, 7 July 1883.

62 McGrath, *"Born in the Cattle,"* 91.

63 McGrath also points out that very few white men were prepared to take responsibility for the children (p. 91).

64 Sylvia Van Kirk, *Many Tender Ties: Women in Fur-Trade Society, 1670–1870* (Norman: University of Oklahoma Press, 1980).

65 Jennifer S.H. Brown, *Strangers in Blood: Fur Trade Company Families in Indian Country* (Vancouver: University of British Columbia Press, 1980).

66 Abbott and Huntington Smith, *We Pointed Them North*, 135–36.

67 Elofson, *Frontier Cattle Ranching*, 124–26.

68 Jane Carey and Claire McLisky, eds., *Creating White Australia* (Sydney: Sydney University Press, 2009). Marguerita Stephens believes that the practice was "exceptional and incidental" but helped to depict Aborigines as "people whose common rights could be morally suspended" ("A word

of evidence: shared tales about infanticide and others-not-us in colonial Victoria," 194).

69 McGrath, *"Born in the Cattle,"* 91.

70 Paul M.C. Hasluck, *Shades of Darkness: Aboriginal Affairs, 1925–1965* (Melbourne: Melbourne University Press, 1988), 50. Hasluck examines the lives of half-castes in the northern part of Western Australia. For Aboriginal circumstances in Western Australia and Queensland, see Gordon Briscoe, *Counting, Health and Identity: A History of Aboriginal Health and Demography in Western Australia and Queensland, 1900–1940* (Canberra: Aboriginal Studies Press for the Australian Institute of Aboriginal and Torres Strait Islander Studies, 2003).

71 McGrath, *"Born in the Cattle,"* 92–93. Margaret D. Jacobs, *White Mother to a Dark Race: Settler Colonialism, Maternalism, and the Removal of Indigenous Children in the American West and Australia, 1880–1940* (Lincoln: University of Nebraska Press, 2009).

72 Reynolds, in *The Other Side of the Frontier*, emphasizes the importance to Aborigines on the Australian continent as a whole of the loss of their hunting lands and traditional food sources as well as their cultural practices. For the modern debate on Native land claims in New Zealand as well as in Canada and Australia, see Louis A. Knafla and Haijo Westra, eds., *Aboriginal Title and Indigenous Peoples: Canada, Australia, and New Zealand* (Vancouver: University of British Columbia Press, 2010).

73 State Library of South Australia, Adelaide, 1079: Arthur C. Ashwin, "Recollections of Ralph Milner's Expedition from Koperamanna to the Northern Territory with Sheep and Horses in 1870/71, with an account of his subsequent experiences in the Northern Territory" (1927), 11–12.

74 "Another Murder in the Victoria River District," *Northern Territory Times*, 21 October 1892.

75 "A Triple Murder," *Northern Territory Times and Gazette*, Friday, 10 February 1905.

76 "Another Murder in the Victoria River District," *Northern Territory Times*, 21 October 1892; "A Triple Murder," *Northern Territory Times*, 19 February 1905.

77 Borroloola Police Station Letter Book: P. Foelsche to G.R. McMinn, 7 July 1883.

78 Baldwin Spencer, "Preliminary Report on the Aboriginals of the Northern Territory," *Bulletin of the Northern Territory* (Melbourne: Department of External Affairs, 7 July 1913),

16; "Police Items," *Northern Territory Times*, 18 October 1907.

79 Aboriginal tomahawk.

80 "Horrible Murder of Chinese by the Blacks," *Northern Territory Times*, 10 June 1882.

81 State Library of South Australia, Adelaide, Alfred Giles papers, PRG 1389/2: Giles, "The First Pastoral Settlement in the Northern Territory compiled principally for his own experiences as an overlander and pioneer pastoralist with special references to the founding of the Springvale, Delamere, Elsey and Newcastle Waters runs, 1870–1895 with extracts from his diary 1879–1895," 106–7.

82 For a discussion of the historiography and the various conflicting views on Native–white conflict, see Bain Attwood and S.G. Foster, *Frontier Conflict: The Australian Experience* (Canberra: National Museum of Australia, 2003). Roberts' views support the evidence originally provided by Reynolds, *The Other Side of the Frontier.*

83 Quarterly Report of G.R. McMinn, Acting Government Resident, 7 July 1883.

84 For one of the few recorded prosecutions of white violence see Borroloola Police Station Letter Book: R. Stott to N. Water, 5 January 1909.

85 Borroloola Police Station Letter Book: C. Power to P. Foelsche, 24 October 1886; "Police Court," *Northern Territory Times*, 31 July 1880; "Police Court," 18 December 1886; "Execution at Fanny Bay," 18 August 1899; "Blacks Again," 3 March 1905; "The Victoria River Tragedy," 10 March 1905.

86 Northern Territory Archives Service, NTC 363.2094 MACL: W.J. McLaren, "The Northern Territory and its Police Forces," 4 vols., 1:226.

87 Peter Forrest, "They of the Never Never" (Darwin: Northern Territory Library Services Occasional Papers 18, 1990), 5.

88 Archer Russell, *A Tramp-Royal in Wild Australia, 1928–1929* (London: Cape, 1934), 254–55, quoted in Richard Kimber, *The End of the Bad Old Days: European Settlement in Central Australia, 1871–1894* (Darwin: Northern Territory Library Services Occasional Papers 25, the fifth Eric Johnston lecture, 1991), 14.

89 Gordon Buchanan, *Packhorse and Waterhole*, 2nd ed. (Sydney: Angus and Robertson, 1934), 117.

90 *Adelaide Register*, 10 January 1890, quoted in Kimber, *The End of the Bad Old Days*, 16.

91 Amanda Nettelbeck and Robert Foster, *In the Name of the Law: William Willshire*

and the Policing of the Australian
Frontier (Adelaide: Wakefield
Press, 2007).

92   The Coniston Massacre of
1928 illustrates that the same
philosophy pertained many
years later. "Over a period of
months and at a number of
sites, more than 60 Aboriginal
men, women and children were
shot and killed" in reprisal
for the murder of one Fred
Brooks. "No charges were
laid against the reprisal party.
A Board of Enquiry set up to
investigate the killings ruled
the party had 'acted in self-
defence.' In evidence to the
Board of Enquiry, Jack Saxby
stated 'I always carry a revolver
on my tours and consider it
necessary. I have had occasion
to shoot at blacks before this
trouble. I have had to shoot to
kill,'" (First Australia, National
Museum of Australia, http://
www.nma.gov.au/exhibitions/
first_australians/resistance/
coniston_massacre).

93   State Library of South
Australia, PRG 247/2, Lewis
family papers, letters from Paul
Foelsche, 1875–1913: Foelsche
to John Lewis, 5 June 1880.
Such an episode was reported
in the Australian newspapers
but several years later
("Tuesday January 19 1886,"
Brisbane Courier, 19 January
1886).

94   Hugh A. Dempsey, "Cypress
Hills Massacre," Montana

Magazine 3, no. 4 (Autumn
1953): 1–9.

95   Paul Sharp somewhat overstates
this point in "Three Frontiers:
Some Comparative Studies
of Canadian, American, and
Australian Settlement," Pacific
Historical Review 24, no. 4
(November 1955): 373–74.
For a recent comparison of
mounted police approaches
to Native subjugation in
Australia and Western Canada,
see Amanda Nettelbeck and
Russell Smandych, "Policing
Indigenous Peoples on Two
Colonial Frontiers: Australia's
Mounted Police and Canada's
North-West Mounted Police,"
The Australian and New Zealand
Journal of Criminology 43 (2010):
356–75.

96   Andrew Graybill, "Rangers,
Mounties, and the Subjugation
of Indigenous Peoples, 1870–
1885," Great Plains Quarterly 24
(Spring 2004): 96. The police
role in supporting government,
big business, and the cattlemen
against Natives and immigrant
workers is explored in Andrew
Graybill, Policing the Great
Plains: Rangers, Mounties, and
the North American Frontier,
1875–1910 (Lincoln: University
of Nebraska Press, 2007).
In the Mounties' defence I
would mention that they were
known at times to side with the
Indians against corporations
such as the Canadian Pacific
Railway; see "In Town and

Out," *Macleod Gazette*, 1 July
1882.

97 James Daschuk, *Clearing
the Plains: Disease, Politics
of Starvation, and the Loss
of Aboriginal Life* (Regina:
University of Regina Press,
2013).

98 "Indian Murderers at Bay,"
Winnipeg Free Press, 20 May
1897; "A Desperate Outlaw,"
Winnipeg Free Press, 1 June
1897; "Siege Incidents,"
Winnipeg Free Press, 7 June
1897.

99 Steele, *Forty Years in Canada*,
277-87; "Charcoal," *Macleod
Gazette*, 30 October 1896;
"Charcoal Adds Another
Victim to his List," 13
November 1896; "Charcoal
on Trial for Murder," 15
January 1897; "Charcoal on the
Gallows," 19 March 1897.

100 Provincial Archives of
Alberta, Edmonton,
70.431/77: J. Martin, "Prairie
Reminiscences," n.d., 6.
For another episode of racial
violence in the Canadian
West, see Steele, *Forty Years in
Canada*, 218-27.

101 Thomas R. Malthus, *An Essay
on the Principle of Population, as
it affects the future Improvement
of Society, with remarks on the
speculations of Mr. Godwin,
M. Condorcet, and other writers*
(Adelaide: eBooks@Adelaide,
2010), http://ebooks.adelaide.
edu.au/m/malthus/thomas/
m26p/index.html; Herbert

Spencer coined the term
"survival of the fittest" in
Principles of Biology (London:
Williams and Norgate, 1864),
1:444.

102 Walter Bagehot, *Physics and
Politics* (part 2, 1872), http://
www.fullbooks.com/Physics-
and-Politics2.html.

103 "The speech of Joseph
Chamberlain, the British
Secretary of State for the
Colonies, at the annual dinner
of the Royal Colonial Institute
on March 31, 1897."

104 Buchanan, *Packhorse and
Waterhole*, vii. Buchanan was
the son of Nathaniel and
Katherine Buchanan who
pioneered the Wave Hill
cattle station in the Victoria
River region of the Northern
Territory.

105 Glenbow Archives, Mrs.
Charles Inderwick, Diary
and Personal Letters from the
North Fork Ranch, M376:
letter of 13 May 1884.

106 "Outrages by the Blacks,"
Northern Territory Times, 4
October 1884.

107 Buchanan, *Packhorse and
Waterhole*, vii; "Outrages by the
Blacks"; Inderwick letter of 13
May 1884, Diary and Personal
Letters from the North Fork
Ranch.

108 Much of this sort of conflict
is found in papers such as the
Macleod Gazette and *Great Falls
Tribune* prior to World War
I, but one searches virtually

in vain for it in the *Northern Territory Times.*

109 Robert Dykstra demonstrates that there has been a tendency to overstate violence in the early cattle towns of Kansas (*The Cattle Towns: A Social History of the Kansas Cattle Trading Centers—Abilene, Ellsworth, Wichita, Dodge City, and Caldwell, 1867–1885* [New York: Atheneum, 1973], 146–48). As in towns farther north, one does, though, detect... a distinct frontier quality about it. Firstly, guns were the main instrument used and most of the men involved in homicides were law enforcement agents, cowboys, or gamblers. Also, single young men often fought over young women, whom they greatly outnumbered.

110 W.R. (Bob) Newbolt, "Memories of Bowchase Ranch," *Alberta History* 32, no. 4 (Autumn 1984): 4.

111 "A Big Drunk," *Macleod Gazette*, 16 February 1886.

112 Glenbow Archives, New Walrond Ranche papers, M8688-5: David Warnock to Duncan McEachran, 23 July 1900.

113 M8688-5: Warnock to McEachran, 29 January 1901.

114 There was the occasional shooting in the cattle camps (E. Hill, *The Territory: The Classic Saga of Australia's Far North*, [Sydney: Angus and Robertson], 1995), 241.

115 Harriet W. Daly, *Digging, Squatting and Pioneering Life in the Northern Territory of South Australia* (London: Sampson, Low, Marston, Searle and Riverington, 1887), 308.

116 An excellent first-hand account is Abbott and Huntington Smith, *We Pointed Them North*, 131–34.

117 Leroy V. Kelly, *The Range Men*, 75th anniversary ed. (Calgary: Glenbow-Alberta Institute, 1988), 174.

118 Henry Ieuch, Charles (Red) Nelson, Frank (Slim, or Left Handed) Jones (Elofson, *Frontier Cattle Ranching*, 90).

119 "Stock News," *Macleod Gazette*, 23 June 1900.

120 "Sale of Unbranded and Wild Cattle," *Northern Territory Times*, 7 December 1900.

121 "Country Notes," *Northern Territory Times*, 11 December 1886.

122 Borroloola Police Station Letter Book: C. Power to P. Foelsche, 22 May 1888.

123 Warren M. Elofson, *Cowboys, Gentlemen and Cattle Thieves: Ranching on the Western Frontier* (Montreal and Kingston: McGill-Queen's University Press, 2000), 3, 113–14.

124 Borroloola Police Station Letter Book: C. Power to P. Foelsche, 28 February 1889.

125 "The Squatter's Troubles," *Northern Territory Times*, 25 December 1896; see also "Expert Opinion of the Wandi

Goldfield and Other Parts," *Northern Territory Times*, 29 May 1896.

126 Ibid.

127 Northern Territory Archives Service, NTRS 298: Writings of H.E. Giles – Springvale Station, 43.

128 Borroloola Police Station Letter Book: C. Power to Lieutenant Constable McGrath, 15 October 1896.

129 Kelly, *The Range Men*, 168. For other such incidents in Canada, see Canada, *Sessional Papers* 41, no. 11 (1906/07), n. 28 (North-West Mounted Police Annual Reports), 63: Report for K division, 1 October 1906.

130 Borroloola Police Station Letter Book: C. Power to Lieutenant Constable McGrath, 15 October 1896, 44.

131 Goldsbrough, Mort and Company papers, National Archives, Canberra, GMRBV/4, 5.

132 Costello, *Life of John Costello*, 130–31.

133 New Walrond Ranche papers, M8688–3: Warnock to McEachran, 8 August 1894.

134 M8688-5: McEachran to Watson, 21 June 1898.

135 Kelly, *The Range Men*, 60–62.

136 Elofson, *Frontier Cattle Ranching*, 61, 88–89, 148.

137 Wilson, "A Force Apart," uses the court records and comes to the conclusion that the Northern Territory was relatively law-abiding (174).

6 PRODUCING "FATS": THE CANADIAN WEST

1 Cox continued: "all these features were not without effect on our supply of native cattle . . . And what was the result of this? Simply that the business was overdone, and the end was what invariably follows over production": *Historical and Biographical Record of the Cattle Industry and the Cattlemen of Texas and Adjacent Territory* (St. Louis, MO: Woodward and Tiernan Printing Co., 1895), 140.

2 See L. Fitch, B. Adams, P. Ag, and K. O'Shaughnessy, *Caring for the Green Zone: Riparian Areas and Grazing Management*, new 3rd ed., http://www.cowsandfish.org/riparian/caring.html, 22; see also Geoff Cunfer, *On the Great Plains: Agriculture and the Environment* (College Station: Texas A&M University Press, 2005), 67.

3 See C. White, *Revolution on the Range: The Rise of a New Ranch in the American West* (Washington: Island Press, 2008), 10.

4 Fitch et al., *Caring for the Green Zone*, 33.

5 "Litter" refers to the organic matter in the form of dead leaves and stems that coat the earth, in this case acting like a sponge both absorbing and holding moisture.

6 See, for instance, "Industrial Activity in Foothills Fescue

Grasslands – Guidelines for Minimizing Surface Disturbance" (Alberta Sustainable Resource Development, Lands Division, March 2010), http://esrd.alberta.ca/lands-forests/grazing-range-management/documents/Grassland-MinimizingSurface Disturbance-2010A.pdf.

7   Warren M. Elofson, *Somebody Else's Money: The Walrond Ranch Story, 1883–1907* (Calgary: University of Calgary Press, 2009), 113 – 39.

8   See, for instance, "Holistic Cow! Why ranchers are going green," www.albertaviews.ab.ca/issues/2003/julaug03/julaug03cow.pdf; "Holistic Management International," http://www.holistic management.org/.

9   Cunfer, *On the Great Plains*, 66–67.

10 See Warren M. Elofson, *Somebody Else's Money: The Walrond Ranch Story, 1883–1907* (Calgary: University of Calgary Press, 2009), 116–38. Except where otherwise noted, the information for the Walrond ranch comes from this source.

11 Terry G. Jordan-Bychkov, *North American Cattle-Ranching Frontiers: Origins, Diffusion, and Differentiation* (Albuquerque: University of New Mexico Press, 1993), 239; R.H. Fletcher, *Free Grass to Fences:*

The Montana Cattle Range Story (New York: University Publishing Corporation, 1960), 87; Leroy V. Kelly, *The Range Men*, 75th anniversary ed. (Calgary: Glenbow-Alberta Institute, 1988), 191; Warren M. Elofson, *Frontier Cattle Ranching in the Land and Times of Charlie Russell* (Montreal: McGill-Queen's University Press, 2004), 135–41.

12 James Cox, *Historical and Biographical Record of the Cattle Industry and the Cattlemen of Texas and Adjacent Territory* (St. Louis, MO: Woodward and Tiernan Printing Co., 1895), 153.

13 Cox, *Historical and Biographical Record of the Cattle Industry*, 140.

14 Kelly, *The Range Men*, 191.

15 Duncan McEachran, *A Journey Over the Plains: From Fort Benton to Bow River and Back* (Montreal: n.p., 1881), 23.

16 They appear monthly in New Walrond Ranche papers in the Glenbow Archives, M8688-3.

17 M8688-4: David Warnock to Duncan McEachran, 9 November 1896.

18 M8688-4: Warnock to McEachran, 20 April 1897.

19 Each year the pattern was about the same at each reserve.

20 Prior to the 1897 sale to Burns, the ranch sold about a thousand each year to the Peigan and Blood bands. In 1898 the company stopped supplying the Indians and sold principally to

Burns or other cattle buyers or else shipped directly to Britain in the fall of each year.

21 The major operational expenses, then, for labour, hay accumulated on the ranch, and custom feeding was $17,550. That is not including the annual dividend or the managerial wages paid to Duncan McEachran himself (Elofson, *Somebody Else's Money*, 105–12).

22 Berry W. Adams, Richard Ehlert, Darlene Moisey, and Ron L. McNeil, *Range Plant Communities and Range Health Assessment Guidelines for the Foothills Fescue Natural Subregion of Alberta, Foothills Fescue Range Plant Community Guide, Alberta* (Lethbridge: Alberta Sustainable Resource Development, 2005), vi, http://esrd.alberta.ca/lands-forests/grazing-range-management/documents/FoothillsFescueSubregionAssessmentGuidelines.pdf.

23 Kelly, *The Range Men*, 151. For the Walrond sales, see M8688-4: "Memo: of sale and agreement between the Walrond Ranche Ltd. and P. Burns and Coy, done in duplicate this the 26th day of June, 1897."

24 In 1898 Duncan McEachran announced that to that point the ranch had paid at least a 5 percent dividend every year since 1883 (M8688-1:

prospectus of the New Walrond Ranche Company, 26 February 1898). We know as well that this convention continued in later years (M8688-2: report of The New Walrond Ranche Company, for the year ending 31 December, 1903; M8688-9: C.W. Buchanan to [Walrond Shareholders], 6 April 1923).

25 M8688-3: Duncan McEachran to Boyle, Campbell, Burton and Coy, 10 July 1887.

26 M8688-3: Duncan McEachran to Boyle, Campbell, Burton and Coy, 10 July 1887.

27 Walrond count books (M8688-37).

28 It was almost certainly the overall drop in value of the Walrond cattle inventory that persuaded the directors to dissolve the Walrond Cattle Ranche Limited and put its assets into the Walrond Ranche Limited, with much lower shareholder value. Shares in the original company had been worth 2,500 pounds sterling, or $12,500. Each of these was now redeemable for 155 shares in the new company worth 50 dollars apiece, or $7,750 (London, National Archives, Walrond Ranche Company papers, BT 31/3925: Memorandum of Agreement, 14 December 1887).

29 The count books are in M8688-37. The numbers in actual counts were invariably

lower than those in the "book count," which was based on numbers bought, those sold, those born, and *estimates* of numbers that had died.

30 Warren M. Elofson, *Cowboys, Gentlemen and Cattle Thieves: Ranching on the Western Frontier* (Montreal and Kingston: McGill-Queen's University Press, 2000), 81–82.

31 Throughout the early to mid-1890s the horse manager David Warnock reported on the devastation wolves were causing to both cattle and horses; on 12 November 1894 he told McEachran that "we have finished rounding-up counting and marking the horses and I am sorry to inform you that we have only gathered forty nine yearlings out of one hundred and one turned out in May last. Myself and Rennie have thoroughly ridden all the surrounding country within a radius of 20 miles from the ranche and are satisfied that we have found all that are alive . . . The number of wolves in this part of the range at present is I think unprecedented, and they are following the foals and yearlings right into the pastures" (M8688-3).

32 M8688-1: prospectus for the New Walrond Ranche Company, 26 February 1898.

33 M8688-3: David Warnock memo, 5 October 1895.

34 M8688-1. In his prospectus he wrote, "the cattle are estimated to number 12,311, but there has not been any actual count since 1890, and although 5 per cent has been written off annually for casualties, this has been a mere estimate, and may or may not be correct."

35 M8688-4: Warnock to McEachran, 20 September 1897.

36 M8688-4: Warnock to McEachran, 2 December 1897. The figure of 9,000 was used to calculate "book numbers" from that point on. In 1898 Warnock told McEachran that "after deducting numbers sold and adding purchases and Fall branding the books show a total of 7,842" (M8688-5: 26 November 1898).

37 M8688-5: Warnock to McEachran, 31 August 1901. The second of the two letters differs from the first largely only in the more detailed explanation of steer numbers. Therefore it is reasonable to assume that Warnock only sent that letter.

38 M8688-29.

39 The people still holding shares in the company at that time were paid back $7.29 for each of their 5041 shares (M8688-9: J.G. Ross to Sir, Madam, 29 April 1908). The contract is in M8688-29. The original price per share had been ten pounds or about fifty dollars.

40 Indeed, there were probably fewer than 2,000 cattle. 2,000 × $26.00 = $52,000.00. $52,000.00 − $36,748.89 = $15,251.11. It seems very unlikely that the ranch would have owed over $15,000.00 for operational expenses. Its two major operating costs – labour and feed – were less than $20,000.00 *annually* (Elofson, *Somebody Else's Money*, 110).

41 M8688-9: J.G. Ross to Sir, Madam, 29 April 1908; M8688-8: McEachran to Walrond, 21 October 1905; M8688-2: report of the New Walrond Ranche Company, for the year ending 31 December, 1903.

42 "Local Notes," *Macleod Gazette*, 7 June 1895.

43 American Heritage Center Archives, Laramie, Frewen papers, MC9529, 3–6: Moreton Frewen to Clare Frewen, 12 September 1884; Elofson, *Frontier Cattle Ranching*, 151–53.

44 "Not in the Air Yet," *Lethbridge Herald*, 22 February 1949; "Author's Book on Famous Ranch Earns Great Community Support," *Medicine Hat News*, 7 November 2008.

45 Elofson, *Frontier Cattle Ranching*, 157.

46 Simon M. Evans, *The Bar U and Canadian Ranching History* (Calgary: University of Calgary Press, 2004), 197.

47 Cox, *Historical and Biographical Record of the Cattle Industry*, 152–53.

48 J.G. Rutherford, *The Cattle Trade in Western Canada*, quoted in Kelly, *The Range Men*, 200.

49 Leland Turner, "Grassland Frontiers: Beef Cattle Agriculture in Queensland and Texas" (PhD diss., Texas Tech University, 2008), 81.

50 Either directly or through middlemen, the most substantial of whom were Patrick Burns of Calgary and Gordon, Ironsides and Fares of Winnipeg (Elofson, *Somebody Else's Money*, 167–88).

51 "A Trip on a Cattle Boat," *Great Falls Tribune*, 4 February 1890.

52 By this time the American railways had special cattle cars with hay and water on board to get the animals from western ranges to Chicago as efficiently and painlessly as possible. Still they figured on a weight loss of 7 percent. On the Canadian railways the loss must have been at least that and for any stock continuing on across the North Atlantic the deficit was greater still.

53 Frewen papers, MC 9529-3-7: Moreton Frewen to Sir, 16 September 1884.

54 J.G. Rutherford, *The Cattle Trade in Western Canada*, quoted in Kelly, *The Range Men*, 200, 201.

55   Max Foran, *Trails and Trials: Markets and Land Use in Alberta Beef Cattle Industry, 1881–1948* (Calgary: University of Calgary Press, 2003), 43; Glenbow Archives, A.E. Cross papers, M1543–470: Clay, Robinson and Company to A.E. Cross, 29 July 1907; Elofson, *Frontier Cattle Ranching*, 93–94.

56   "Yesterday's Markets," *Edinburgh Courant*, 12 September 1885.

57   "Yesterday's Markets," *Edinburgh Courant*, 18 September 1885.

58   "Yesterday's Markets," *Edinburgh Courant*, 30 October 1885.

59   Foran, *Trails and Trials*, 24–25.

7 PRODUCING "FATS": THE NORTHERN TERRITORY

1   "The S.A. Premier and the Territory," *Northern Territory Times*, 21 October 1904.

2   Gordon Buchanan, *Packhorse and Waterhole*, 2nd ed. (Sydney: Angus and Robertson, 1934), 112.

3   South Australia State Library, Adelaide, Alfred Giles papers, 1389/1: Diary, 26 January 1882, "Cattle at Delamere doing very well but not fattening so quickly as I thought they would – neither did the horses fatten." Giles attributed this to the myriad of flies, which "give them no rest night or day." 2 July 1882,

"Rode up to the telegraph station to send telegram to Pickford," the butcher in Palmerston, he wrote in his diary. The next day he "cut out and sent 30 heavies and 20 lights."

4   Giles Diary: 4 November 1882.

5   Giles Diary: 13 November 1882.

6   Giles Diary: 26 January 1882.

7   National Archives, Canberra, Goldsbrough Mort and Company papers, 2/872: "Letters Received from H.W.H Stevens, Port Darwin 1877–91."

8   He proceeded to award the contract to MacIlwraith, McEachern and Company.

9   F.H. Bauer, *Historical Geography of White Settlement in Part of Northern Australia 2*, "The Katherine Darwin Region" (Canberra: Commonwealth Scientific and Industrial Research Organization, 1964), 136–42; National Archives, Canberra, Goldsbrough, Mort and Company papers, GMC 2/872: Memorandum titled "*Singapore shipment of bullocks*" states that "during months December 1892 and February, March, April, May, June 1893, the returns from Singapore sent by Mr. K.A. Stevens show that during these months 857 bullocks were killed or disposed of. 97 died, mostly from red water. 954 realized 36,189.06 dollars . . .

almost 37.93 dollars per head. Allowing 38 [Singaporean] dollars per head at 2 [shillings] 9 [pence] per dollar equals about 5 [pounds] 4 [shillings] and 6 [pence] per head. Those cattle were mostly purchased at 3 [pounds] 10 [shillings] each and with steam freight of not less than 2 [pounds] 10 [shillings] the cost landed at Singapore will be 6 [pounds] or a loss of 15 [shillings] 6 [pence] per head independent of charges of all sorts in Singapore."

10 GMC 2/874-876: January stock returns 1893, signed in Singapore by K.A. Stevens.

11 January stock returns 1893.

12 From 1 to 15 January 1893 the average weight of another fifty-one bullocks was a mere "367 lbs.," and from 15 to 31 January 1893 fifty-one bullocks weighed "479 lbs" (GMC 2/874-876).

13 GMC 2/878B: "Stock Returns for the Month of May 1893 at the North Australian Butcher Company, Singapore."

14 GMC 2/872: Thomas Maldrum to R.M. Watson, 27 October 1897.

15 GMC 2/872: Maldrum to Watson, 27 October 1897.

16 GMC 2/872: Maldrum to J. Davis, 27 November 1897.

17 GMC 2/872: memorandum titled "Goldsbrough, Mort and Company Ltd. Letters Received from H.W.H.

Stevens, Port Darwin, 1877–1897," 2.

18 GMC, GMRBV/4, 6: "This transcript is probably part of the evidence given to the 1895 Royal Commission into N.T. affairs conducted by SA govt."

19 GMC, GMRBV/4, 6.

20 In his letter of 27 October, Maldrum told Watson that those were the numbers they needed.

21 Australia, *The Northern Territory Beef Cattle Industry: An Economic Survey, 1962–63 to 1964–65* (Melbourne: Commonwealth Scientific and Industrial Research Organization, 1968), 28. However, "generally speaking," the report reads, "the amount of supplementary feeding undertaken was negligible."

22 "Northern Territory Meat Trade," *Western Mail*, 10 July 1909. This article estimated the distance from Victoria River Downs to Pine Creek at "about 320 miles."

23 GMRBV/4, 6.

24 GMRBV/4, 6.

25 F.A.C. Bishop, *Report on an Inspection of the Pastoral Holdings, Stock Routes, Bores and Dips on the Barkly Tableland, Northern Territory* (Melbourne: Government Printer, 1923), 19.

26 For the extensive nature of the industry and lack of control over breeding, see Australia, *The Northern Territory Beef Cattle Industry*, 19–31.

27 Chapter 10.

28 "Rural Industries," *The Register*, 13 May 1905; "Pastoral Intelligence," *The Sydney Morning Herald*, 17 October 1895; "Stock Items," *The Northern Miner*, 25 April 1908; "Stock Movements," *The Register*, 21 July 1908; "Stock Movements," *Chronicle*, 5 September 1908. The south was the highly urbanized portion of Australia, the states of South Australia (of which Adelaide was and is the capital), New South Wales (Sydney), and Victoria (Melbourne).

29 "Stock Movements and State of the Country," *The Queenslander*, 20 November 1886.

30 Between 1891 and 1902 overall, Australian pastoralists reduced their herds by 50 percent. Queenslanders lost 4.5 million of their seven million cattle (Sheena Coupe, ed., *Frontier Country: Australia's Outback Heritage*, vol. 1 [Willoughby, NSW: Weldon Russell, 1989], 168; Stuart McIntyre, *A Concise History of Australia* [Cambridge: Cambridge University Press, 1999], 23–27).

31 "Stock Items," *Northern Territory Times*, 24 August 1906. In the same year, some 700 were trailed from the Lake Nash area to Adelaide. By the mid-1890s virtually all the animals were taking that route to market.

32 "Rural Industries," *The Register*, 15 May 1905; "Rural Industries," *The Register*, 13 April 1908; "Stock Movements," *Chronicle*, 11 June 1910; "Stock Movements," *The Advertiser*, 14 June 1910; "Cattle for Adelaide," *The Advertiser*, 29 October 1910.

33 "Pastoral Intelligencer," *The Sydney Morning Herald*, 17 October 1895; "Stock Movements," *The Register*, 21 July 1906; "Stock Items," *The Northern Miner*, 25 April 1908; "Stock Movements," *Chronicle*, 11 June 1910; "Stock Movements," *The Advertiser*, 14 June 1910; "Stock Movements," *The Advertiser*, 29 October 1910.

34 "A Long Droving Trip," *Northern Territory Times*, 25 January 1907.

35 Ibid.

8 THE HORSE TRADE

1 Northern Territory Archives Service, South Australian Government and Administrators Reports, "Government Resident's Half-Yearly Report on Northern Territory to June 30th, 1886."

2 Keith R. Binney, *Horsemen of the First Frontier (1788–1900) and the Serpent's Legacy* (Neutral Bay: Volcanic Publications, 2005), xv: "In 1788, the First Fleet, of eleven ships brought

out nine horses from the Cape of Good Hope, English horses having perished on the perilous sea journey. Subsequent ships also brought out Cape horses, such as the Britannia, which landed in 1795 with thirty-three horses. English horses also began arriving safely, the influential thoroughbred stallion, Rockingham, was brought out in 1799. About this time, the Governor of New South Wales asked for more heavy horses, specifying Scottish Clydesdales. Timor ponies were shipped over from northern Islands. Increasing demand for saddle and workhorses led to the migration of the best of old English breeds, which combined with the Cape horses and the Timor pony, went into the melting pot that produced a unique Australian horse, the Waler. The notable English breeds were Thoroughbred, Clydesdale, Suffolk Punch, Cleveland Bay, Lincolnshire Trotter, Norfolk Roadster, Yorkshire Coacher, Hackney, Arab and Percheron, which although a French breed, had its own English studbook, including Shire, and native British ponies." An important progenitor of the Waler was the Timor Pony, which was brought to Australia early and recognized for its hardiness, stamina, and agility. Wild herds of these ponies continue

to survive on the Coburg Peninsula.

3 Fiona Carruthers, *The Horse in Australia* (Sydney: Random House, 2008), 59–79, 259–85.

4 "Horse," http://www.feral.org.au/pest-species/horse/.

5 Binney, *Horsemen of the First Frontier*, xv–xxviii; Carruthers, *The Horse in Australia*, 59–79.

6 "Whoas, Wild Horses of Alberta Society," http://northernhorse.com/wildhorses/.

7 "Alberta has too many wild horses, forester says," http://www.cbc.ca/news/technology/story/2011/08/04/calgary-wild-horses-forestry.html.

8 Glenbow Archives, New Walrond Ranche papers, M8688-3: McEachran to Boyle, Campbell, Burton and Co., 10 July 1887.

9 M8688-3: Warnock memo, [November 1893]; [2 July] 1894.

10 M8688-3: Warnock to McEachran, 19 September 1894.

11 The ranch kept Native "wolfers" at work poisoning and trapping but in 1896, when McEachran made the decision to quit the horse business, significant eradication had still not been achieved (M8688-4: Warnock to McEachran, 18 April 1896).

12 M8688-3: 12 November 1894.

13 M8688-3: Warnock to McEachran, 12 November 1894.

14 M8688-3: Warnock to McEachran, 12 November 1894.

15 M8688-3: Warnock to J.G. Ross, 16 May 1894.

16 M8688-3: J.F. Scott to McEachran, 3 August 1892.

17 M8688-3: J.W. Mathison memo, 7 November 1888.

18 M8688-3: Warnock to McEachran, 23 January 1894.

19 M8688-4: Warnock to McEachran, 25 March 1895.

20 M8688-4: Warnock to McEachran, 25 March 1895.

21 M8688-3: Warnock to Major Bell, 6 April 1894.

22 M8688-3: Warnock to J.G. Ross, 16 May 1894.

23 M8688-3: Warnock to McEachran, 2 February 1894.

24 M8688-3: Warnock to McEachran, 14 November 1894.

25 M8688-4: Warnock to McEachran, 22 April 1895.

26 M8688-4: Warnock to McEachran, 2 April 1895.

27 M8688-4 Warnock to J.G. Ross, 11 November 1895.

28 M8688-4: Warnock to McEachran, 15 April 1895.

29 M8688-3: David Warnock to McEachran, 13 November 1893. "We have all WR. Horses on the North side of the river and I have instructed Murray to" use "the greatest vigilance in preventing Coy. Horses from going south and strange horses from coming north of the river."

30 M8688-3: Mathison memo, 27 April 1889; M8688-4: Warnock to McEachran, 15 April 1895.

31 In early 1898 McEachran decided to liquidate the Walrond Ranche Company and put its assets into the New Walrond Ranche Company Limited. To further the latter objective, he composed a prospectus that he hoped would attract investors (M8688-1: "The New Walrond Ranche Company, Limited," 26 February 1898). In that document he announced that the horse business had not paid financially, and he promised that the new company would have nothing further to do with it. He indicated that its downfall had principally been "competition from electric motors." Evidence from the ranch correspondence strongly suggests that this was only one of the problems.

32 M8688-1: Warnock memo, 2 May 1896; Warnock memo, 25 July [1896]; Warnock memo, 1 August 1896. In all three cases the vast majority of the fifty-two head are listed as "aged." For the rest, see M8688-1: Warnock memo, August 1896; Warnock memo, 17 October 1896; Warnock memo, 28 November 1896.

33 M8688-1: "Memo of sale and agreement between the Walrond Ranche (Ltd) and Messrs W.H. Fares and P.

Burns re the draught horses the property of the Ranch Company," 26 June 1897.

34 M8688-1: Warnock reported to McEachran on 18 April 1896 that he had bought 15 saddle horses "well broken and sound at $40."

35 Frederick Ings, *Before the Fences (tales from the Midway Ranch): Autobiography*, ed. J. Davis (Calgary: McAra Printing, 1980), 78.

36 Simon M. Evans, *The Bar U and Canadian Ranching History* (Calgary: University of Calgary Press, 2004), 149–70.

37 Glenbow Archives, A.E. Cross papers, M8780-112: Cross to A.R. Springett, 10 November 1902.

38 He once told a neighbour that horses "do well in almost every part of this district, but require careful management and plenty of experience with a natural gift of looking after them, in order to make them a success" (M8780: Cross to A.R. Springett, 10 November 1902).

39 M8780-112: Cross to Mr. Hodson, November 1900. The emphasis of the word "local" is the author's alteration.

40 Warren M. Elofson, *Cowboys, Gentlemen and Cattle Thieves: Ranching on the Western Frontier* (Montreal and Kingston: McGill-Queen's University Press, 2000), 27–29, 48–49, 147. Some western breeders, who closely monitored the local market, also mated their Cayuse mares with Percheron or even Clyde or Shire stallions to give them still greater size and strength.

41 "Horses for South Africa," *Macleod Gazette*, 21 February 1902.

42 Ings, *Before the Fences*, 78; Leroy V. Kelly, *The Range Men*, 75th anniversary ed. (Calgary: Glenbow-Alberta Institute, 1988), 94, 109.

43 The positive assessments kept coming throughout the frontier period. As late as 1908, for instance, a newspaper editor offered the opinion that "the tablelands in the Northern Territory, where horses thrive 'on nothing a year,' are the natural breeding ground for Indian remounts. Not only are animals reared in that part of the country as 'tough as nails,' but the similarity of the climate to that of north west India gives to Australian-bred horses a decided advantage over those imported from Europe or North America" ("Horse Breeding," *The Register*, 6 August 1908).

44 State Library of South Australia, Adelaide, Alfred Giles papers, 1389/1: Diary, 26 January 1882.

45 State Library of South Australia, Adelaide, Alfred Giles papers, 1389/2: Giles, "The First Pastoral Settlement

in the Northern Territory compiled principally for his own experiences as an overlander and pioneer pastoralist with special references to the founding of the Springvale, Delamere, Elsey and Newcastle Waters runs, 1870–1895 with extracts from his diary 1879–1895," 149.

46 "The Northern Territory. Half-Yearly Report by Government Resident," *South Australian Register*, 4 October 1886.

47 The outfit brought in as many horses as cattle ("The Northern Territory. Half-Yearly Report by Government Resident").

48 "The Condition of our Cattle Industry," *South Australian Register*, 15 September 1893.

49 Jill Bowen, *Kidman: The Forgotten King* (Sydney: Harper Collins, 2007), 77–78.

50 National Archives, Canberra, NT 13/9606–13/11631: Commonwealth of Australia, "Department of External Affairs, File of Papers, Subject: Batchelor Demonstration Farm Report on results of operations conducted at Darwin, 19 July 1913," 28–29.

51 Ross Duncan, *The Northern Territory Pastoral Industry, 1863–1910* (Melbourne: Melbourne University Press, 1967), 160.

52 "Horsing the Guns," *The Register*, 11 March 1911.

53 National Archives, Canberra, NT, 011631: Commonwealth

of Australia, "Report of the Department of Agriculture for year ending December 31" (1912), 60.

54 "Northern Territory," *The Argus*, 19 September 1913.

55 State Library of South Australia, Adelaide, Lewis family papers, PRG 247/10/1: John Lewis to H. Grainger, 23 September 1908; "Rockhampton, Tuesday, February 6, 1900, The Horse Supply," *Morning Chronicle*, 6 February 1900; "Snaring Brumbies, Wild Horses of the Northern Territory," *The Register*, 19 December 1906.

56 "Department of External Affairs, File of Papers, Subject: Batchelor Demonstration Farm," 28–29.

57 Duncan, *The Northern Territory Pastoral Industry*, 160.

58 All types of cattle in all of Alberta and Assiniboia, Simon M. Evans, "Stocking the Canadian Range," *Alberta History* 26, no. 3 (Summer 1978): 1; Canada, *Fourth Census*, 1901, vol. 2, 52 –53.

59 "Are Horses Deteriorating in Australia?" *The Brisbaine Courier*, 20 October 1877; "Raising Horses in Australia," *The Daily News*, 13 July 1889; "Draught Horses in Australia," *Western Star and Roma Advertiser*, 5 November 1910.

60 "Horses Required in Australia," *Rockhampton Bulletin*, 5 September 1873.

61 "Horse-breeding in Australia," *Northern Territory Times*, 22 November 1884. "From the returns for the last ten years I find that the numbers of horses have increased or otherwise in the various colonies as follows: In South Australia, in 1873–4, the number of horses was 87,451; in 1882–3, 162,400. During the same time in Victoria the number increased from 180,342 to 280,874; in Queens-land from 99,243 to 229,124; in New Zealand from 99,859 to 161,736; whilst in New South Wales the number decreased from 328,014 to 326,964."

62 A recent PhD dissertation explores the development of the cattle industry in Queensland and Texas (Leland Turner, "Grassland Frontiers: Beef Cattle Agriculture in Queensland and Texas," Texas Tech University, 2008).

63 "The Horse Supply," *Morning Bulletin*, 6 February 1900; see also "Draught Horses in Australia," *Western Star and Roma Advertiser*, 5 November 1910.

64 Jeannie Gunn, *We of the Never-Never*, 10th ed. (2003), 75, http://www.gutenberg.org/ebooks/4699.

65 Gunn, *We of the Never-Never*, 200.

66 "A New Disease in Horses," *The Queenslander*, 25 February 1882; "The Resources of Northern Territory of South Australia," *South Australian Register*, 3 May 1882; "The Northern Territory," *Warwick Examiner and Times*, 22 May 1912; "Red Gulf Grass," *The Sydney Morning Herald*, 14 August 1912; "Buffel Grass Shows Much Promise," *The Central Queensland Herald*, 27 November 1952.

67 Michael J. Costello, *Life of John Costello, Being the Adventures of a Pioneer, Pastoralist and Explorer in Queensland and the Northern Territory* (Sydney: Dymock's Book Arcade, 1930), 196–98.

9 DIVERSIFICATION IN WESTERN CANADA: THE TRIUMPH OF THE FAMILY RANCH/FARM

1 Geoff Cunfer makes this point regarding the American Great Plains (*On the Great Plains: Agriculture and the Environment* [College Station: Texas A&M University Press, 2005], 69–112).

2 Warren M. Elofson, *Cowboys, Gentlemen and Cattle Thieves: Ranching on the Western Frontier* (Montreal and Kingston: McGill-Queen's University Press, 2000), 18–19.

3 This is assuming that the cow would have had to be fed during the worst 100 days of weather and the steer the worst 150 days to keep it at least maintaining – but, hopefully, gaining – weight. The cows

would have needed about 20 pounds of dry hay a day and the steers, depending on age and size, would average about 20 pounds.

4 This included the yearling heifers from previous calf crops that were bred to replace older or poorer cows as they were sold off.

5 1.5 × 8,500.

6 It can be assumed that had the Walrond put up all its own hay without contract the costs would have been very close to the same. The management would have had to hire many more men, purchase a great array of haying, hauling, and stacking equipment, and provide housing and a food supply for the men.

7 With horse-drawn equipment one man could put up about 60 tons of hay.

8 There were two waves of settlement: the first started in the 1890s and brought farmer/ranchers to the area, many of whom took 160-acre homesteads supplemented by free range or small grazing leases. It was the second wave, beginning in the early years of the twentieth century, that brought homesteaders, most of whom initially settled on 160-acre parcels, which they later doubled through pre-emption. This wave eventually produced modern density levels in the countryside but, of course, not

in the urban centres (Elofson, *Cowboys, Gentlemen and Cattle Thieves*, xviii, 149).

9 See Wallace Stegner, *Wolf Willow: A History, a Story, and a Memory of the Last Plains Frontier* (New York: Penguin Books, 1955), 137. "The net effect . . . was to make stock farmers out of ranchers. Almost as suddenly as the disappearance of the buffalo, it changed the way of life of the region."

10 A section is 640 acres, a quarter section is 160 acres.

11 H.F. Lawrence, "Early Days in the Chinook Belt," *Alberta Historical Review* 13, no. 1 (Winter 1965): 11.

12 Pincher Creek Historical Society, *Prairie Grass to Mountain Pass* (Pincher Creek, AB: Pincher Creek Historical Society, 1974), 128.

13 Canada, *Sessional Papers* 22, no. 13 (1889), nn. 17, 20: Annual Report of the Commissioner, 13 December 1888.

14 Glenbow Archives, Mrs. Charles Inderwick, Diary and Personal Letters from the North Fork Ranch, M376: letter of 13 May 1884, 24.

15 "All Over the Range," *Macleod Gazette*, 4 August 1885.

16 Canada, *Sessional Papers* 42, no. 14 (1907–8), n. 28, 56: Annual Report for D Division, 1 November 1907.

17 Clay Chattaway and his family operate the Bar S ranch, which Rod Macleay bought in

1919; see Clay Chattaway and Warren Elofson, *The Rocking P Gazette in Canadian Ranching History*, https://ucalgary.ca/rocking-p-gazette/.

18 Bar S Ranch, Chattaway Notes, 30 October 2013, "Chattaway Section 2 cleaning."

19 Elofson, *Cowboys, Gentlemen and Cattle Thieves*, 133–49.

20 "Local and General," *Pincher Creek Echo*, 10 May 1904.

21 "Mange," *Pincher Creek Echo*, 24 May 1904.

22 See Warren M. Elofson, *Frontier Cattle Ranching in the Land and Times of Charlie Russell* (Montreal and Kingston: McGill-Queen's University Press, 2004), 159–74.

23 Canada, *Sessional Papers* 28, no. 9 (1895), nn. 13, 26.

24 Canada, *Sessional Papers* 33, no. 12 (1899), nn. 15, 19: Report of the Commissioner, 20 December 1898.

25 Elofson, *Frontier Cattle Ranching*, 159–74.

26 Fred Ings of Trails End Ranch on the east side of the Porcupine Hills was one such operator. Monica and Bill Hopkins near Millarville and Claude Gardiner homesteaded in the hills northwest of Macleod where they pastured their stock. They then acquired further holdings on lower elevations on which to plant and harvest crops.

27 Bar S Ranch, Nanton, AB, Macleay family papers: "John Ware Ranch."

28 Macleay family papers: "remarks by Clay Chattaway," 30 October 2013.

29 Glenbow Archives, Burns papers, M160-202: Riddell, Stead, Graham & Hutchison to P. Burns, April 13, 1925. At this time Macleay had 7,889 cattle, 346 horses and 51 hogs. Macleay's operation was family owned and operated, but it was one of the very biggest of that type in Alberta and Saskatchewan at the time.

30 Elofson, *Cowboys, Gentlemen and Cattle Thieves*, 27–29, 48–49, 147; Alberta, Department of Agriculture, *Annual Report*, 1913, 136. Prior to the war, the peak marketings in the Pincher Creek area were in 1906 when 683 sales were recorded (Alberta, Department of Agriculture, *Annual Report*, 1906, 77).

31 For the death rate on the big ranches in the earlier period, see Warren M. Elofson, *Somebody Else's Money: The Walrond Ranch Story, 1883–1907* (Calgary: University of Calgary Press, 2009), 17.

32 This is about what cattlemen expect to get today. It is also what I normally achieved when running my own cow/calf operation in the 1970s and 1980s.

33 A live steer weighing 1,400 lbs. at three cents per pound, which was about average in the early twentieth century.

34 Mary Neth, *Preserving the Family Farm: Women, Community, and the Foundations of Agribusiness in the Midwest, 1900-1940* (Baltimore: Johns Hopkins University Press, 1955), 17-70.

35 Teachers in 1911 were paid between $641 and $973 per annum and farm labourers got on average $421 per annum ("Canada Farm Labour Higher than Here," *New York Times*, 2 April 1911).

36 Macleay family papers: Clay Chattaway's notes, 30 October 2013.

37 Elliott West, "Families in the West," reprinted from the *Organization of American Historians Magazine of History* 9 (Fall 1994).

38 Porter family, in Pincher Creek Historical Society, *Prairie Grass to Mountain Pass*, 338.

39 Clay Chattaway's notes, 30 October 2013. A democrat was, and is, a light farm or ranch wagon with at least two seats, usually pulled by two horses. A stone boat was a flat wooden platform on skids that could be pulled by one or two horses.

40 May family, in Foothills Historical Society, *Chaps and Chinooks: A History West of Calgary* (Calgary: Foothills Historical Society, 1976), 273.

41 Clay Chattaway's notes.

42 I am indebted to Rachel Herbert for this reference and for notes 43-48 below. ("Ranching Women in Southern Alberta, 1880–1930," MA thesis, University of Calgary, 2011).

43 Pedersen family, in Pincher Creek Historical Society, *Prairie Grass to Mountain Pass*, 797.

44 Bateman family, in Foothills Historical Society, *Chaps and Chinooks*, 257.

45 Halton family, in Pincher Creek Historical Society, *Prairie Grass to Mountain Pass*, 52.

46 Halton family, in Pincher Creek Historical Society, *Prairie Grass to Mountain Pass*, 67.

47 Monica Hopkins, *Letters from a Lady Rancher* (Halifax: Formac Publishing, 1983), 37.

48 Ibid.

49 The progression is visible in the population figures. Calgary and vicinity had 43,204 males and 37,214 females in 1916. In 1911 it had 39,657 males and 25,529 females. Macleod and vicinity had 19,379 males and 14,504 females in 1916. In 1911 it had 18,213 males and 12,548 females. Maple Creek and vicinity had 28,126 males and 19,424 females in 1916. In 1911 it had 12,322 males and 7,408 females (Canada, *Census of Prairie Provinces, 1916: Population and Agriculture*, 44–127).

50 West, "Families in the West."

51 "Women Ranchers," *Calgary Herald*, 21 October 1902.

52 William H. McIntyre, *A Brief History of the McIntyre Ranch* (Lethbridge: *Lethbridge Herald*, 1948).

53 Macleay family papers.

54 Macleay family papers: "Rocking P Gazette," January 1924.

55 "Rocking P Gazette," September 1924.

56 "Rocking P Gazette," January 1924.

57 Macleay family papers; Burns papers, M160-215: "Agreement made this 27th day of July, A.D. 1928 between Roderick R. Macleay and Mrs. Laura Sturtevant Macleay and Burns Ranches Ltd."; R.R. Macleay, "Statement of Amount Re '76' Ranch," 18 October 1926; "Bill of Sale Roderick R. Macleay and Laura Sturtevant Macleay to Western Ranches Limited," 2 February 1929.

58 Macleay family papers.

59 Ibid.

60 Henry C. Klassen, "A Century of Ranching at the Rocking P and Bar S," in *Cowboys, Ranchers and the Cattle Business: Cross-Border Perspectives on Ranching History*, eds. Sarah Carter, Simon Evans, and Bill Yeo (Calgary: University of Calgary Press, 2000), 112, 113.

61 Quoted in Leroy V. Kelly, *The Range Men*, 75th anniversary ed. (Calgary: Glenbow-Alberta Institute, 1988), 197–98.

62 *The Pincher Creek Echo*, 19 January 1911. The editor wrote: "In this district we should not complain of full harvests and the cowboy having to turn his lariat into a hay fork that is what we want and what makes for genuine prosperity."

63 In 1922 the United Grain Growers Ltd. set up a co-operative cattle export pool to Great Britain. This was designed to provide a new market for Canadian cattle, to share risk, and to ensure a steady stream of cows to mitigate fluctuations in British prices, which were notoriously unstable (Macleay family papers: Letter to Roderick Macleay from the United Grain Growers Ltd., 1922). In 1931 Roderick Macleay took a chance on the British market since the Canadian market was very poor, and in 1933, 53,000 Canadian cattle were marketed in England; however, as the Depression dwindled this market dwindled (Macleay family papers: "John Ware Ranch," handwritten notes [compiled history, date unknown]).

64 Ended with the 1995 Western Grain Transition Payment Program. For marketing generally, see Max Foran, *Trails and Trials: Markets and Land Use in the Alberta Beef Cattle Industry, 1881–1918* (Calgary: University of Calgary Press, 2003).

10 THE TEXAS SYSTEM AT HOME IN NORTHERN AUSTRALIA

1   As against less than 10,000 years for most soils in Europe, Asia, North America, and New Zealand, which have been formed from recent mountain building or glacial scouring of the land.

2   "A Northern Territory Policy; Pastoral and Agricultural," *Northern Territory Times*, 10 August 1989.

3   "Christmas," *Northern Territory Times,* 24 December 1881.

4   State Library of South Australia, Adelaide, Lewis family papers, PRG 247/10/1: [John Lewis] to H. Grainger, 23 September 1908.

5   "Current Topics," *Chronicle*, 5 October 1907.

6   "Kapunda Horse Sale, a Capital Start, Indian Buyers Busy," *The Register*, 29 September 1909; "Pastoral Items," *The Northern Miner*, 19 October 1908.

7   "Horsing the Guns," *The Register*, 11 March 1911.

8   "To The Editor," *Northern Territory Times*, 7 July 1883.

9   Northern Territory Archives Service, South Australian Government and Administrators Reports, "Government Resident's Report on Northern Territory for the Year 1891," statement by J.S. Little at Austral Downs.

10 R.A. Perry, *Pasture Lands of the Northern Territory, Australia* (Melbourne: Commonwealth and Industrial Research Organization, 1960), 21.

11 Australia, *The Northern Territory Beef Cattle Industry: An Economic Survey, 1962–63 to 1964-65* (Melbourne: Commonwealth Scientific and Industrial Research Organization, 1968), 20–50.

12 Ibid.

13 Ibid., 26.

14 Ibid., 27

15 Ibid., 26.

16 Ibid., 25.

17 Ibid., 27.

18 Ibid., 27–28.

19 Ibid., 27. The Government Resident's Report for 1890 quoted in Australia, "Report of Preliminary Scientific Expedition to the Northern Territory," *Bulletin of the Northern Territory* 1 (Melbourne: Department of External Affairs, March 1912): 32, stated: "it is generally stated redwater (so-called) does not attack acclimatized or Territory-bred cattle. The chief complaint throughout is that overlanded cattle (travelling from Queensland especially) alone exhibit the symptoms of the disease, and die therefrom."

20 Australia, *The Northern Territory Beef Cattle Industry*, 27–28.

21 Present-day cattle graziers in both Queensland and the Northern Territory have interbred their British cattle with the Brahman or

Zebu species originally from Southeast Asia – particularly the Indian subcontinent – mainly because of their tolerance to extreme heat but also because they are resistant to ticks due to the thickness of their hide.

22 Australia, *The Northern Territory Beef Cattle Industry*, 29–31, 32–39.

23 F.A.C. Bishop, *Report on an Inspection of the Pastoral Holdings, Stock Routes, Bores and Dips on the Barkly Tableland, Northern Territory* (Melbourne: Government Printer, 1923), 9.

24 Northern Territory Archives Service, NTRS 636 BUC: Graeme Bucknall, "A Documented Short History of Undoolya: The First Legal Cattle Station in the Northern Territory" (National Trust of Australia, Northern Territory, 1983), 11.

25 Perry, *Pasture Lands of the Northern Territory*, 21.

26 "In contrast to the other . . . districts, the Alice Springs district is served by direct rail link to a stable market at Adelaide and this is reflected in the general efficiency and prosperity of the industry in that district. All the properties are relatively close to the rail trucking centres, which means that cattle of any age can be turned off and weight losses en route to market are relatively low. In recent years road transport from property to railhead has proved economical compared with walking and is rapidly gaining in popularity" (Perry, *Pasture Lands of the Northern Territory*, 23). Today the rail trains have been replaced by so-called "road trains"– huge trucks with up to three trailers that can haul as many as 120 bullocks at a time from station to destination.

27 "In all districts, breeders comprised at least 50% of the herd, the highest proportion being in the Alice Springs and Barkly Tableland districts where they were 57% and 60% respectively" (Australia, *The Northern Territory Beef Cattle Industry*, 23). Branding rates: at Alice Springs – 44 percent, Barkly – 40 percent, Victoria River – 40 percent (Australia, *The Northern Territory Beef Cattle Industry*, 25). "About three quarters of the turnoff from stations was steers and bullocks (older steers) the remaining one-quarter being a mixture of breeders, calves, and bulls. Purchases by the majority of the stations were usually confined to bulls for replacement purposes in the breeding herd." Average number sold in the districts in the three years: Alice Springs – 463, Barkly – 2,049, Victoria River – 2,029 (Australia, *The Northern Territory Beef Cattle Industry*, 29). "In both the Barkly Tableland and Alice

Springs Districts there is little surface water; most of the water on stations comes from bores, dams, earth tanks or wells. Bores were important on most stations but the difficulty of finding adequate underground water was marked by the large number of unsuccessful bores on some stations" (Australia, *The Northern Territory Beef Cattle Industry*, 30). Note: cattle numbers in the Alice Springs district declined from about 350,000 to 139,000 due to a long and prolonged drought (Australia, *The Northern Territory Beef Cattle Industry*, 50).

28   Australia, *The Northern Territory Beef Cattle Industry*, 24–25.

29   "While it was not possible to estimate the mortality rate for individual classes of stock, including newborn calves, estimates were obtained of mortalities in all branded cattle. The reported average mortality of the survey period ranged from 8 to 13 %" (Australia, *The Northern Territory Beef Cattle Industry*, 24).

30   National Archives, Canberra, Goldsbrough, Mort and Company papers, GMRBV/4, 6: "This Transcript is probably part of the evidence given to the 1895 Royal Commission into N.T. affairs conducted by SA govt."

31   A. Grenfell Price, *The History and Problems of the Northern Territory, Australia* (John Murtagh Macrossan Lecture, Brisbane: University of Queensland Press, 1930), 30.

32   Amanda Nettelbeck and Robert Foster, *In the Name of the Law; William Willshire and the Policing of the Australian Frontier* (Kent Town: Wakefield Press, 2007), 15–112.

33   Baldwin Spencer, "Preliminary Report on the Aboriginals of the Northern Territory," *Bulletin of the Northern Territory* 7 (Melbourne: Department of External Affairs, July 1913), 21. "The native morality is such that the disease, once contracted, is bound to be widely disseminated amongst both aboriginals and white men of low morality."

34   Spencer, "Preliminary Report," 16.

35   Spencer, "Preliminary Report," 9. "Pastoral areas, such as the Victoria River Downs, Willeroo, Messrs. Bradshaw's station, and Newcastle waters on the west of the telegraph line, and others such as Brunette, Corella, Eva Downs, the McArthur river Station, Nutwood Downs, Tanumbirini, Hodgson Downs, etc. on the east, occupy great stretches of country over which the natives roam more or less freely. A limited number of them are employed on the stations, where they are well treated, and do most useful

work, for which they receive food, clothes, tobacco etc."

36 Nettelbeck and Foster, *In the Name of the Law*, 112.

37 Australia, "Report of Preliminary Scientific Expedition to the Northern Territory," 8. "It is not too much to say, that, under existing conditions the cattle stations" in all three of the pastoral districts "could not be worked without their aid." See also Gordon Buchanan, *Packhorse and Waterhole*, 2nd ed. (Sydney: Angus and Robertson, 1934), 118.

38 Australia, "Report of Preliminary Scientific Expedition to the Northern Territory," 8.

39 Goldsbrough, Mort and Company papers, GMC 87/2/1: company account books.

40 For the numbers for the 1960s see Australia, *The Northern Territory Beef Cattle Industry*, 53.

41 Spencer, "Preliminary Report," 22.

42 "Six Years in the Territory," *Northern Argus*, 3 February 1899; "Our Black Brothers, Roper River Mission, Northern Territory, Stagnant. A 'White' Nigger," *The Sydney Morning Herald*, 26 October 1909; "The Aboriginal Past and Present," *Northern Standard*, 5 June 1934.

43 "Sketcher, Northern Territory, II," *The Queenslander*, 10 February 1917. For other accounts of the work of Aboriginal women, see also "On the Track of the Roper," *Northern Argus*, 3 February 1899; "In Dark Australia," *Northern Territory Times*, 10 June 1904.

44 Mary Durack, *Kings in Grass Castles* (London: Constable, 1959), 355–56. A "wurlie" is an Aboriginal shelter of branches and leaves.

45 Glenbow Archives, New Walrond Ranche papers, M8688-3: Bell to McEachran, 9 April 1887.

46 Thus the wages for Indian cowboys were about half those for white cowboys. The wage figures for the ranch are in M688-28.

47 Goldsbrough, Mort and Company papers, GMC 2/876/7: B. Blair to Goldsbrough, Mort and Company, 24 October 1889.

48 "The Northern Territory," *South Australian Chronicle*, 25 August 1894; "Cattle Raising on the McArthur River," *Cairns Post*, 22 February 1910; "Cattle Distributions 1912," in Griffith Taylor, *Railways and stock routes, with later additions, also shown* (Commonwealth Bulletin II), quoted in A. Grenfell Price, *The History and Problems of the Northern Territory, Australia* (Adelaide: A.M. Acott, 1931), 36.

49 Lewis family papers, PRG 247/10/1: V.V. Brown to Messers Drew and Greaves, 6 July 1906.

50 Glen McLaren and William Cooper, *Distance, Drought and Dispossession: A History of the Northern Territory Pastoral Industry* (Darwin: Northern Territory University Press, 2001), 55–56. After the Commonwealth of Australia took over the administration of the Northern Territory on 1 January 1911, new bores would be drilled and old ones repaired along all the major cattle trails.

51 Lewis family papers, PRG 247/10/1: H.J. Rose to Hon. John Lewis, 12 June 1909.

52 PRG 247/10/1: H.J. Rose to Hon. John Lewis, 12 June, 1909.

53 PRG 247/10/1: H.J. Rose to John Lewis, 21 July 1909.

54 "The Explorer," *The Queenslander*, 16 August 1924.

55 PRG 247/10/1: "Memo," 2 January 1908.

56 James Cox, *Historical and Biographical Record of the Cattle Industry and the Cattlemen of Texas and Adjacent Territory* (St. Louis, MO: Woodward and Tiernan, 1895), 85.

57 This was the cost in 1887 for rail transportation from Montana to Chicago (Cox, *Historical and Biographical Record*, 143).

58 I have not been able to find dependable cost analyses for the Canadians at that time. However, in 1930 Rod Macleay sent 58 head to Manchester. His costs per head were about $40.00 – the main difference being the CPR freight charge from Cayley in Alberta to Montreal at $15.53/head (Bar S Ranch, Nanton, AB, Macleay family papers: account of cattle sales to Great Britain).

59 The owners sometimes eschewed railway transportation because of its known failure to keep to schedules and because of the hardships it placed on the animals (Richard Maurovic, *The Meat Game: A History of the Gepps Cross Abattoir* (Kent Town: Wakefield Press, 2007, 222). Thus they were unlikely to pay much more for the service than droving charges.

60 Lewis family papers, PRG 247/10/1: Hy Grainger to John Lewis, 6 January 1906; see also PRG 247/10/1: W.T. Bache to John Lewis, 19 October 1909. Lewis would probably have put the cattle on the train at Hergott Springs, 280 miles north of Adelaide. But one can assume he was not prepared to pay much more than a shilling a mile for that.

61 Lewis family papers, PRG 247/10/1: Charles N. Turner to John Lewis, 3 July 1906 and 6 July 1906. See also Australia, *The Northern Territory Beef Cattle Industry*, 27–28; Margaret

Kowald and William Johnston, *You Can't Make it Rain: The Story of the North Australian Pastoral Company 1877–1991* (Brisbane: Boolarong Publications with North Australian Pastoral Company, 1992), 43.

62 State Library of South Australia, Adelaide, PRG 1079: "Arthur C. Aswhin's Recollections of Ralph Milner's Expedition from Kopperamanna to the Northern Territory with sheep and Horses in 1870/71 with an account of his subsequent experiences in the Northern Territory" (1927), 29.

63 Buchanan, *Packhorse and Waterhole*, 139.

64 Ibid., 65.

65 The common Asian dingo (canis lupus dingo) only gets to about 60 centimetres high and 15 kilograms. The grey wolf varies in height from 60 to 95 centimetres, and varies in weight between 25 to 38.5 kilograms, depending on the species. However, the Australian dingo is traditionally larger than the Asian dingo and the larger dingoes are of very similar size to smaller wolves.

66 Lewis family papers, PRG 247/10/1: Hy Grainger to John Lewis, 6 January 1906.

67 P.C. Thomson, "The behavioural ecology of dingoes in north-western Australia, III, Hunting and Feeding behaviour, and diet," *Wildlife Research* 19, no. 5 (1992): 531–41, doi:10.1071/WR9920531; P.C. Thomson, "The behavioural ecology of dingoes in north-western Australia, IV, Social and spatial organization, and movements," *Wildlife Research* 19, no. 5 (1992): 543–63, doi:10.1071/WR9920543; L.R. Allen and P.J.S. Fleming, "(American Sheep Industry Association, 3 May 2009), http://www.sheepusa.org/; Lee Allen, Peter Thomson, and Alan Lisle, "Pack size and prey behaviour affects prey selection and the predation of livestock by dingoes" (Australian Government, Department of Agriculture, Fisheries and Forestry, 3 May 2009).

68 Leroy V. Kelly, *The Range Men*, 75th anniversary ed. (Calgary: Glenbow-Alberta Institute, 1988), 132.

69 Canada, *Sessional Papers* 26, no. 9 (1893), n. 15, 83: Annual Report for K Division, 1 December 1892.

70 Kelly, *The Range Men*, 132.

71 Ibid., 137.

72 Glenbow Archives, Canadian Agricultural, Coal and Colonization Company papers, Stair Ranch Letterbook, M-2384, 416–17: D.H. Andrews to C. Akers, 15 March 1893.

73 Canada, *Sessional Papers* 33, no. 12 (1899), nn. 15, 19: Report

of the Commissioner, 20
December 1898.

74 Canadian Agricultural,
Coal and Colonization
Company papers, Stair Ranch
Letterbook, M-2384, 461–65:
Andrews to C. Akers, 5 June
1893.

75 Kelly, *The Range Men*, 42–43.

76 Glenbow Archives, A.E. Cross
papers, M8780-450: Selkirk
Cross to A.E. Cross, 5 June
1903.

77 Canada, *Sessional Papers* 28, no.
11 (1904), n. 28, 14: Annual
Report for A Division, 30
November 1903.

78 "Losses at Crane Lake," *Macleod
Gazette*, 13 April 1904.

79 Kelly, *The Range Men*, 191. The
McIntyre ranch, for instance,
had only 300 tons of hay for
some 9,000 cattle (William H.
McIntyre, *A Brief History of the
McIntyre Ranch* [Lethbridge:
Lethbridge Herald, 1948] 25).

80 *Fort Macleod – Our Colourful
Past: A History of the Town of
Fort Macleod from 1874 to 1924*
(Fort Macleod History Book
Committee, 1977), quoted in
Hugh A. Dempsey, *The Golden
Age of the Canadian Cowboy*
(Calgary: Fifth House, 1995),
145.

81 E.C. Abbott and H.
Huntington Smith, *We Pointed
Them North: Recollections of a
Cowpuncher*, 2nd ed. (Norman:
University of Oklahoma Press,
1955), 176.

82 Warren M. Elofson, *Cowboys,
Gentlemen and Cattle Thieves:
Ranching on the Western Frontier*
(Montreal and Kingston:
McGill-Queen's University
Press, 2000), 85.

83 Provincial Archives of Alberta,
Edmonton, 72,27/SE: Violet
LaGranduer, "Memoirs of a
Cowboy's Wife," 5.

84 Michael J. Costello, *Life of John
Costello, Being the Adventures of
a Pioneer, Pastoralist and Explorer
in Queensland and the Northern
Territory* (Sydney: Dymock's
Book Arcade, 1930), 209

85 Northern Territory
Archives Service, South
Australian Government and
Administrators Reports,
"Government Resident's
Report on Northern Territory
for the Year 1890."

86 "Central Australian cattle
stations struggle to survive,"
7 July 2006, reporter Sara
Everingham, http://www.
abc.net.au/stateline/nt/
content/2006/s1686232.htm.

87 See also "Pastoral Industry of
the Northern Territory," *South
Australian Register*, 5 April 1894.

88 "Drought relief in the red
centre," 30 March 2007,
reporter Adrienne Francis,
http://www.abc.net.au/
stateline/nt/content/2006/
s1886279.htm.

89 Leland Turner, "Grassland
Frontiers: Beef Cattle
Agriculture in Queensland and

Texas" (PhD diss., Texas Tech University, 2008), 92–95.

90 Perry, *Pasture Lands of the Northern Territory*, 24.

91 *Texas Stockman*, 17 November 1886, 3.

92 Perry generally urged more diversification (*Pasture Lands of the Northern Territory*); See also Australia, *The Northern Territory Beef Cattle Industry*, 23.

11 CONCLUSION: THE FRONTIER LEGACY

1 Northern Territory Archives Service, NTRS 636 BUC: Graeme Bucknall, "A Documented Short History of Undoolya: The First Legal Cattle Station in the Northern Territory" (National Trust of Australia, Northern Territory, 1983), 10.

2 "A Remarkable Man. The Late Mr. W.P Hayes, Sen.," *The Register*, 19 November 1913.

3 "A Life of Toil," *The Register*, 19 November 1913.

4 "Old Stock and Other Notes," *The Northern Miner*, 2 December 1905, quoted from the *Rockhampton Bulletin*.

5 Max Cartwright, *The Never Never Country: A History of the Roper River and Urapunga* (Alice Springs: M. Cartwright, 1999).

6 *Brisbane Daily Mail*, 31 October 1920, quoted in Barbara James, *No Man's Land: Women of the Northern Territory* (Sydney: Collins Australia, 1989), 238.

7 "Sketcher, Northern Territory, II," *The Queenslander*, 10 February 1917. The reporter continued: "Mrs. Rogers, as the intrepid horsewoman that she is, is very particular in her horse flesh, and is always mounted on stylish, upstanding animals with plenty of fire in them. It is told of Mrs. Rogers that there is not one stockrider on the Roper and few in the Territory that can do cutting out with such neatness and coolness as she can, and that is certainly a feather in any stockrider's cap. During the year, mostly spent in camping out, this lady, with her staff, gets over thousands of miles of country mustering."

8 Average *net* income over the three years: Alice Springs (−1,214), Barkly (21,137) Victoria (19,378) (Australia, *The Northern Territory Beef Cattle Industry: An Economic Survey, 1962–63 to 1964–65* [Melbourne: Commonwealth Scientific and Industrial Research Organization, 1968], 51). *Net* farm income is the amount available to provide a return to the operator's labour, management, and capital. This amount is obtained by adding to net cash income the interest paid and cattle inventory gain, and subtracting depreciation. The figures were: Alice Springs −4,109, Barkly 38,344, Victoria 34,193 (52).

9   The return on investment in the Alice Springs area was estimated at –3.5 percent, the Barkly 6.6 percent, and the Victoria River 4.5 percent. Few company businesses today would be satisfied with such returns.

10 Statistics Canada: http://www.statcan.gc.ca/tables-tableaux/sum-som/l01/cst01/agri119j-eng.htm.

11 http://www.statcan.gc.ca/tables-tableaux/sum-som/l01/cst01/agri119i-eng.htm.

12 For the Turner debate, see George F.G. Stanley, "Western Canada and the Frontier Thesis," *Canadian Historical Association* 19, no. 1 (1940): 105–17; Kerwin Lee Klein, "Reclaiming the 'F' Word, or Being and Becoming Postwestern," *The Pacific Historical Review* 65, no. 2 (May 1996): 179–215; Patricia Nelson Limerick, "Turnerians All: The Dream of a Helpful History in an Intelligible World," *American Historical Review* 100, no. 3 (June 1995): 697–716; Patricia Nelson Limerick, "Going West and Ending Up Global," *Western Historical Quarterly* 32, no. 1 (Spring 2001): 4–23; Slatta, Richard, "Taking Our Myths Seriously," *Journal of the West* 40, no. 3 (2001): 3–5.

13 For the best book illustrating the impact of the frontier environment on all aspects of life in a grain farming community in western Canada see Paul L. Voisey, *Vulcan: The Making of a Prairie Community* (Toronto: University of Toronto Press, 1988).

14 "Kind of Men Canada Needs," *Calgary Herald*, 1 February 1904.

15 Glenbow Archives, A.E. Cross papers, M8780-458: May 1895.

16 "The Remittance Men," *Calgary Herald*, 26 November 1904.

17 "Came out to be a Cowboy," *Calgary Herald*, 12 April 1904.

18 Leroy V. Kelly, *The Range Men*, 75th anniversary ed. (Calgary: Glenbow-Alberta Institute, 1988), 129.

19 Monica Hopkins, *Letters from a Lady Rancher* (Halifax: Formac Publishing, 1983), 23–24, letter of October 1909.

20 Glenbow Archives, New Walrond Ranche papers, M8688-5: David Warnock to Duncan McEachran, 23 January 1899.

21 Glenbow Archives, Canadian Agricultural, Coal and Colonization Company papers, Stair Ranch Letterbook, 196: D.H. Andrews to John Clay Jr., 11 May 1891.

22 "The Barr Colony," *Calgary Herald*, 25 April, 1903.

23 Cross papers, M8780-498: A.E. Cross to W.M. Bell, 16 November 1906.

24 Glenbow Archives, Herbert M. Hatfield papers, M 480:

Hatfield to provincial librarian in Edmonton, 10 December 1908.

25 Kelly, *The Range Men*, 78.

26 Ibid.

27 Ibid.

28 Ibid., 88.

29 Ibid., 54, 91, 95, 107.

30 Grant MacEwan, *John Ware's Cow Country* (Nanoose Bay, BC: Greystone Books, 1995), 80–81.

31 "The Sundance Kid in Alberta," *Alberta History* 42, no. 4 (Autumn 1995): 10–15.

32 It should be said that not all Englishmen failed horribly in the West. Simon Evans's work in particular shows that many British people settled on the frontier and actively pursued the profession of ranching for a considerable period of time. The Hopkinses were two of them. They became proficient at all aspects of ranching and stuck with it until they retired. Numerous others learned the trade of the cowboy and successfully worked the ranges for the big ranching outfits. What does seem evident, however, is that for people from more developed societies the adjustment to frontier life was anything but easy. There was a tendency for some to come out ill prepared and with very unrealistic expectations about what was going to be required. A significant proportion gave up rather quickly and went home.

33 "Ranching at a Profit," *Regina Leader*, 11 June 1896.

34 Theodore Roosevelt, *Ranch Life and the Hunting Trail* (London: T. Fisher Unwin, 1888), 7, 9–10.

35 H.S. Canfield (New York: Century, 1902).

36 M. Howe, afterwards Elliott (Boston, Cambridge: Roberts Brothers, 1884).

37 H.L. Williams (London: General Publishing, 1890).

38 H.L. Williams (New York: R. Midewitt, 1870).

39 St. George Rathborne (London: Shumen Sibthorp, 1902).

40 *The Virginian: A Horseman of the Plains* (New York: Macmillan, 1902).

41 R. Connor, *Sky Pilot: A tale of the Foothills* (Chicago: R.H. Revell, 1899), 27, 31–32.

42 S.S. Hall, *Stampede Steve; or, the Doom of the Double Face* (New York: Beadle and Adam, 1884), 2–3.

43 "Gum Leaves," *The Brisbane Courier*, 27 February 1904.

44 "Original Poetry," *Western Star and Roma Advertiser*, 3 October 1885.

45 "Gum Leaves."

46 "The Stockman," *Clarence and Richmond Examiner*, 7 July 1910.

47 "The Stockman," *The Wallaroo Times and Mining Journal*, 13 October 1875. See also "Ned the Stockman," *Australian Town*

and Country Journal, 18 June 1887; "Penrith Rowing Club," *Napean Times*, 17 August 1889; "Colonial Art Criticism," *Australian Town and Country Journal*, 19 July 1894.

48 Even in Australia the extraction of natural resources (whether maritime or gold and other minerals), wool production, local manufacturing, and construction expanded throughout most of the nineteenth century. Growing populations concentrated increasingly in the main urban centres – Melbourne, Sydney, Adelaide.

49 See, for instance, "The Prayer of Nature" and "There Is Pleasure In The Pathless Woods."

50 See, for instance, "The Mask of Anarchy Written on the Occasion of the Massacre at Manchester," and "Ode to the West Wind."

51 See, for instance, "Intimations of Immortality from Recollections of Early Childhood."

52 Belford, Clarke and Co., 1883.

53 London: Sampson, Low, Marston, Low and Searle, 1874.

54 Hartford: American Publishing Co., 1869.

55 Vardon and Pritchard, 1905.

56 Sydney: Angus and Patterson, 1895; Sydney: Angus and Anderson, 1906. A.B. (Banjo) Patterson became a national celebrity in the 1890s.

57 For a few of the many articles that circulated through Australian newspapers, see "The Bushman," *Napean Times*, 22 December 1888; "Jimmie the Bushman," *Clarence and Richmond Examiner*, 26 March 1901; "A Peerless Bushman's Skill," *The Cumberland Angus and Fruitgrowers Advocate*, 12 December 1907; "The Australian Bushman," *The Cumberland Argus and Fruitgrowers' Advocate*, 12 May 1915; "The Wily Bushman," *The Cumberland Argus and Fruitgrowers' Advocate*, 20 October 1917.

58 "There is a broad range of styles, from *bluegrass*, to *yodelling* to *folk* to the more popular. The genre has been influenced by Celtic and English folk music, by the traditions of *Australian bush* balladeers, as well as by popular *American country music*. Themes include: *outback* life, the lives of *stockmen*, *truckers* and *outlaws*, songs of romance and of political protest; and songs about the "beauty and the terror" of the *Australian bush*. Pioneers of a more Americanized popular country music in Australia included *Tex Morton* (known as *The Father of Australian Country Music*) in the 1930s and other early stars like *Buddy Williams*, *Shirley Thoms* and *Smoky Dawson*. In 1932, Tex Morton arrived from New Zealand, aged 16,

and humped his swag around outback stations, where he began to earn a name as a performer. In 1936 he cut his first commercial records in Australia. He went on to establish a distinctly Australian *bush ballad* style, shifting from American songs to songs about Australia. He attained national popularity in the 1930s and formed a traveling "Rodeo and Wildwest Show" in the 1940s. In 1949 he travelled to North America and Europe enjoying great success as a stage hypnotist, working in film and with artists such as *Hank Williams*. He returned to Australia in the early 1960s, by which time a generation of performers had carved a place for the Australian themed country music he pioneered" ("History of Country Music," http://www. historyofcountrymusic.com.au/ tributetotex.html).

59 Warren M. Elofson, *Frontier Cattle Ranching in the Land and Times of Charlie Russell* (Montreal and Kingston: McGill-Queen's University Press, 2004), 96–118.

60 Samuel Steele, *Forty Years in Canada: Reminiscences of the Great North-West, with some account of his service in South Africa,* ed. M.G. Niblett, 2nd ed. (Toronto: Prospero Books, 2000), 270–71.

61 "Australian Rough Riding," *The Maitland Mercury & Hunter River General Advertiser,* 21 November 1889; "Australian Rough-Riding," *Kilmore Free Press,* 17 January 1884; "Rough-Riding in Victoria," *The Brisbane Courier,* 17 November 1884.

INDEX

· ·

A

American Civil War, 7
American cowboy. *See also* heroic image
  esteem, 118, 202
  in public imagination, 3
American cowboys in Canada, 9–10, 199
American West, 8
  cowboys in Canada learned their trade
    in, 10
  racial violence, 77
Americans as role models, 199
Andrews, D.H., 182–83, 198–99
Angus, 7, 16, 91, 152
Anthony Lagoon Cattle Station, 35
Anthony's Lagoon, 37
Arizona, 3
Armour, Philip D., 105
Ashwin, Arthur, 74, 179
Asian market, 112, 114–15
Assiniboia, 3, 7, 9, 58
  big grazing operations with 21-year
    closed leases, 8
  livestock recorded in Canadian census
    reports, 162–63
  pasture abuse, 100
  reserve system, 77
Austin, Fred, 157
Austin, Katherine, 157
Austral Downs, 45, 117
Australia
  colonization, 79
  disdain for Old World types who could
    not adapt, 201
  Northern Territory (*See* Northern Terri-
    tory of Australia)
  wild horse population, 123–24
Australian owners
  early ones underestimated magnitude of
    problems, 195
  grasslands capacity, 35
  losses, 25–26
  poor choices of land to lease, 40, 44, 56
  previous grazing experience, 25, 32, 35
  realistic ambitions, 25, 116
  reasonable grasp of climate and pastoral
    conditions, 5, 25, 27, 40
Australian rodeo, 204

Australian stations, 172. *See also* Texas
    system in Northern Australia
  bad shape before international depres-
    sion (1890s), 57
  calves lost to heat, 172
  improvements in form of wells, 169–70
  like large mixed farms in southern
    regions, 35
  only modest attempts at quality control
    in the herds, 168–69
  opium to build labour force, 69–70
  steps to improve transportation, 176
  vast holdings, 27, 33–37, 168
  weaker position financially than in Ca-
    nadian West, 58
Australian stockmen
  high respect for, 118
Australian writers
  vivid descriptions of heroes' style and
    dress, 202
Australians who financed the industry. *See*
    Australian owners
Auvergne station, 83
Avon Downs, 34, 45
"axle grease," 203

B

Bagehot, Walter, 78
Bagot, E.M. (Ned), 25, 31–32
Balfour, Arthur, 17
Banka Banka Station, 167
Bar S, 161–62
Bar U, 9–10, 17, 22, 105, 131, 199
  land purchases, 101
  size, 34
Barkly Tableland, 33, 35, 37, 56
  average farm income (mid-1960s), 194
  few sustainable water surfaces, 29
  grazing grass, 28
  losses among early pastoralists, 26
  rainfall, 29
  redwater disease, 53
  sheep, 45
  trailing in initial herds, 47

Burns, Patrick, 104, 130
Burrandilla feeding station, 118
Butler, W.F., *The Great Lone Land,* 203
Byron, George Gordon Byron, Baron, 203

C

Calgary, 9–10, 43, 71
Calgary Herald, 198
Cameron, Evelyn, 157–58
Campbell, Duncan, 76
Campbell, Jim, 84
Canada Land & Ranche Company, 105
Canada Packers, 164
Canadian Agricultural Coal and Coloniza-
    tion Company, or 76, 9, 105
Canadian barroom shoot-outs, 80
Canadian cattle industry. *See also* Texas
    system in western Canada
  British owners of, 3, 9, 16, 198
  "cattle kings" of the corporation era, 16
  corporation ranches in Canada, 8,
    11–12, 35, 59, 143–45
  Eastern capitalists, 3, 16, 18
  "great ranches," era in western Canada,
    8, 11
  investors paid little attention to quality,
    21
  men who underwrote the cattle compa-
    nies, 17, 20
  start-up challenges, 40
Canadian federal government influence on
    the ranching industry, 5
Canadian Pacific Railway, 43, 89, 106, 179
Canadian ranchers, 3, 14–16, 43–44
  chronic cash shortage, 101
  difficulties upgrading herds (*See* beef
    herd quality in western Canada)
  forced to purchase land, 101
  forced to send cattle to Europe in un-
    der-finished state, 108
  ignorance of conditions in their new
    land, 94
  naivety of some, 90

not familiar enough with their sur-
    roundings, 194
trailing in cattle, hauling in materials
    and supplies, 51 (*See also* cattle
    drives)
unable to sell cattle in US because of
    duty, 108
Canadian Veterinary General, 105
Canadian West. *See* western prairie Canada
carcass weights. *See* dressed weights
carrying capacity, 28, 35
cartage, expense of, 39, 49–51, 55, 57
  Canada continues to have advantage, 176
  out-cartage, 177
Cartwright, E.A. (Aubrey), 161
casinos, 70
cattle drives, 8, 51, 58. *See also* trailing
  cattle
Cattle Export Service, 112, 116
cattle grazing
  only one of several techniques (with
    diversification), 163
cayuses, 132
CC ranch, 157
Chamberlain, Joseph, 78–79
  wife and daughter able to take over
    (after his death), 160–61
Charcoal (member of the Blood tribe), 78
Charleville, Queensland, sales ring in, 117
Chattaway, Clay, 148
Chicago, 43, 71, 179
Chicago auction rings, 107
Chicago packinghouses, 7
chickens, 154–55
The Chief of the Cowboys, 200
Chinese in Australia, 69–70, 75, 166
Chinook, 15, 146–47
Chisholm Trail, 7
Circle Diamond outfit, 9
Circle ranch, 181
Clarke, S.J., 68
Clarke, Terri, 204
Clearing the Plains (Daschuk), 77
Cloncurry, 120
clover, 148
Clydesdales, 13, 125–26, 129, 136–37

dime and romance novels, 200
heroic image of the frontiersman, 10,
201
dingoes, 45, 180
diet, 180–81
dipping for mange, 14
dipping for ticks, 54
disease, 4–5, 40, 195. *See also* names of
specific diseases
diversified operating techniques, 145, 162
almost totally lacking in Northern Territory, 166, 168
Canadian West, 143–64, 189
dividend payments, 101–2, 105, 116
"doggie," 203
doggies (imported yearlings), 103
death due to winter, 183–84
Downer, A.G., 25
draught horses, 48, 133, 138, 167, 179
dressed weights of cattle, 96, 100, 112, 116
lightweight carcasses a problem, 112–15
small size reduced total ranch income,
100
drinking and gambling (Canada), 69–70
driving cattle. *See* cattle drives; trailing
cattle
drought, 27, 29, 35–36
cattle owners designed means for handling it, 186–88
damage to pastures from, 187
list of officially declared droughts,
219–21
not as damaging as sever winters faced
on northern Great Plains, 181,
185–86, 188
threat when droving stock along overland routes, 177
drought-resistant grasses Nature selected
were not replaced with less hardy ones,
188
drovers' wages, 179
dry season, 28
scorching heat, 29
dry spells, 30. *See also* drought

dry spells alternating with heavy rains and
floods, 166
dry stream beds, 48
"duffer," 204
duffing, 65, 81–82, 195. *See also* Native
depredations of livestock; rustling
building herds by stealing neighbours'
cattle, 84
use of "running iron," 84
white Australian, 83
Duncan, Ross, 5
Dunlap, Jim, 10, 199
Durack, Mary, 175
Dutch Henry gang, 81

E

Edinburgh, 8
Edinburgh sales ring, 106
eggs, 154, 156
Elder, Smith & Co., 32
Elder, Thomas, 32, 134
elite horses. *See* well-bred horse business
Elsey River, 49, 53
Elsey station, 134, 141
Emerson, George, 8, 10, 146, 198
Emily Gap on Undoolya, 31
England, 17, 106
Englishmen of a specific kind, 196, 206
bias against, 196–97
environment
establishing appropriate agricultural
techniques for, 5
impact on human behaviour, 1
environmental challenges, 15, 23, 27, 115.
See also drought; winter
environmental reasons for the failure of
great ranches, 11–13, 15
Eva Downs, 34, 186
Evans, Simon, 131

F

families setting societal norms, 89, 196
family approach in northern Australia, 191–93
  collaboration to fend off creditors, 192–93
  man and wife co-managed some corporation stations, 193
family ranch/farm in western Canada, ix, 11, 143–64, 195
  better rate of reproduction out of their stock, 154–55
  children incorporated into production, 160–62
  collaboration to fend off creditors, 162
  emerging as main production unit in Canada, 191
  getting off horses, 146–47
  got by with little money, 156
  open range for summer, keeping home in winter, 148
  roughage and grain to finish beef, 154
  selective breeding programs, 154
  sidelines such as poultry and eggs, 154
  women working off the ranch, 157
  women's contributions, 157–62
  working out (working off the farm), 156–57
fan-tan, traditional Chinese game of, 70
Fares, W.H., 130
farm incomes, 194
fattening cattle, 7. *See also* finishing cattle
  farmers in Ontario and Quebec finishing western cattle, 164
  producing fats in the Canadian West, 89–109
feather top grass, 28
feed to augment natural grasslands, 169
feedlot business, 154
fenced yards or corrals needed for sheep, 47
fences, 131, 148, 150
  allowed for proper sorting of cattle, 152
  costs, 50
  losses kept to a minimum, 163
  Northern Territory, 170

  outside bulls from getting in, 152
  regulate breeding, 151–52
financial pressures, 109
finishing cattle, ix, 154. *See also* fattening cattle; marketing cattle prematurely
  barriers to, 89–96
  fats in Northern Territory, 111–22
  grain finishing, 107–8, 111, 116, 122
finishing cattle on southern feedlots (Australia), 188
Finke River, 25–26, 30
First World War, 124
Fisher, Charles, 32, 34, 41, 57
  forced to seek shareholders in Britain, 33, 41
  shipping to the Dutch East Indies, 112
fishing, 158–59
Five Mile creek, 30
"fixin' to," 204
flash flooding, 29, 45, 56
Fleming, Martin, 84
Flinders grasses, 29
flooding, 30
fly time, 135–36
Foelsche, Paul, 77
Foran, Max, 5–6
Forrest, Alexander, 32
Forrest, William, 29
Fort Benton, Montana, 43, 51
Fort Macleod, 7, 182, 185
Fortescue River, 45
Foster, Robert, 173
Franklin, John, 198
freight rates, 164
Frewen, Morton, 105
frontier, ix, 1–2, 47, 79, 194
  as a concept, 195
  literature extolling, 52
  not orderly and law abiding, 86
  popular image of individualism and self-reliance, 160
  process of selection imposed by, 196, 198, 201–2
  racial violence and, 78
  raised some types of people to heroic stature, 196 (*See also* heroic image)

N

N Bar N, 9, 12, 58
Napplebar creek, 30
National University archives in Canberra, 52
Native bands in Alberta and Assiniboia. *See also* Aboriginal People
  beef for, 7, 22, 96, 100
Native depredations of livestock, 39, 45, 56, 82, 172
  Australia *vs.* Canada, 52, 84–85
Native people working in the cattle industry
  essential and brought down expenses, 173–74
  women (lubras), 175–76, 192–93
Native prostitution, 71–72
Native sex providers, 73
  kidnapped for sexual pleasure, 52, 72, 74
  mixed marriages in the Canadian West, 73
  not always exploited in either continent, 72
Native trackers, 83
Nebraska, 107
needle and thread grass, 96
Nelson-Jones gang, 81
Neth, Mary, 155
Nettelbeck, Amanda, 173
New Mexico, 8
New South Wales, 47, 117
  ban on importation of infected cattle, 54
  bred Walers, 124
  large mixed farms, 35
"New World" conditions, 2
New York, 8
Newcastle River, 49
Newcastle Waters, 32, 35, 54, 177–79
  operated into the modern era, 42
  sheep, 45
Niedringhaus, Fredrick, 9
Niedringhaus, William, 9
No. 6 creek, 30
"no English need apply," 196
North Fork ranch, 11

North-West Mounted Police, 81, 129
  efficient job of keeping Indians on reserves, 53, 77, 85
  former officers who took up ranching, 8
  heavy drinking by young males, 68
  kept white ranchers from taking law into own hands, 85–86
Northern Australia Pastoral Company, 34
Northern Great Plains. *See* western prairie Canada
Northern Star, 34
Northern Territories Commission (1895), 39
Northern Territory betting business, 70
Northern Territory Government, 187
Northern Territory of Australia, 1
  Aborigines (*See* Aboriginal People (Australia))
  under administrative control of South Australia, 27, 66
  animal husbandry, ix
  cattle being bought by grain farmers from south, 117
  challenges to frontier graziers, 27–37
  difficult to get animals fat (*See* finishing cattle)
  distances, 40, 51, 121
  domestic crops risky in, 166
  duffers, 84
  feral horses, 124
  first round of leaseholders failed, 37, 55, 187
  gender imbalance, 68
  government intervention, 5, 41, 43
  open range cattle stations (*See* Texas system in Northern Australia)
  police (under-equipped with many duties), 66–67
  remoteness from markets, 55, 121
  small population, 52, 168
  start-up costs, 39, 55
  traditional farming sub-industries not attempted, 166
  water issues, 36 (*See also* drought)
  watering facilities on trails, 171
Northern Territory Pastoral Company, 33

A book in the Campus Alberta Collection, a collaboration
of Athabasca University Press, the University of Alberta Press
and the University of Calgary Press.

a PROUD
PARTNER in

Campus Alberta

UNIVERSITY OF CALGARY
Press

AU PRESS
Athabasca University

THE UNIVERSITY
of ALBERTA PRESS

Upgrading Oilsands Bitumen and Heavy Oil
by Murray R. Gray
978-1-77212-035-6 (hardcover)

Alberta Oil and the Decline of Democracy in Canada
Edited by Meenal Shrivastava and Lorna Stefanick
978-1-77199-029-5 (paperback)

*So Far and Yet So Close: Frontier Cattle Ranching in Western Prairie
Canada and the Northern Territory of Australia* by Warren M. Elofson
978-1-55238-794-8 (paperback)

www.ingramcontent.com/pod-product-compliance
Lightning Source LLC
Chambersburg PA
CBHW050334270326

41926CB00016B/3454